BECOMING A
CRITICAL THINKER

EIGHTH EDITION

VINCENT RYAN RUGGIERO

CENGAGE
Learning·

Australia • Brazil • Mexico • Singapore • United Kingdom • United States

CENGAGE
Learning

**Becoming a Critical Thinker,
Eighth Edition**
Vincent Ryan Ruggiero

Product Director: Monica Eckman

Product Manager: Kate Derrick

Managing Content Developer:
Megan Garvey

Associate Content Developer:
Rachel Smith Kerns

Product Assistant:
Cailin Barrett-Bressack

Marketing Manager: Lydia Lestar

Rights Acquisitions Specialist:
Ann Hoffman

Manufacturing Planner:
Betsy Donaghey

Art and Design Direction,
Production Management,
and Composition:
Cenveo® Publisher Services

Cover Image:
© iStockPhoto.com/Ayk Kokcu

Photo for chapter openers,
background image for the front
matter, back matter, inside
front cover, inside back cover,
"Good Thinking" box, and page
numbers is © iStockPhoto.com/
Ayk Koku.

For product information and
technology assistance, contact us at **Cengage Learning
Customer & Sales Support, 1-800-354-9706**

For permission to use material from this text or product,
submit all requests online at www.**cengage.com/permissions**.
Further permissions questions can be emailed to
permissionrequest@cengage.com.

Library of Congress Control Number: 2013948731

ISBN-13: 978-1-285-43859-7

ISBN-10: 1-285-43859-0

Cengage Learning
200 First Stamford Place, 4th Floor
Stamford, CT 06902
USA

Cengage Learning is a leading provider of customized learning solutions with office locations around the globe, including Singapore, the United Kingdom, Australia, Mexico, Brazil, and Japan. Locate your local office at: **international.cengage.com/region**.

Cengage Learning products are represented in Canada by Nelson Education, Ltd.

For your course and learning solutions, visit
www.cengage.com.

Purchase any of our products at your local college store or at our preferred online store **www.cengagebrain.com**.

Instructors: Please visit **login.cengage.com** and log in to access instructor-specific resources.

Printed in the United States of America
1 2 3 4 5 6 7 17 16 15 14 13

CONTENTS

3   Improving Your Investigative Skills   47

4   Strengthening Your Individuality   71

ACKNOWLEDGMENTS

Many people have contributed to the eighth edition of this book. I would especially like to thank Sarah Turner and Margaret Leslie for their thoughtful suggestions during the development of this edition, and Anupriya Tyagi for careful attention to the details of the production process.

I also wish to acknowledge the contributions of the following professors, whose advice has been of great help to me in preparing this and previous editions of the book:

Marcia Anderson, Metropolitan State University (MN)

Susan Anderson, Northern Illinois University (IL)

Robert Arend, San Diego Miramar College (CA)

Valeria Becker, University of North Dakota (ND)

John Bird, Winthrop University (SC)

Judy Bowie, DeVry University (IL)

Joel R. Brouwer, Montcalm Community College (MI)

Susan F. Corl, Louisiana State University, Eunice (LA)

Marilyn Corzine, Southwest Florida College of Business (FL)

Ozzie Dean, DeVry Institute of Technology, West Hills (CA)

Gina Firenzi, San Jose State University (CA)

Kathleen J. Fitzgerald, Columbia College (MO)

Catherine Gann, Missouri Western State College (MO)

Glennon Graham, Columbia College, Chicago (IL)

Fran Gray, Southwest Florida College of Business (FL)

Joshua Hayden, Cumberland University (TN)

Cynthia Henderson, College of Lake County (IL)

Marion Hernandez, MassBay Community College (MA)

Gail Herring, McLennan Community College (TX)

David Houston, South College (TN)

Melvin A. Jenkins, Indiana University of Pennsylvania (PA)

Martha Johnson, Texas A&M University (TX)

Eric Knickerbocker, Missouri State University (MO)

John Kowalczyk, Ferris State University (MI)

Patsy Krech, The University of Memphis (TN)

Kevin J. Kukla, SUNY Oswego (NY)

Cynthia H. LaBonne, Fairleigh Dickinson University (NJ)

Carol E. Lacey, Metropolitan State University (MN)

Nancy L. LaChance, DeVry Institute of Technology, Phoenix (AZ)

Helen Laurence, Umpqua Community College (OR)

Marcel Lebrun, Plymouth State University (NH)

Joe LeVesque, Northwood University (TX)

Hakim J. Lucas, Medgar Evers College (NY)

Evelyn Martinez, Pima Community College—Desert Vista Campus (AZ)

Becky Lee Meadows, St. Catharine College (KY)

Louise L. Myers, Naugatuck Valley Community College (CT)

Linda J. Nelson, Davenport University (IN)

Rebecca R. Noel, Plymouth State University (NH)

Sharon Occipinti, Florida Metropolitan University—Tampa (FL)

Mary O'Shaughnessy, DeVry Institute of Technology, Long Beach (CA)

Jim Pollard, Spokane Falls Community College (WA)

Diane Rielly, Naugatuck Valley Community College (CT)

Margie Robertson, Manatee Community College (FL)

Anita Rosenfield, DeVry Institute of Technology, Pomona (CA)

Marni Sanft, Utah Valley State College (UT)

Tracey Schaub, Massasoit Community College (MA)

Penny Schempp, Western Iowa Tech Community College (IA)

Matt Schulte, Montgomery College (MD)

Andrew Scoblionko, DeVry Institute of Technology (NJ)

Jill Silos, Hesser College (NH)

Karen Sookram, Doane College (NE)

Dianna Stankiewicz, Anderson University (IN)

Jeffrey D. Swanberg, Rockford Business College (IL)

Eric Sun, Macon State College (GA)

Mary Vacca, Briarcliffe College (NY)

Lynn E. Walker, Katherine Gibbs School, New York City (NY)

Joyce White, Mayville State University (ND)

Sheri L. Yarbrough, Kennedy-King College (IL)

TO THE INSTRUCTOR

When first published in 1989, this book was designed to meet a then unmet need—to provide an introduction to critical thinking for students whose programs of study did not require or allow for a standard, philosophical introduction to critical thinking.

This design permitted greater latitude than would have been possible with a standard text. I was able to omit some topics that would have been expected in a standard text. A notable example is the distinction between inductive and deductive thinking, which many thinkers, including a fair number of logicians, have come to regard as a distinction without a meaningful difference. They believe that the terms *inductive argument* and *deductive argument* are essentially artificial and tend to obscure the fact that most arguments include *both* inductive elements (movements from the particular to the general) *and* deductive elements (movements from the general to the particular).

The greater latitude also permitted the inclusion of topics that are thought to "belong" to fields other than philosophy or logic. For example, the subject of Chapter 4 is individuality and the role that habits and attitudes commonly associated with psychology play in shaping our thinking. I have also been able to address more expansively the various *applications* of critical thinking (see Chapter 7).

Over the years, some instructors in standard critical thinking courses have found that this book is more appropriate for their students than one of the many standard critical thinking texts. Where their syllabi have required coverage of a topic not covered here (such as the inductive and deductive distinction), they have provided their students with supplementary material or created Internet research assignments.

SIGNIFICANT CHANGES TO THE EIGHTH EDITION

- **Investigating issues.** The treatment of investigating issues (Chapter 3) has been expanded.
- **Individuality and the W.I.S.E. approach.** The connection between using the W.I.S.E. approach and the strengthening of individuality has been reinforced.

- **Linking chapters.** The concepts and approaches in several chapters have been linked by the use of a single extended illustration: the highly publicized case of the White Plains, New York, *Journal News*'s publication of the names and addresses of more than 33,000 legal gun owners. The case is introduced in Chapter 1 and then revisited and expanded in Chapters 3 and 4.

- **New exercises.** A number of timely new cases have been added as exercises for students' critical thinking. They include the following:

    Governmental bans on soft drinks, trans fats, bake sales, and lemonade stands, and new mandates for school lunches

    Multitasking pros and cons

    Party-line voting vs. issue voting

    A North Dakota woman marrying herself

    Apparent decline of leadership in government

    Government "redistribution of wealth"

    Proposed expansion of U.N. powers

    Effect of communications technology on conversation

    Social justice

Fundamentals of Thinking 1

WHAT IS INTELLIGENCE?

In a scene from the movie *Forrest Gump*, Forrest is sitting on a bench next to an old man who asks him rudely, "Are you stupid?" Forrest gives the man his most dignified look and responds politely, "Stupid is as stupid does, Sir." This isn't just a clever comeback; it is a profound truth. And the corollary is also true: "Smart is as smart does." Intelligence isn't just something we *have*. It is, more importantly, something we *do*. Unfortunately, this has not always been understood.

A century ago, most prominent psychologists believed that intelligence is fixed and unchangeable—that everybody is born with a certain "amount" that can never be increased. These psychologists argued that since the mind cannot be improved, education should not try to teach students *how* to think but should instead *tell them what to think*.[1] Not surprisingly, this belief had

---

[1] The most influential of these individuals included H. H. Goddard, Lewis Terman, Edward Thorndike, and Robert Yerkes. To learn more about their ideas, go to www.google.com and enter their names. Incidentally, Terman was the creator of the Scholastic Aptitude Test (SAT).

Digital Vision/Photodisc/Getty Images

a significant effect on instruction. Education associations urged teachers to lecture students and emphasize memorization and regurgitation of information rather than evaluation and judgment.[2]

The psychologists theorized that some nationalities and races are "intellectually inferior" and conducted tests to prove their thesis. The most widely publicized efforts were the Army's Alpha and Beta Intelligence Tests.[3] Though later revealed to be unscientific and badly flawed, at the time their pessimistic conclusions were considered the definitive measure of human intelligence and influenced every social agency. Legislators enacted immigration laws that discriminated against entire nations and regions. Business leaders demanded that workers follow procedures set by industrial engineers and "leave their minds at the company gate." Advertisers aimed at people's emotions rather than their minds. Journalists avoided complexity and simplified their reporting.

The effects of this negative view of intelligence lasted for decades and in some ways are still with us. That is why you, like many others, may have learned to associate intelligence only with *factual knowledge*. In this view, the mind is little more than an information warehouse, with the size varying from person to person; those with the greatest capacity are "walking encyclopedias" who can answer all the questions in class and win prizes on game shows.

There's nothing wrong with possessing information, of course. (It certainly beats ignorance.) But the human mind is capable of much more than passively receiving and storing information. It has the potential to seek out and evaluate ideas, then use them to solve problems, resolve issues, and meet everyday life challenges. In a word, the human mind has the potential for *thinking*. And the more a person develops this potential, the more intelligent he or she becomes. This is not mere wishful thinking. Over the last century, many scholars and researchers have proved it to be true.[4]

---

[2] See, for example the especially significant *Cardinal Principles of Secondary Education*, advanced by the National Education Association in 1918, which can be found on the Internet using the search term "NEA Cardinal Principles."

[3] For more information, do an Internet search using the terms "Army Alpha and Beta Tests" and "Robert Yerkes."

[4] Here are a few of the individuals whose contributions you may wish to explore further: Bernadine Schmidt, Reuven Feuerstein, J. P. Guilford, Mary Meeker, Alma Brewer, Howard Barrows, E. Paul Torrance.

GOOD THINKING!

The Story of Albert Einstein

Few people deserve the title "genius" more than Albert Einstein. His theory of relativity is one of the greatest intellectual achievements in human history.

Academically, however, Einstein was less than mediocre. One teacher told him he would "never amount to anything." Eventually, he was asked to leave school.

After spending some time traveling in Italy, Einstein applied to the Zurich Polytechnic School. He failed the admissions exam, and was required to return to high school for a year before being accepted. On graduating from Zurich he was rejected for an assistantship because no professor would give him a recommendation. He managed to get a job as a tutor but was soon fired.

Some years later, while working at odd jobs, Einstein submitted a doctoral thesis to the University of Zurich, but it was rejected. He eventually got a job in the patent office. In his spare time, he continued his studies, quietly earned a doctorate, and began publishing his scientific findings. Finally, after many years in relative obscurity, his work won him the recognition he deserved.

If Einstein had accepted his teachers' assessment of his intelligence, he would undoubtedly have lost the motivation to pursue his studies, and the world would be unimaginably poorer.

For more information on Albert Einstein, see www.nobel.se/physics/laureates/1921/einstein-bio.html.

Are there limits to intellectual potential? Undoubtedly. Do some people have greater potential than others? From all indications, yes. But the more salient fact is that we can never know our potential until we have tried to develop it. This entails working beyond initial failures. After all, how many of us became proficient at jumping rope, riding a bike, playing tennis or the clarinet, or driving a car after one or two—or one hundred and two—attempts?

WHAT IS THINKING?

Imagine that you are staring into space, picturing yourself heading for the airport. You see yourself ready for a month's cruise in the Caribbean, your pockets stuffed with cash. Would this mental process be thinking?

Now imagine that you're discussing politics with friends. "It's always the same with politicians," you say. "They're full of promises until they're elected. Then they develop chronic amnesia." Would you be thinking in this case?

Thinking, as we will define it in this book, is a purposeful mental activity. You control it, not the reverse. For the most part, thinking is a conscious activity. Yet the unconscious mind can continue working on a problem after conscious activity stops—for example, while you sleep.

Given this definition, your ruminations about a Caribbean cruise are not thinking but daydreaming; you are merely following the drift of your fantasies. On the other hand, your discussion of politics could constitute thinking, as long as you aren't just repeating something you've said or heard before.

There are three broad dimensions of thinking: the *reflective* dimension ponders experience and identifies challenges; the *creative* dimension produces relevant ideas for meeting challenges; and the *critical* dimension evaluates the ideas and decides which is best. Although the three dimensions are sometimes considered separately, the term "critical thinking" is often used to refer to them collectively. That is how we will use it in this book. Chances are you received little or no critical thinking instruction in high school. If so, your teachers were not to blame; they, and their teachers before them, were probably denied such training, largely because of the false notion that thinking can't be taught, or the equally false notion that some subjects teach thinking automatically.

Thinking can be taught, and not just to "gifted" students but to all students. No course automatically teaches thinking, though any course can teach it when teachers make thinking skills a direct objective and give students regular practice in producing and evaluating ideas.[5] Such instruction benefits students in their studies, their careers, community service, and personal relationships. According to psychologist Albert Ellis, "[People] can live the most self-fulfilling, creative, and emotionally satisfying life by intelligently organizing and disciplining [their] thinking."

Unfortunately, shallow, illogical thinking is common. For example, a drug or alcohol abuser may tell himself, "I'm not addicted—I can quit any time I want." A painfully thin anorexic may persuade herself that she is grossly overweight. Even highly educated people may reason that they can never contract a sexually transmitted disease if they have sex only with "nice people." Abusive parents may think that screaming and hitting are appropriate ways of disciplining children.

---

[5] In *An Experiment in the Development of Critical Thinking*, first published in 1941, Edward Glaser cited more than 340 studies bearing on this and related questions. In subsequent decades, hundreds more studies on critical and creative thinking confirmed his conclusion.

"I never heard of anyone pulling a
muscle while thinking."

Marty Bucella/Cartoon Bank.Com

There are even worse examples of poor thinking. A woman doused her husband with rubbing alcohol and set him on fire because he had been acting crazy and refusing to work. She reasoned that by setting him on fire, she'd get him into the hospital for some help. A father kept his 18-year-old daughter chained in the basement because he was afraid she would become a prostitute. An elderly woman robbed a bank, then jumped on her *three-wheel bike* and pedaled away, believing that police could never catch her. (They caught her a couple of blocks from the scene.)

Thinking errors as extreme as these are easy to recognize. Others are more difficult, especially when the ideas are our own rather than other people's. And the most difficult to discern are those enshrined in popular culture. It's easy to assume that other people have examined such ideas and found them worthy, when that may not be the case. For this reason, we should question most vigorously the ideas we are tempted to take for granted—familiar, fashionable ideas.

KEY PRINCIPLES OF THINKING

Thinking is like building a house or a skyscraper—the success of the enterprise depends on the firmness of the foundation. The foundation of thinking, of course, is not concrete and steel but *principles*—ideas that have survived rigorous testing and proved trustworthy. The following principles of thinking are among the most important:

Truth is discovered, not created

You have probably heard it said that truth is subjective and personal, or that each person creates truth to his or her own specifications. This belief is common today, and it means that believing something is so *actually makes it so.* In other words, reality is whatever we wish it to be.

This idea directly contradicts the view that has been generally accepted since ancient times—the view that *truth is the accurate representation of objective reality.* In this view, reality is unaffected by our wishes, preferences, and assumptions.

Is the new view that truth is created and subjective more reasonable than the traditional view that truth is objective? Perhaps the best way to tell is to consider what the new view of truth implies about everyday issues. *If truth is created by each person, then. . .*

. . . Galileo's assertion that the sun is the center of the solar system, a view that shocked most people of his time, is not true for everyone but just for those who want to believe it.

. . . those who believe that the earth is flat, the Holocaust never happened, and Saddam Hussein was a benevolent leader of his people are correct. And so are those who take opposite views.

. . . when a drunk falls into an empty swimming pool thinking that it is full, water will suddenly appear and save him from a hard landing.

. . . the standard courtroom oath—"I swear to tell the truth, the whole truth, and nothing but the truth"—is outdated. Witnesses should be allowed to testify to their own personal truth, and no one's truth should be considered superior to anyone else's. Moreover, since defendants' pleas of not guilty are equal to prosecutors' claims of guilt, all court cases should be dismissed.

. . . it is a waste of time for archeologists to dig for proof of lost civilizations, for medical researchers to search for the causes and cures of diseases, for historians to pore over dusty manuscripts for clues to the past, and for students to read textbooks like this one. Instead, they should simply decide what they want to believe and—presto!—it will become reality.

. . . all your incorrect answers on past true or false tests should be marked correct and your grade-point average raised accordingly.

As even these few examples make clear, the notion that truth is created by each individual does not hold up under scrutiny. But the Good Thinking profile of Nellie Bly on this page adds another example. When she traveled about the world doing her investigative work, she was clearly not looking to create the truth but, rather, to discover it.

GOOD THINKING!

The Story of Nellie Bly

Her real name was Elizabeth Cochrane, and she was born in 1864 in Pennsylvania. When she was six years old her father died, and her mother had to raise Elizabeth and her fourteen brothers and sisters by herself. At sixteen, Elizabeth moved to Pittsburgh to find work. One day in 1885 she read a newspaper article advancing the traditional argument that "a woman's place is in the home." She wrote a response that so impressed the editor that he hired her. She then took the name Nellie Bly and began her remarkable career.

Nellie had an active, inquiring mind that served her well in her specialty, investigative reporting. She wrote articles on marriage and divorce, and helped to initiate important legal reforms. She traveled in Mexico and wrote about exposing the political corruption and widespread poverty. She had herself committed to a New York asylum for ten days so that she could expose the terrible conditions and the inhumane treatment of the inmates. Later she traveled around the world hoping to set a new speed record. She succeeded.

Nellie left journalism to marry an industrialist. When he died ten years later, she took control of his company and won praise for her enlightened treatment of her employees. At a time when workers typically labored long hours in unhealthy sweatshops for low pay, she provided her workers with health care, libraries, and gymnasiums.

Eventually, Nellie returned to reporting. While she was on holiday in Europe, the First World War broke out, and she immediately volunteered to be a war correspondent for the *New York Journal*. She became the first female correspondent to cover a war from the front lines. After the war, Nellie returned home and wrote a newspaper column until her death of pneumonia in 1922.

For more information on Nellie Bly, see http://az.essortment.com/nellyblybiogra_rsls.htm or www.library.csi.cuny.edu/dept/history/lavender/386/nellie.html.

Ideas are interrelated[6]

When one idea is expressed, closely related ideas are simultaneously conveyed, logically and inescapably.[7] In logic, this kinship is expressed by the term *sequitur*, Latin for "it follows." (The converse is *non sequitur*, "it does not follow.")[8]

Consider, for example, the idea that many teachers and parents express to young children as a way of encouraging them: "If you believe in yourself, you can succeed at anything." From this it follows that *nothing else* but belief—neither talent nor hard work—is necessary for success. The reason the two ideas are equivalent is that their meanings are inseparably linked. (Note: The statement "belief in oneself is *an important element* in success" is different because it specifies that belief is not the only element in success.)

In addition to conveying ideas closely linked to it in meaning, an idea can *imply* other ideas. For example, the idea that there is no real difference between virtue and vice implies that people should not feel bound by common moral standards. Samuel Johnson had this implication in mind when he said: "But if he does really think that there is no distinction between virtue and vice, why, Sir, when he leaves our houses let us count our spoons."

If we were fully aware of the closely linked meanings and implications of the ideas we encounter, we could easily sort out the sound ones from the unsound, the wise from the foolish, and the helpful from the harmful. But we are seldom fully aware of the linkages. In many cases, we take ideas at face value and embrace them with little or no thought of their associated meanings and implications. In the course of time, our actions are shaped by those meanings and implications, whether we are aware of them or not.

To appreciate the influence of ideas in people's lives, recall the series of events that followed the psychologists' declaration that intelligence is fixed and unchangeable. Teachers changed their classroom methods, legislators changed immigration laws, business leaders changed their attitude toward workers, and advertisers and journalists changed their approaches to the public.

The influence of the psychologists' idea about intelligence did not end there. It also encouraged eugenicists to intensify their efforts to save the human

---

[6] This section is copyright © 2010 by MindPower, Inc. Used with permission.

[7] Peggy Rosenthal offers a slightly different explanation of the same phenomenon: "Even when we think we are choosing our words with care and giving them precise meanings, they can mean much more (or less) than we think; and when we use them carelessly, without thinking, they can still carry thoughts. These thoughts we're not aware of, these meanings we don't intend, can then carry us into certain beliefs and behavior—whether or not we notice where we're going." *Words and Values: Some Leading Words and Where They Lead Us* (New York: Oxford University Press, 1984), viii.

[8] One example of *non sequitur* is a child's answer to his teacher's question "Why do you get so dirty during playtime?" He responded, "Because I'm closer to the ground than you are." Another is the conclusion of a medical authority in 1622 about the treatment of a wound: "If the wound is large, *the weapon* [emphasis added] with which the patient has been wounded should be anointed daily; otherwise, every two or three days." The medical quotation is from Christopher Cerf and Victor Navasky, *The Experts Speak: The Definitive Compendium of Authoritative Misinformation* (New York: Villard, 1998), 38.

race from people presumed inferior. Margaret Sanger's Planned Parenthood urged the lower classes to practice contraception. Others succeeded in legalizing forced sterilization, notably in Virginia. The U.S. Supreme Court upheld the Virginia law with Justice Oliver Wendell Holmes, Jr., declaring, "Three generations of imbeciles are enough."[9] Over the next five decades 7,500 women, including "unwed mothers, prostitutes, petty criminals and children with disciplinary problems," were sterilized.[10] In addition, by 1950, more than 150,000 supposedly "defective" children, many relatively normal, were held against their will in institutions. They "endured isolation, overcrowding, forced labor, and physical abuse including lobotomy, electroshock, and surgical sterilization."[11]

The innumerable ideas you have encountered may not affect your life quite so dramatically, but they will influence your beliefs and behavior, for better or worse, even if you do not *consciously* embrace them.

A statement can't be both true and false at the same time and in the same way

This principle is known as the principle of contradiction. The following examples demonstrate the validity of this principle:

Statement: My roommate borrowed my sweater without permission.

Comment: If this statement were both true and false at the same time in the same way, it would mean that you simultaneously *gave* your permission and *didn't give* your permission. That is impossible. You must either have given your approval or not given it. This example confirms the principle of contradiction.

Statement: During World War II the Nazis killed millions of Jews in concentration camps.

Comment: Either the Nazis did this horrible deed or they didn't. Since there is no way they did it and didn't do it, this example also supports the principle of contradiction.

Statement: Capital punishment is a deterrent to crime.

Comment: Let's assume for the sake of discussion that capital punishment was once a deterrent to crime but no longer is—in other words, that this statement was true at one time but is false today. Does this situation challenge the principle of contradiction? No. The principle specifies that a statement cannot be both true and false *at the same time* in the same way.

Statement: Edgar is richer than Clem.

Comment: If Edgar has more money than Clem, but Clem surpasses him in moral character or satisfaction, then the statement would be both

---

[9] See *Buck v. Bell*, 1927.

[10] Stephen Jay Gould, *The Mismeasure of Man* (New York: W. W. Norton, 1981), 335.

[11] Michael D'Antonio, *The State Boys Rebellion* (New York: Simon & Schuster, 2004), 5, 18.

true and false but not *in the same way*. It would be true in one sense and false in another. (To be a contradiction, it would have to say Edgar has more money than Clem *and* does not have more money than Clem.) Thus, this example also confirms the principle of contradiction.

A note of caution: The principle of contradiction applies whenever opposing statements make *exactly opposite* assertions—for example, *she is* versus *she isn't*, *he did* versus *he didn't*, *they have* versus *they haven't*. In such cases, it is certain that one statement must be true and the other false. However, when the assertions made are not exactly opposite but merely different, both could be false. For example, if you say "Sally got the highest mark on the exam" and I say "Luke got the highest mark," it is possible that we are both mistaken. (Bertha or Juwan may have gotten the highest mark.)

Everyone makes mistakes, even experts

It's a shame that there are no official accuracy statistics available for experts in the various fields of knowledge. If there were, you could check the experts' "batting averages." You might be shocked to learn just how often experts are wrong. Bennett Cerf and Victor Navasky have compiled an interesting collection of wrong judgments and predictions made by experts. Many are so far off the mark that they are laughable. Here is a brief sampling:

A British scientist in 1895: "Heavier-than-air flying machines are impossible."

A London professor at the dawn of the railroad, when the top speed was 25 mph: "Rail travel at high speed is not possible because passengers, unable to breathe, would die of asphyxia."

The commissioner of the U.S. Office of Patents, arguing for the abolition of his office in 1899: "Everything that can be invented has been invented."

The President of the British Royal Society in 1900: "X-rays are a hoax."

A banker, in 1903, advising against investing in Ford Motor Co: "The horse is here to stay, but the automobile is only a novelty—a fad."

A famous movie studio head, commenting on the future of TV: "People will soon get tired of staring at a plywood box every night."

Variety magazine's assessment of rock and roll in 1955: "It will be gone by June."

An editor, in 1957, turning down a book on computers: "[I have it] on the highest authority that data processing is a fad and won't last out the year."

This is not to say that the "batting averages" of experts are lower than those of nonexperts. As a rule, they are considerably higher. The most sensible approach is therefore not to settle for a single expert's opinion but to seek a second, and perhaps a third, expert opinion before making up your mind.

In addition, since advanced degrees are not awarded with crystal balls, be especially wary when any expert attempts to predict the future.

Ideas can be examined without being embraced

Some people refuse to consider an idea that differs from their own out of loyalty to their convictions. This refusal is especially strong in political and religious matters.

For example, a conservative might refuse to read an article by a liberal, and a Christian might refuse to listen to a lecture on Judaism, Buddhism, or Islam. Such people prevent themselves from deepening their understanding. In addition, because knowledge is as essential to thinking as air is to breathing, they stifle their intellectual development and do themselves a disservice.

Whenever you are tempted to deny a fair hearing to unfamiliar or opposing ideas, remind yourself that examining an idea is not the same as embracing it. If, after applying critical thinking, you decide that an idea is faulty, you will have a substantial basis for rejecting it. Moreover, you will be in a better position to explain its flaws to others.

Feeling is no substitute for thinking

Following feelings, impulses, and impressions is fashionable today. Some people go so far as to say that feelings are a *better* guide than thoughts. This is a comforting idea, but in order to believe it you have to overlook the many times when feelings have led you astray.

Consider a time when you were trying to lose weight and your feelings said, "Order the double hot fudge sundae." Or another time when you felt the urge to tell your instructor or the boss what you *really* thought of her. Or occasions when you felt the impulse to go to a party instead of studying for a test, charge an expensive item you didn't need and couldn't afford, or drive 30 miles an hour over the speed limit to avoid being late. No doubt you can think of many additional examples of feelings that, if followed, would have caused you pain or misfortune.

Louis L'Amour, vagabond and author of dozens of western novels, tells a story from his days as a laborer in an Oregon lumber mill. The story illustrates the danger of relying on feelings, impulses, and impressions:

> They put a number of us to digging holes four feet square and down to hardpan for concrete piers to support a building soon to be erected. There were at least a dozen of us on the job and the ground was partly frozen. After we got down a short distance, water had to be bailed out, so progress was slow. There was a husky young German, a couple of years older than I, and we got into a contest to make the work more fun. The average was two and a half holes per day, while several were doing three. The German and I were doing four holes apiece.

Our boss was an easygoing Irishman who saw what was going on and wisely stayed out of it, but the management in its wisdom decided he was not gung-ho enough as a boss and brought in a new man.

Knowing nothing of any of us, he came suddenly into the area and found the German and me leaning on our shovels, having just finished our second holes for the day, while nobody else had finished one. He promptly fired both of us for loafing along with another chap who had been doing three holes a day. In his first day on the job he had fired his three best men. (L'Amour, 105)

The problem with following feelings, urges, and impressions is not that they always lead us astray—they don't—but that they aren't consistently reliable. Sometimes they advise us well, and sometimes they don't. In L'Amour's example, the new boss's mistake was to act on his immediate impression instead of examining it critically.

Rather than mindlessly following your feelings, think about them carefully and decide whether they *deserve* to be followed.

KEY HABITS AND SKILLS OF THINKING

The first step in making the most of your intellectual potential is to strengthen the habits and acquire the skills associated with effective thinking. The sections that follow cover the most fundamental of these habits and skills.

The habit of curiosity

Most children are filled with curiosity. They are constantly asking, "What's that, Mommy?" and "Why, Daddy?" Alas, parents soon tire of such questioning and discourage it, and teachers are too impatient or too busy keeping pace with the curricula to answer. So, many children learn to stifle their curiosity. That is most unfortunate because small and great achievements alike can be traced to curiosity. This is true not only in science and technology but also in the humanities, the social sciences, and business. Virtually every invention has its origin in someone asking "Why is it made (or done) that way?" or "Could there a better way?" And every new insight begins similarly, in someone wondering if things are as they seem or as common opinion holds. The Good Thinking profile of Paul Vitz on page 13 is an example.

The good news is that, though your curiosity may be dormant, it can be revived. All you need to do is be more observant of what people are saying and what is happening around you, ask probing questions, and when time permits seek answers. Before long, you will have made curiosity a habit.

Skill in distinguishing facts from opinions

Facts are ideas whose accuracy is clearly and amply documented and affirmed by knowledgeable people. Opinions are ideas that have not yet been sufficiently documented and are therefore still open to dispute.

Despite the clarity and simplicity of these definitions, the task of distinguishing facts from opinions can be difficult. One reason is that not every *statement* of fact is factual. The most obvious example is a lie—for example, a child saying she didn't eat the cookies when she did, or the perpetrator of a crime swearing he is innocent. In addition to lies, there are honest mistakes. A person might misread a memo and tell a colleague a meeting is scheduled for 3:00 pm today when it is actually scheduled for tomorrow. Or an art expert might declare a painting to be the work of a master and only later discover it is a brilliant forgery. For years it was considered a fact that the earth is flat. (Believe or not, there is still a Flat Earth Society composed of people who cling to this discredited "fact.")

Another reason that facts and opinions can be difficult to distinguish is that opinions are often stated *as if* they were facts. Consider these statements: "The death penalty constitutes cruel and unusual punishment"; "The cause of children committing crimes is irresponsible parenting." Each statement appears to be factual because of the way it is stated. Yet informed people continue to disagree about each. Therefore, each statement is an opinion. (This is not to say that either of these statements is false, only that neither issue has been settled.)

Over time some opinions acquire the status of facts. For example, in the nineteenth century it was standard practice for physicians to handle cadavers in the hospital morgue and then, without washing their hands, make their rounds and visit patients. When one perceptive physician, Ignaz Semmelweiss, expressed the opinion that this practice might be responsible for spreading infections, he was ridiculed and ostracized. Today his "absurd" opinion is universally recognized as a fact.

GOOD THINKING!

The Story of Paul Vitz

Paul C. Vitz is a professor of psychology and the author of many articles and several books, including *Faith of the Fatherless: The Psychology of Atheism*. The story behind this book illustrates how a simple question can lead to new insights.

For much of his life, Vitz had been an atheist, but at age 38 he embraced religion and became interested in the historic tension between psychology and religion. He learned that "even in intellectual and academic circles, atheism did not become respectable until about 1870 . . . and it continued to be restricted to small numbers of intellectuals into the twentieth century." From his training as a psychologist he also knew that "many atheists are famous for arguing that [religious] believers suffer from illusions, from unconscious and infantile needs, and from other psychological deficits." Freud, for example, argued that belief in God is nothing more than a projection of the believer's desire for security.

As he reflected on these facts, he began to wonder whether this "projection theory" might apply to atheists as well as to believers, or perhaps even apply *better* to atheists than believers. Eager to find out, he decided to study the lives of famous atheists and famous religious believers and see if any interesting patterns emerged. The atheists he chose included Freud, Nietzsche, Hume, and Sartre; the theists included Pascal, Berkeley, de Tocqueville, Kierkegaard, and Buber.

The study revealed that every famous atheist had a weak, dead, or abusive father, and almost every theist had a positive relationship with his father. After analyzing the data, Vitz concluded that the projection theory of religious belief is not only unscientific but also a form of the logical fallacy known as *ad hominem*—in other words, it focuses on the believer personally rather than on the evidence for or against religious belief.

Vitz writes as follows: "Since *both* believers and nonbelievers in God have psychological reasons for their positions, one important conclusion is that in any debate as to the truth of the existence of God, psychology should be irrelevant. A genuine search for evidence supporting, or opposing, the existence of God should be based on the evidence and arguments found in philosophy, theology, science, history, and other relevant disciplines. It should also include an understanding of religious experience."

Paul Vitz's research could pave the way for a more scholarly approach to the study of religion.

For more information on Paul Vitz, see Paul Vitz, *Faith of the Fatherless: The Psychology of Atheism* (Dallas, TX: Spence Publishing Co., 1999).

The following examples illustrate the challenge of separating facts from opinions.

Statement: The 2000 Summer Olympic Games were held in Tokyo.

Comment: This statement has the form of a fact, yet it is not factual. The 2000 Summer Olympic Games were held in Sydney, Australia.

Statement: Camel's hair brushes are made of Siberian squirrel fur.

Comment: The statement appears ridiculous, yet it is factual.

Statement: Stalin was more brutal than Hitler.

Comment: This statement is an opinion, but it is so well supported by historical evidence that many would consider it a fact.

Statement: Eyewitness testimony is generally unreliable.

Comment: Anyone unfamiliar with the relevant research would consider this an opinion, and a wrong one at that. Yet it is a fact.

The following simple guidelines will help you decide whether any statement is a fact or an opinion:

1. **If a statement is common knowledge, it is a fact and need not be supported.**

   Example: Both John and Robert Kennedy were assassinated.

   Example: The cost of a college education is significantly higher today than it was twenty years ago.

   Comment: Both statements are common knowledge, so no support is needed.

2. **If a statement is not common knowledge yet has been confirmed to be accurate, it is a fact and need not be supported. However, the source of the confirmation should be cited.**

   Example: The gray reef shark uses unusual body language to signal that it feels threatened.

   Comment: This fact is not well known, at least among laypeople, so the source should be cited. (It is Bill Curtsinger, "Close Encounters with the Gray Reef Shark," *National Geographic*, January 1995, 45–67.)

3. **If the statement is neither common knowledge nor confirmed to be accurate, it is an opinion and should be supported with evidence— that is, with reliable information.**

   Example: More Americans are victimized by chronic laziness than by workaholism.

   Comment: Some people will disagree, and others may ask, "Why does the author think this? What reasons does he or she have for holding this view rather than some competing view?" The person making the statement should provide answers to such questions.

4. **If it is not clear whether a statement is a fact or an opinion, treat it as an opinion.** In other words, support it with evidence as explained in point #3 above.

Remember another important point about opinion. As used in critical thinking, the term *opinion* refers only to matters of judgment, not to matters of taste or personal preference. The ancient Romans used to say that there is no way to argue profitably or think critically about matters of taste. Their view is as wise today as it was a couple of millennia ago.

Do you favor a slender figure or a full figure? Do you find long or short hair more appealing? Do you prefer fitted jeans or ones with the crotch down around the knees? Do you regard the Lincoln Town Car as beautiful or ugly? Do you enjoy sitcoms more than soap operas? All of these are matters of personal preference or taste that cannot be supported by facts.

As long as you express matters of taste *as matters of taste* you need not defend them, even if others find your tastes odd. Thus, you should say "I prefer long hair" rather than "Long hair is more attractive than short hair," "I prefer the look of the Lincoln Town Car" rather than "The Lincoln Town Car is the most stylish car on the road," and "I enjoy sitcoms more than soap operas" rather than "Sitcoms are superior entertainment."

The habit of checking facts and testing opinions

One reason for checking the facts about an issue is that people sometimes misstate them. Another is that they sometimes *omit* important facts. It doesn't matter whether the misstatement or omission is accidental or on purpose. Either way, if we fail to check, our evaluation may be flawed.

Often you will be able to check the facts of an issue by consulting an appropriate reference book, such as an encyclopedia, an almanac, a newspaper archive, or a dictionary. At other times, you will have to consult the research literature in the field. Chapter 3 includes detailed advice on doing library and Internet research. You may wish to skim those sections now and refer to them whenever you are doing an exercise that calls for research.

The idea of testing opinions may seem odder than checking facts because it has become fashionable to think of opinions as something sacred and above criticism. Many people reason, "I have a right to my opinion—therefore my opinion must be right." They would be shocked to learn that for centuries, opinion was not so highly regarded.

Almost 2,000 years ago the Greek philosopher Epictetus wrote: "Here is the beginning of philosophy: a recognition of the conflicts between men, a search for their cause, *a condemnation of mere opinion* . . . and the discovery of a standard of judgment." [Emphasis added.] Nineteenth-century British author Sir Robert Peel termed public opinion "a compound of folly, weakness, prejudice, wrong feeling, right feeling, obstinacy, and newspaper paragraphs."

American author John Erskine sarcastically termed opinion "that exercise of the human will which helps us to make a decision without information." American philosopher George Santayana observed that "people are usually more firmly convinced that their opinions are precious than that they are true." And one humorist suggested that many opinions that are expressed ought to have been sent by *slow freight* instead.

If you reflect on these skeptical views of opinion, you will appreciate that they underline an important reality—not all opinions are equally sound. Some are wise, others are foolish, and most fall somewhere between the two extremes. Unfortunately, most of us tend to forget this when forming opinions. Armed with little more than a sketchy news report, an assertion by a celebrity, or a fleeting impression, we may form opinions on complex subjects, such as the causes of child abuse, the reason for dinosaur extinction, or the health benefits of the latest diet.

Some time ago, a roving reporter took his tape recorder into the street and asked passersby, "How serious is racial tension in New York?" Among those who responded were a porter, two teachers, a truck driver, a film editor, a security guard, and a secretary. Chances are that at least some of these people lacked sufficient knowledge to form an opinion, but that didn't stop them from expressing one. (Perhaps they never heard the old saying, "It's better to remain silent and be thought a fool than to express your thoughts and remove all doubt.")

To be a critical thinker, you will need to develop the habit of testing opinions—your own as well as other people's—before trusting them. Here are seven effective ways of doing so.

Consult everyday experience   Consider your personal experience as well as what you know to be the experience of other people. If the opinion in question challenges that experience, it is almost certainly mistaken, at least in part. For example, Wayne Dyer, a popular author of self-help books, says that guilt is "not a natural behavior," that it is "useless" and should be "exterminated" (Dyer, 90–91). Yet, experience suggests that most people—particularly kind and considerate ones—feel guilt when they offend others. It's precisely their guilty feelings that motivate them to apologize for their bad behavior and to make amends. Dyer's idea is, at best, an overstatement.

Consider the opinion's likely consequences   One way to recognize that an opinion is flawed is to observe that it leads to unintended—and sometimes *undesired*—consequences. Not long ago zealous advocates of African American studies courses expressed the opinion that only African Americans should be allowed to teach such courses. But then Arthur Schlesinger, Jr., a well-known historian, pointed out that such a prohibition would have unintended consequences. He wrote: "The doctrine that only blacks can teach and write black history leads inexorably to the doctrine that blacks can teach and write only black history as well as to inescapable corollaries: Chinese must be restricted to Chinese history, women to women's history, and so on" (Schlesinger, 105).

Suppose you were evaluating this opinion: "The welfare system that continues to drain our tax dollars should not be gradually phased out but ended immediately." Among the consequences you would identify would be (1) some able-bodied welfare recipients would seek work and find it; (2) others would be less successful in their search; (3) those who are too old or too ill to work would be left with no source of income; (4) the living conditions for some children on welfare would decline; and (5) private agencies such as the Salvation Army would increase their giving. After examining these consequences, you would no doubt conclude that the opinion, as stated, is unreasonable.

Consider the implications   This approach entails identifying and examining related ideas suggested by the opinion. Let's say the opinion is "What people view in movies or on television has no effect on their behavior." (Media spokespeople often say this in response to complaints that graphic sex and violence have a negative social impact.)

The implications of this conclusion are that viewing films and television programs cannot degrade, inspire, or motivate us. If this were really the case, then public service announcements to drive only when sober and practice safe sex would be pointless and advertisers would be wasting millions of dollars on them.

Think of exceptions   This approach is useful when you are evaluating an opinion that expresses a general rule. The more exceptions you can think of, the more suspect the opinion is. Carl Rogers, a famous psychologist, wrote: "One of the basic things which I was a long time in realizing, and which I am still learning, is that when an activity feels as though it is valuable or worth doing, it is worth doing" (Rogers, 22). To test this idea, think of activities that someone might feel are worth doing but really aren't. Here are just a few: shoplifting, lying on a résumé, and expressing to an instructor your negative assessment of his teaching ability.

Here is another example of thinking of exceptions. A commonly expressed opinion is "If you are strongly motivated, you can be anything you want to be." A notable exception is Michael Jordan's attempt to be a major league baseball player. He certainly did not lack motivation, and his basketball career proved he was a gifted athlete. Despite these advantages, however, he was unable to succeed in baseball. Jordan's case raises questions about the soundness of the opinion.

Think of counterexamples   Suppose an author claims that parents should not give children responsibilities until they are in their teens, and supports her view with a number of case histories like this one: "I know a person who was given responsibilities such as picking up his clothes and toys at age 3; taking out the garbage at age 6; and raking leaves, washing dishes, and doing laundry at age 10. Today he's in his mid-thirties and resents having had all those chores." A counterexample would be the case of someone (perhaps you) who had similar responsibilities in childhood and now regards the experience as valuable. The more counterexamples you identify, the more justified you are in wondering about the reasonableness of the author's opinion.

Scholars in every field use the technique of finding counterexamples. Some time ago the issue of repressed memory was in the news. People undergoing therapy suddenly recalled horrible incidents of physical or sexual abuse they had supposedly suffered as children. Some therapists said they were suffering from "traumatic amnesia" and that victims of multiple instances of abuse were more likely to suffer from it than were victims of a single instance. This opinion sounded logical. But at least one critical thinker offered some powerful counterexamples—slaves, survivors of concentration camps in World War II, and victims of torture and political persecution. She noted that all these people suffered intense abuse for years yet never for a moment forgot it (Hagen, 39). These counterexamples did not disprove the idea that memories of abuse can be repressed, but they did suggest the possibility that some claims of repressed memories, though perhaps sincere, are nevertheless false.

Reverse the opinion   This test consists of taking the exact opposite of the opinion you are examining and determining if a case can be made for it. Consider the popular opinion "People must feel good about themselves before they are able to achieve." The reverse of that idea would be "People must achieve before they can feel good about themselves." A little investigation will reveal that this is not a new belief but the one that prevailed for hundreds, even thousands, of years before the self-esteem movement became dominant. To decide which of the two opinions is more reasonable, you might consider ordinary achievements in your own life—such as learning how to tie your shoes, whistle, ride a bike, dribble a basketball, drive a car, surf, or use a computer—and then decide whether self-esteem preceded or followed the achievement.

Look for relevant research   Every subject from agriculture to zoology has its devoted students, individuals who have spent decades learning everything they can about it and sharing their knowledge with others. These individuals are as near as the library or the Internet. One of the best ways to test any opinion is to see what these knowledgeable people have to say about it. (Chapter 3 explains how to conduct research. If you wish, you may look ahead and read that explanation now.)

THE NEED FOR A SYSTEMATIC APPROACH

Chapter 2 will present a step-by-step approach to thinking. But before doing that, it may be helpful to demonstrate the value of such an approach. The easiest way to do that is in the context of an actual situation. The situation we will use is the growing concern over mass murder in the United States.

Between 1982 and 2012, there were 62 mass murders in the United States with a combined loss of almost 1,000 lives. Among the most notable incidents were those in Tucson, Arizona; Fort Hood, Texas; Blacksburg, Virginia; Columbine and Aurora, Colorado; and Newtown, Connecticut. The Newtown incident was especially troubling because the great majority of the 26 victims were little children.

Concerned individuals and groups naturally wondered how such wanton violence could be ended. The editors of the White Plains (New York) *Journal News* decided that a partial solution would be to publicize information on gun ownership. Taking advantage of the Freedom of Information Act (FOIA), they searched public records for the names and addresses of legal gun owners in two local counties and published their findings—33,614 in all—with an interactive map.

The newspaper's action immediately triggered strong reactions. The county clerk of a third county refused to provide the gun ownership information to the newspaper, claiming it would create a danger for law-abiding citizens. New York State Senator Greg Ball agreed, and went so far as to call the editors "asinine." Commentators from around the country offered a variety of criticisms of the *Journal News*. Many pointed out that criminals could use the information on gun ownership to plan their robberies, entering the homes of gun owners while they are away and stealing their guns, or targeting the homes of people not on the list because, without guns, they would be more vulnerable.

Publishing the list had a number of unintended consequences. Prison guards reported receiving threats from inmates saying "we now know where you and your family live." A woman who had previously been stalked for years started receiving disturbing phone calls again. A battered wife who had left her husband and started a new life was terrified that her published address would enable him to find her. Retired judges and police officers became fearful that criminals they had dealt with over the years would use the published information to find them and exact revenge.

Perhaps the most ironic unintended consequence concerned the editors of the *Journal News* themselves. Their own personal information was posted on line. They and their staffs received threatening phone calls, some so serious they were forced to hire armed guards for protection. Gun owners and their supporters published a list of the newspaper's advertisers and urged people to boycott them.

A number of critics found it odd that the *Journal News* focused its investigation on law-abiding individuals rather than, for example, convicted sexual predators or people who didn't pay child support. And virtually all of the critics agreed not only that the publication of gun ownership information was a violation of the privacy of legal gun owners and that it produced a number of unfortunate consequences, but also that it contributed nothing to solving the problem of gun violence in general or the Newtown, Connecticut, shootings in particular.

This *Journal News* case is a classic case of poor thinking. The editors intended to be helpful and to solve a problem, but in fact they did the opposite. The saddest fact is that all the difficulties could have been avoided if they had approached the issue more thoughtfully—for example, if they had taken the time to wonder whether factors other than legal gun ownership might be contributing to the epidemic of mass shootings in America and, if so, whether those factors might be more important and more newsworthy than the names and addresses of legal gun owners.

This case of deficient thinking may be more obvious and dramatic than most, but it is certainly not an isolated example. Other examples could be cited in school, at work, and in personal lives. The best way to avoid thinking lapses in all these areas is to adopt a systematic approach to thinking. Chapter 2 will introduce such an approach.

EXERCISES

1.1. Throughout this century, a famous painting entitled *The Man with the Golden Helmet* was believed to be the work of the Dutch master Rembrandt. Some years ago it was proved to have been painted by someone else. Some people would say that the truth about this painting changed. Do you agree? Explain.

1.2. Examine each of the following cases in light of what you've learned about truth in this chapter. State your view and explain why you hold it.

a) Ira is a journalist. Will the belief that he can create his own truth make him more or less likely to value accuracy in his reporting?

b) Bruce is prejudiced against minorities and women. Which of the following beliefs would be more helpful in overcoming his prejudice: the belief that truth is subjective and created or the belief that truth is objective and discovered? Explain your reasoning.

c) Most students can use additional motivation to learn. Will the belief that they can create their own truth help or hinder their motivation? Explain.

1.3. Classify each of the following exchanges as (a) an actual contradiction or (b) a near contradiction. Briefly explain each choice.

MAVIS: *Big time college sports are corrupt.*

CORA: *You're absolutely wrong, Mavis.*

KAREN: *There are very few real heroes today.*

HANNA: *I think there are more today than there have ever been.*

BRAD: *Look at that new Lincoln across the street.*

CLARA: *That isn't a Lincoln—it's a Mercury.*

1.4. Indicate whether each of the following statements is

    a) clearly a fact.

    b) possibly a fact, but not clear without documentation.

    c) an opinion.

    d) a personal preference expressed as a personal preference.

    e) a personal preference incorrectly expressed as an opinion.

Remember that it is sometimes difficult to separate facts and opinions. There may be room for disagreement over some answers, so be prepared to explain your choices.

   1. I find blue-eyed redheads appealing.

   2. The Chevrolet Camaro is the most stylish car on the market.

   3. All religions share the same fundamental truths.

   4. Darwin's theory of evolution continues to be controversial.

   5. Pornography is an insult to women.

   6. Black people are the victims of crime more often than white people.

   7. Prostitution should be legalized.

   8. People who need organ transplants greatly outnumber organ donors.

   9. The publicity given to suicides leads to most "copycat" suicide attempts.

  10. Comic books are as instructive about life as novels are.

  11. Most students who drop out of school lack the intelligence to succeed.

  12. Surgical procedures have been performed on fetuses while they were still in the uterus.

1.5. Now take the statements in the previous exercise and do as follows:

- For each that you classified as (b), possibly a fact, state one or more reliable sources that could be cited to support the statement (assuming that the statement is factual).

- For each that you classified as (b), write questions that might be raised about the statement.

- If you classified any statement as (e), rewrite it as a personal preference rather than as an opinion.

1.6. Evaluate these opinions applying the lessons you learned in this chapter.

A famous movie actress explained why she nursed her daughter for two years: "That's a particular philosophy I have . . . allowing her to make her own decisions. I feel she is a better judge than I am."

Line from a bumper sticker: "Guns don't kill people; people kill people."

A New Age author tells his readers: "You are the only thing that is real. Everything else is your imagination."

1.7. State an opinion you have heard expressed (or expressed yourself) about a current local, national, or international issue and evaluate it as you did the statements in Exercise 1.6.

1.8. In each of the following cases, decide whether the reason offered is both good and sufficient to support the opinion or action. Explain your decision.

"Your Honor, I believe I was justified in hitting my wife. She kept nagging me about getting a job."

"I didn't sign that petition. The person who asked me to sign refused to support my proposal last year."

"I oppose government funding for abortions. It requires taxpayers to finance a procedure that many of them believe is a moral outrage."

Students who are caught cheating should receive a failing grade in the course. Cheating is a serious violation of scholarly integrity.

Women should not take their husbands' names when they marry. Doing so is a sign of subjugation.

1.9. What lessons can you draw from the "good thinking" profiles of Albert Einstein, Nellie Bly, and Paul Vitz presented in this chapter? Explain how you can use each of those lessons in your career or personal life.

1.10. Describe an occasion on which you or someone you know acted without thinking through the matter sufficiently. Explain what happened as a result of this failure. What could you done in the thinking stage to anticipate and avoid what happened?

QUIZ

1. Define the term *intelligence*.

2. Name the three broad dimensions of thinking.

3. Thinking can be taught but only to gifted students. True or false?

4. Every idea is distinct from all others and its meaning is unrelated to theirs. True or false?

5. Explain the error in this statement: "I create my own truth. What I believe to be true is true for me."

6. State the principle of contradiction. Then explain how this principle aids us in critical thinking.

7. Respond to this statement: "I have a right to my opinion, so you have no business challenging it."

8. Is it useful to argue about matters of taste? Explain.

9. Feeling is no substitute for thinking. True or false?

10. One effective way to test opinions is to consult your personal experience. True or false?

Answers to this quiz are available at www.cengagebrain.com.

The W.I.S.E. Approach to Thinking[1]

2

IN THIS CHAPTER

▶ Introducing the W.I.S.E. approach — *The acronym stands for Wonder, Investigate, Speculate, Evaluate.*

▶ Examples of problem solving — *These cases show how W.I.S.E. is used with problems.*

▶ Examples of issue resolution — *These cases show how W.I.S.E. is used with issues.*

▶ An important relationship — *Often issues are identified while solving problems, and problems while resolving issues.*

▶ A caution about bias — *Be alert for three forms of bias in your thinking.*

Scholars and practitioners of critical thinking agree that knowing the principles, habits, and skills of thinking is just the first step in becoming a critical thinker. The next step is to put this knowledge into practice. For that, you will need a strategy or approach to guide your efforts. Numerous strategies have been developed in various fields of study. Examples include "The Scientific Method," "A Sociological Heuristic," "The Process of Invention," and the "Creative Problem Solving Process."[2] Three of these strategies have seven steps, one has eight.

Having to learn a different strategy for each subject area is impractical and can be confusing. Fortunately, it is not necessary to do so. All such strategies are remarkably similar in the thinking processes they specify and even in the arrangement of steps. The strategy you will learn in this chapter is

---

[1] The W.I.S.E. approach is Copyright © 2002, 2010 by Vincent Ryan Ruggiero. The term itself and the explication presented in this chapter are used with permission.

[2] For explanations of these approaches, see, respectively: *Wikipedia*, the Free Encyclopedia, http://en.wikipedia.org/wiki/Scientific_method; James M. Henslin, *Sociology: A Down-to-Earth Approach*, 7th ed. (New York: Pearson, 2005), 144; Joseph Rossman, *The Psychology of the Inventor* (Washington, DC: The Inventor's Publishing Co., 1931), 57; Alex Osborn, *Applied Imagination* (New York: Scribner's Sons, 1957), 115.

"Every time I start to see the light, the bulb
burns out."

Mark Anderson/Andertoons.com

simpler and easier to remember than most, and it can be used for challenges
in every field of study.

INTRODUCING THE W.I.S.E. APPROACH

The W.I.S.E. approach to thinking incorporates all three kinds of thinking—
reflective, creative, and critical. It consists of four steps:

Wonder   This step entails reflecting on our experiences and observations and identifying challenges that are worth addressing. Unlike the
other steps, this one does not begin or end with particular challenges but
is ongoing.

Investigate   This step consists of gaining information about the challenges identified by wondering. It helps us gain the information and reach
the understanding needed to solve problems and resolve issues.

Speculate   This step consists of identifying possible solutions to problems
and possible resolutions of issues.

Evaluate   This step consists of testing the possible solutions to problems or the various arguments about issues and deciding which one(s) are
most worthy.

Let's look more closely at each of these steps and consider how to master
them.

GOOD THINKING!

The Story of Frank and Lillian Gilbreth

This remarkable husband and wife team, both of whom were born in 1868, became pioneers in the science of time management. As a young apprentice, Frank studied master bricklayers and noted that they all used different motions. He also noted that each of their assistants had an individual way of placing the bricks and mortar; some did less bending, reaching, and lifting than others and were more efficient.

Gilbreth realized that having all the workers imitate the more efficient ones would result in a considerable cost saving. He wondered how he could achieve maximum efficiency and, after considering various changes, decided to fit each scaffold with a shelf for the bricks and mortar and a convenient stacking system. Ultimately his changes reduced the number of motions required to lay a brick from 18 to 4 1/2. Gilbreth then became a building contractor and, later, a management engineer.

Eventually, Frank met and married Lillian, who had studied literature but then obtained a Ph.D. in industrial psychology. Both lectured at Purdue University and worked as management consultants, helping a wide variety of workers, including surgeons, save time, improve performance, and reduce fatigue. Their basic approach was to film workers at their jobs and then conduct exacting motion studies to determine optimum motion patterns.

Frank Gilbreth died in 1924. After his death, Lillian continued to use their approach to help injured individuals become productive despite their handicaps and to improve household efficiency. She died in 1972.

This amazing couple made all their contributions while raising twelve children. Their best-selling book, *Cheaper by the Dozen*, was made into a classic movie that is still shown from time to time on TV. A more recent version of their story starred Steve Martin.

For more information on the Gilbreths, see http://gilbrethnetwork.tripod.com/bio.html.

Step 1: Wonder

Almost 2,500 years ago, Socrates noted that wonder is the beginning of wisdom. What inspires wonder? One inspiration is a desire to improve things. In the early days of the railroad, tracks were made with a flange (lip) so that the trains would not fall off. Millions of tons of steel were required to make that flange. Years later, someone wondered whether there was a less expensive way of keeping cars on the tracks and eventually thought of putting flanges on the trains' *wheels* instead of the tracks. That approach has been standard ever since.[3]

An even greater spur to wonder is negative experience. For Levi Strauss the experience was *failure*. During the California Gold Rush in the mid-nineteenth century, Levi Strauss received a shipment of heavy cloth and attempted, unsuccessfully, to sell it as material for tents. He wondered how he might use all that cloth and eventually invented Levi jeans.

For Robert Kearns, the experience was *frustration*. Bothered that the slowest setting on his wipers was still too fast, requiring him to listen to the thump-thump even in light drizzle, he wondered how the annoyance might be overcome and in time invented the variable speed wiper.

For businessman Frank McNamara, the experience was *embarrassment*. One day in 1949, he was having lunch in an expensive restaurant with some friends. When he went to pay, he discovered that he had left his wallet at home and needed to call his wife and ask her to bring it to him. After wondering how to avoid such situations in the future, he invented the credit card.

One of the strongest motivations to wonder is *controversy*. Every dispute is a challenge to find the most informed and reasonable view. There are local controversies such as campus parking and grading policies, international controversies such as trade embargos, and national controversies, including health care legislation, illegal immigration, medical marijuana, the auto company bailout, Social Security privatization, vaccines for children, and the drinking age, to name but a few.

Stay alert for events or situations that you find frustrating or annoying, and listen to what people complain about in conversation. Then, instead of grumbling, wonder about how the situations can be improved. Also be alert for issues that people disagree about and recognize them as opportunities to gain new insights.

Step 2: Investigate

Investigation aims to satisfy the curiosity expressed in wondering. The focus of investigation is slightly different for problems than for issues because problems are seldom controversial,[4] whereas issues are always controversial.

Problems   In investigating a problem, the aim is to understand (1) how the process in question works or how the implementation is designed;

---

[3] George Iles, *Inventors at Work* (New York: Doubleday & Page, 1906), 370.
[4] Of course, specific proposals for *solving* problems can be controversial.

(2) why people are dissatisfied with the process or the implementation—for example, a process may be too time-consuming or an implementation may not work as intended; (3) and why previous attempts to solve the problem, if any, failed.

Issues In investigating an issue, there are two aims. The first is to acquire the evidence necessary for you to form a judgment (see Step 4). Following are the most common kinds of evidence, with a comment on the comparative reliability of each.

Anecdotes. Perhaps the most common form of evidence, anecdotes are brief or extended accounts of something that happened. If verified, they can be valuable, but tracing their origin and verifying them can be difficult. (Anecdotes often prove to be empty rumors or hoaxes.)

Eyewitness testimony. Eyewitness testimony is a report of what someone observed firsthand. Such testimony is popularly regarded as highly reliable. After all, there is something persuasive about a seemingly honest person who says "I saw it happen" and goes on to provide the details of who, how, and where. However, research has shown that eyewitness testimony is sometimes false. Preconceived notions can distort perception, and the memory of an earlier event can be corrupted by subsequent events. Therefore, eyewitness testimony varies in reliability.

Laboratory or field experiments. Laboratory experiments are performed under controlled circumstances; field experiments take place in natural surroundings. For example, one might observe a group of children at play, participants at a political convention, or Amish farmers raising a barn. For the results of the observation to be reliable, the observer must not have influenced the behavior of the group. Also, the period of observation must have been of reasonable duration. Both kinds of experiment are reliable if replicated—that is, duplicated by one or more independent sources.

Statistical studies. Statistics usually refers to quantitative information obtained about every individual in a group or category. Examples of statistics are the percentage of deaths caused by drunken driving, the comparative college admissions scores of various racial and ethnic groups, and the voting records of members of Congress. If the statistical sources are reputable, the statistics are generally highly reliable. But it is prudent to check that they are quoted accurately.

Surveys and opinion polls. This type of information is a subdivision of statistics. However, it is obtained in a special way—by a sampling of the group. The sample may be random or systematic (e.g., every 50th name in the phone book). It may also be done in person, by telephone, by post, or by email. Such sampling is generally highly reliable if these conditions are met: All members of the group must have an equal chance of being contacted, and the questions must be clear, unambiguous, and unbiased. Keep in mind that the way survey questions are phrased can influence the responses. (Caution: Surveys measure only how many people hold a viewpoint, not whether the viewpoint is correct.)

Expert opinion. This kind of testimony has the advantage of being grounded in extensive knowledge of the subject and understanding of what is typical in most cases. This kind of evidence can be highly reliable, especially if the opinion is shared by most experts. (Remember, though, that experts are human and can be mistaken even when they agree.)

Research reviews. Research reviews examine the general body of research information on a topic. It is not uncommon for such a review to cover dozens, even hundreds, of independent research studies. When research reviews do not omit any significant studies, they are among the most highly reliable types of evidence.

The second aim of investigation is to identify the conflicting arguments about the issue. An argument is defined as a rationale or line of reasoning consisting or two or more assertions[5] that are offered as true, plus a conclusion that purportedly follows logically from them. When members of Congress disagree over a piece of legislation, they offer conflicting arguments. So do prosecution and defense attorneys when they make their summations to the jury, and scholars when they engage in formal debate. Arguments can vary in length from a single sentence to a brief essay or even to a 400-page book. Complex arguments contain a network of assertions.

As you examine the arguments people present on an issue, you will encounter the evidence they believe supports their assertions. (The types of evidence will be the same as those listed previously.) Responsible individuals will offer significant, and often substantial, evidence. Irresponsible individuals will offer little or no evidence, sometimes because of carelessness, and sometimes because they mistakenly believe that their ideas deserve to be accepted on their own say-so.

The more thorough your investigation, the more prepared you will be for the next step, speculation. Remember that the purpose of investigation is to *understand* and not to judge. Judgment is a separate step and comes later. (Note: The next chapter explains how to conduct investigations. Feel free to look ahead to that chapter if you have any questions.)

---

[5]Logicians call such assertions *premises*.

GOOD THINKING!

The Story of Elizabeth Loftus

The majority of men and women engaged in scholarly research are not invited to the talk shows or written about in popular magazines, even when their work has a significant effect on people's lives. Psychologist Elizabeth Loftus is an exception. One reason is that her research has challenged some longstanding beliefs about human memory. Another is the relevance of that research to some prominent controversies of the last decade or two.

The traditional view is that memory is like a videotaped record of events etched into the grooves of our minds. According to this theory, a particular record may become hidden, even from ourselves, but it is never lost. Given our desire and, in some cases, the assistance of people experienced in recovering such "data," we can recover any memory, however traumatic. And what we recover will be accurate to the smallest detail.

A number of researchers have challenged this traditional view of memory, but none as effectively as Loftus. She devised her own research projects and proved that real memories can be altered, and that fictitious memories can be created. In experiments with children and adults, she first showed them short films and later discussed their recollections of what they saw. In one experiment, by merely asking "Did you see a bear?" or "Did you see a boat?" she was able to make them remember details that were not present in the film.

In another case, by using the word "smash" instead of "hit" she was able to change people's estimate of the speed of cars *and* to create a memory of broken glass where there had been none.

For more information on Elizabeth Loftus, see Elizabeth Loftus and Katherine Ketcham, *Witness for the Defense* (New York: St. Martin's Press, 1991) or Elizabeth Loftus, *Eyewitness Testimony* (Cambridge, MA: Harvard University Press, 1996).

Step 3: Speculate

The aim of this step is to consider, in light of your investigation, various responses to the problem or issue. Because of the difference between problems and issues, we will discuss each separately.

Problems   With problems, speculation aims at identifying a broad range of possible solutions. Begin by asking a variety of "How can . . . ?" questions. (These questions are recommended because, unlike others, they point to solutions.) Take, for example, the problem of communicating with people over distances. During America's westward expansion, the problem was expressed, "How can we expedite mail delivery to the West Coast?" That question led to development of the Pony Express. Another question, "How can we communicate messages without transporting them?" led to an even better solution—the invention of the telegraph. Slightly different "How can . . . ?" questions led to other communications innovations, including the typewriter, the telephone, the computer, and the Internet.

Consider, too, the problem hotels had with long checkout lines during peak morning hours. Managers asked, "How can we handle the long lines at the checkout desk more efficiently?" and thought of adding clerks and posting "Be sure to allow time for checkout" reminders in guests' rooms. But only when managers dared to ask the seemingly outrageous question "How can we eliminate the formal checkout procedure altogether?" did they think of placing the final bill under the door on the day of checkout and offering instant video display of guests' accounts on the TV screen.

When the massive oil spill occurred in the Gulf of Mexico in early 2010, the questions asked included "How can the break in the pipe be sealed?" "How can the spilled oil be captured?" "How can the oil be prevented from reaching the coastal areas?" "How can animals caught in the oil be saved?" and "How can people whose businesses have been harmed by the spill be compensated?"

Notice that each "How can . . . ?" question in the previous paragraphs opened a different avenue of thought and thus led to a different kind of solution. So, be sure to ask many different "How can . . . ?" questions. The key to doing so is to choose your verbs carefully. For example, if the problem concerns a process (such as registering for classes), you might ask "How can we *simplify* the process?" "How can we *speed up* the process?" and "How can we *shorten* delays in the process?" For other types of problems, you might choose verbs such as *combine, reduce, eliminate, repair, streamline,* or *enhance.*

After you have expressed the problem in a number of "How can . . . ?" questions, think of as many possible answers as you can for each question. The first answers you think of are likely to be common and predictable, but if you persevere, you will produce some uncommon and therefore more interesting possibilities. As people familiar with the technique of brainstorming will tell you, it is best to separate this idea *production* from idea *evaluation* (Step 4 of the W.I.S.E. process). The reason is that stopping to evaluate each idea breaks the flow of thought and necessitates beginning again. Also, be sure to devote sufficient time to idea production. The more possible solutions you consider, the better your chances of producing a satisfactory, or even a great, one. Skimping on idea production will lessen your chances of solving the problem.

Issues With issues, speculation aims at considering possible resolutions of the controversy. (These possibilities will be compared and narrowed down in the final stage, evaluation.) First, summarize the arguments on both sides of the issue, as revealed in your investigation. Keep in mind that there may be a number of different arguments for both the pro and the con side of an issue. In some cases you may be able to think of new arguments that you did not encounter in your investigation; summarize these too. Include in each summary the main assertions and the conclusion.

Next, turn all the conflicting assertions and conclusions into questions, using words like "Is?" "Does?" "Could? "Should?" and "Would?" The advantage of this approach is that it forces you to analyze every assertion and not simply *assume* that the ones you are most familiar with are correct. (This assumption, common among careless thinkers, is a serious obstacle to critical thinking.)

The simplest way to perform these steps is by dividing a sheet of paper into three columns. Figure 2.1 illustrates this approach with three examples, each from a different issue.

Step 4: Evaluate

The aim of this step is to decide on the best solution to the problem or resolution of the issue.

Problems For problems, review all the possible solutions you produced in response to your "How can . . . ?" questions and decide which is the *best* solution. For example, for the problem of the Gulf oil spill, there were many possible solutions offered for *each* of the main questions—"How can the break in the pipe be sealed?" "How can the spilled oil be captured?" "How can the oil be prevented from reaching the coastal areas?" "How can animals caught in the oil be saved?" and "How can people whose businesses have been harmed by the spill be compensated?"

Next, test the possible solutions against the relevant criteria and decide which solution is best. Here is a comprehensive list of criteria helpful in finding solutions to problems. (Some may not apply to the particular problem you are addressing.) After considering the relevant criteria, decide which of your possible solutions best fits them.

Comprehensiveness. Will any of these solutions solve the entire problem? If not, which one will solve most of it?

Longevity. Which solution is likely to last the longest? In the case of products, the kind of materials and their design will be relevant.

Practicality. Which solution is the most workable? Simplest? Least confusing? In the case of a product, how simple or complex will its function be? In the case of a process, how many steps will be required to perform it?

Safety. Which solution is safest—in other words, which poses the least risk to those involved in its implementation?

Efficiency. Which solution requires the least time and effort to implement? For example, which involves the fewest steps and the fewest people to implement it?

Economy. Which solution costs the least? Both the initial cost and the continuing cost should be considered. Sometimes the initial cost—say, for training of staff—may be low, but the continuing cost—say for salaries and utilities—may be prohibitively high.

Compatibility. Which solution is most compatible with existing approaches and procedures?

Appearance. If the solution is something that will be seen—for example, a product—does it have aesthetic appeal?

Morale. Which solution will have the most positive (or least negative) effect on the people involved in implementing it?

Legality and morality. Which solution is most consistent with existing legal obligations and moral requirements—for example, to people and the environment.

Issues For issues, your goal is to find the most defensible point of view. To do this you must decide which assertions are true, and which conclusion flows logically from those assertions. The most defensible view may be exactly what someone has already expressed, or a different view that you construct from the insights on both sides of the issue.

Begin by addressing each of the questions you raised about the various arguments (as illustrated in Figure 2.1). In the case of an assertion, check the kind and quality of the evidence that was offered in support, or that you discovered.

For **anecdotes**, consider: Is the author's presentation of the anecdote or case faithful to the facts? If so, are the experiences described typical or untypical? How plausible are they? Are they verifiable?

For **eyewitness testimony**, consider: Does the person have anything to gain by misrepresenting the facts? Were the conditions favorable to observation—for example, did the event occur in the day or at night, in good weather or bad? Did the event occur slowly or quickly? Was the person in a state of mind conducive to accurate observation? Could the person's memory have been confused by something that occurred after the event but before the testimony was given?

For a **laboratory experiment**, consider: Have the findings of the experiment been confirmed by other, independent researchers?

For a **field experiment**, consider: Did the presence of the investigator influence the outcome?

FIGURE 2.1

Sample Arguments	Counterarguments	Relevant Questions
Issue 1: Self-esteem is essential to learning. High self-esteem increases academic achievement; low self-esteem decreases academic achievement. Certain educational practices tend to lower self-esteem—for example, criticizing students' thought and expression on essay questions and withholding credit for wrong answers on math questions. Therefore, such practices should be abandoned.	**Issue 1:** Self-esteem is not essential to learning. The level of self-esteem, whether high or low, has no significant effect on academic achievement. Practices such as criticizing students' thought and expression on essay questions and withholding credit for wrong answers on math questions help students correct their mistakes and learn. Therefore, such practices should be encouraged.	**Issue 1:** Is self-esteem essential to learning? Does high self-esteem increase achievement? Does low self-esteem decrease it? Do criticism of essay answers and losing credit for wrong answers lower self-esteem? Are such practices harmful or helpful? Should they be abandoned or encouraged?
Issue 2: Spanking is a form of violence. Its consequences are always negative. It teaches children that aggression is a legitimate response and that might makes right. Anyone who is spanked in childhood is more likely than others to be an abusive spouse and parent in adulthood. Therefore, parents who spank their children are guilty of child abuse and should be so charged.	**Issue 2:** Spanking is not a form of violence. If done without anger when children are young, it can have a positive influence. It teaches that actions have consequences and that we must take responsibility for what we say and do. Children who are spanked in a context of love and caring are likely to be more respectful of rules and others' rights in adulthood. Their parents deserve our appreciation.	**Issue 2:** Is spanking a form of violence? Are its consequences positive or negative? Do the circumstances matter? Does it teach children that aggression is legitimate and might makes right or that they are responsible for their behavior? Are those who are spanked more likely to be better or worse in adulthood for the experience? Is spanking equivalent to child abuse? Should it be discouraged or encouraged?
Issue 3: In all forms of athletic competition, injuries can occur. But in boxing alone, injuring the opponent is the very purpose of the contest. Furthermore, no amount of training and no protective gear can control the risk of serious injury. Therefore, boxing is not a sport but a form of brutality, and it should be outlawed.	**Issue 3:** Boxing is one of the most ancient forms of athletic competition. Like other forms, it demands coordination, quick reflexes, and high levels of strategy. Before boxers are permitted to compete, they must undergo rigorous training and be cleared by medical doctors. To outlaw boxing would be a disservice to the many poor people for whom it has provided a livelihood.	**Issue 3:** Is boxing an ancient form of competition? Does it demand coordination, quick reflexes, and high levels of strategy? Are boxers rigorously trained and examined medically? Do more injuries occur in boxing than in other competitions? Is injuring one's opponent the boxer's aim? Do training and gear offer sufficient protection? Is boxing properly classified as a sport? Would outlawing boxing be a disservice to the poor? Should boxing be outlawed?

For **statistical evidence**, consider: Is the source of the data reliable? How long ago were the statistics compiled? Have conditions changed since then?

For a **survey** or **opinion poll**, consider: Was the sample representative of the larger group? Were the questions clear and objective? For mail surveys, did too few people respond for the survey results to be trusted?

For **expert opinion**, consider: Does the person have specific expertise in the subject in question? (It is not uncommon these days for experts to offer opinions far outside their areas of expertise.) Does the expert's view represent the majority or minority view among experts in the field? In other words, do other experts agree with the person in question?

For a **research review**, consider: Were any important studies omitted?

When the evidence supporting an assertion is both sufficient and credible, you should accept it. (It is not uncommon to find that each side of the dispute has some correct and some mistaken assertions.) When you have finished checking all the assertions and identified those that are true to the facts, your final step is to determine what conclusion they best support—in other words, the most worthy viewpoint on the issue.

If at this point the W.I.S.E. approach seems formidable, it is only because of the explanatory material necessary to introduce it and answer the most obvious questions. As with any other new process, once you become familiar with it, you will appreciate how easy it is to use.

EXAMPLES OF PROBLEM SOLVING

Any number of examples could be offered to show the relevance of the W.I.S.E. approach to problem solving, but space limitations permit only two.[6]

The uncooperative page markers

Art Fry was a chemical engineer employed in the product development department of 3M Corporation. However, his best-known breakthrough idea didn't occur in the workplace but in his church choir.

Fry enjoyed singing in his church's choir and, like members of choirs everywhere, was in the habit of marking the scheduled hymns with little

---

[6] I am not suggesting that the individuals in the problem and issue examples *consciously employed* the W.I.S.E. approach. (How could they have? It was developed after the achievements noted here.) I am saying, rather, that their cases *exemplify its relevance* to real life challenges.

pieces of paper. This way he could turn to the appropriate hymn quickly and be ready to sing when the choirmaster gave the signal. Unfortunately, the little pieces of paper had a way of falling out, leaving him to hurriedly flip through the pages searching for the correct hymn.

Fry wondered how he could get the slips of paper to stick to the page so that they wouldn't fall out but could be easily removed when he was through with them. He remembered a peculiar adhesive a fellow researcher had concocted a few years earlier. At that time no one had been able to think of a use for it.

Fry checked the files, got the formula, and made a batch of adhesive. It turned out to be too strong for his purposes. So he experimented with the formula and finally produced a glue that was like the little bear's porridge in the Goldilocks story—not too strong, not too weak, but just right. He took the idea to management and got approval to test-market the sample product, and the "Post-it®" was born.

The librarian's lament

Imagine how difficult it would be to use a library if there were no system for shelving the books. If you wanted a particular book, you'd have no idea how to find it. It might be on the top shelf of aisle #1, the bottom shelf of aisle #40, or anywhere in between. The larger the library, the more difficult it would be to use. A large university library would be virtually *impossible* to use.

The situation was never quite that bad, but up until 1876 the system in use was inflexible and cumbersome. Each book had a designated place on the library shelves. A book on astronomy might be between a book on woodworking and another on medieval architecture. To make matters worse, each library had its own system.

Melvil Dewey, a student assistant in the Amherst College library, lamented the difficulty of reshelving books. He wondered if there were a better way, and set out to devise one. His investigation and experimentation led to the system known as the Dewey decimal system.

The Dewey system has ten main divisions: 000 is Computers, information, and general reference; 100, Philosophy and psychology; 200, Religion; 300, Social sciences; 400, Language; 500, Science; 600, Technology; 700, Arts and recreation; 800, Literature; 900 History and geography. Each division has a series of subdivisions. Dewey's system made the library much easier to use. Today Dewey's system is used in more than 135 countries and has been translated into more than 30 languages. It is also proving useful in classifying Internet resources.[7]

---

[7] For more information on Melvil Dewey, see www.oclc.org/dewey/resources/biography.

EXAMPLES OF ISSUE RESOLUTION

Is venting anger healthy?

For centuries, the prevailing view was that, though it can sometimes be appropriate to express anger, as an everyday rule it is better to suppress it. But in the 1960s and 1970s a dramatically different view became popular among many psychologists and the general public—the view that suppressing anger is emotionally unhealthy. "Express your anger," the experts said, "and it will dissipate, and with it a lot of harmful tension, stress, and even neurosis."

Carol Tavris, a psychologist, wondered about this issue: Was the centuries old view, with its emphasis on restraint, really so mistaken? Are people who control their urges and treat others with civility really in danger of becoming neurotic?

She set out to answer these and related questions by conducting her own observational studies and by consulting others' research into anger and its effects. She noticed that people expressing anger seem to grow angrier, not calmer. Moreover, research confirmed her observation and proved that "talking out an emotion doesn't reduce it, [but instead] . . . rehearses it." The research also established that overexpressed anger is more likely to contribute to disease, in particular heart disease, than is suppressed anger.

In reviewing her considerable research, Tavris concluded that the belief that expressing anger promotes health is a combination of misunderstanding, oversimplification, and myth. The appropriate use of anger, she decided, "requires an awareness of choice and an embrace of reason. It is knowing when to become angry. . . and when to make peace; when to take action and when to keep silent. . . ."[8]

What causes yellow fever?

By 1900 the United States had suffered 90 epidemics of yellow fever. One in 1793 killed 10 percent of the population of Philadelphia. Napoleon reportedly sold the Louisiana Territory to the United States because the disease claimed 90 percent of the forces he had stationed there. The disease began with chills and a headache, then progressed to severe pain, high fever, and vomiting. Next came jaundice, followed in extreme cases by internal bleeding and death.

For a long time medical experts disagreed about the cause of the disease. Some said it was bacterial; others thought it was transmitted by insects. In time the former view prevailed, but outbreaks of the disease continued. Walter Reed, a young army surgeon who was also trained in bacteriology and pathology, noted that one member of a family would be stricken while

---

[8] For more information on this issue, see Carol Tavris, *Anger: The Misunderstood Emotion* (New York: Simon & Schuster, 1982).

others were not. Noting that the disease was neither contagious nor airborne, he wondered if the older, discredited view might be correct.

Reed's investigation took the form of an ingenious experiment. He had one group of army volunteers sleep on the clothing and beds of yellow fever patients in a screened room (to keep mosquitoes out). No one in this group became infected. Meanwhile, he kept another group completely apart from infected people and their belongings. But this group he exposed to mosquitoes that had been in the rooms of infected people. These volunteers became infected.

Having proved how yellow fever was transmitted, Reed had the army install mosquito nets and wipe out mosquito breeding grounds in and around Havana. These efforts were so successful in ending the scourge that the same approach was used in Panama, thus removing a major obstacle to the construction of the Panama Canal.

Walter Reed was awarded the Congressional Medal of Honor for his contribution to the eradication of yellow fever. He also became the first physician to be elected to the Hall of Fame of Great Americans at New York University. The Walter Reed Army Medical Center in Washington DC is named after him.[9]

AN IMPORTANT RELATIONSHIP

Because of the differences in dealing with problems and issues, we have separated them. But it is important to understand that we often find problems while dealing with issues, and vice versa. The following example will clarify this relationship.

Suppose that on your way to work each day you drive by a defunct low-cost apartment project. When new, it was heralded as a great step forward in meeting the needs of the poor. Now it is a monument to failure. You see graffiti on the walls, boarded-up entrances, broken windows, and garbage and other litter on the lawns. In short, it is an eyesore that cries out for demolition.

You begin to *wonder*: Why didn't it succeed? Is this project typical or atypical of government programs? You realize that this is an issue rather than a problem because it evokes conflicting responses. (You probably have heard or read some of the responses.) Intrigued, you *investigate*. First you check the origin of the housing project and find that it was part of the Great Society program of the 1960s and 1970s, a massive attempt to wipe out poverty. Digging deeper, you find that implementing the program cost hundreds of billions of dollars without having any lasting effect on poverty, and that it has supported a number of food and medical assistance programs as well as low-cost housing projects. You learn, too, that many housing projects have gone

---

[9] For more information on Walter Reed, see www.wramc.amedd.army.mil/welcome/history/index1.htm.

through the same stages as this one—that is, they first became run-down, then drug- and gang-infested, and finally scheduled for demolition.

Next you *speculate* about the possible reasons for the failure of the government's efforts to help the poor. Perhaps the programs are at fault. For example, they might be insufficiently funded or poorly designed and managed, in which case they would need to be redesigned, more generously funded, or placed under different (perhaps private) management. Or perhaps the people being helped lacked certain attitudes and skills necessary for self-sufficiency and successful living. The programs might have done little if anything to remedy this deficiency or might even have aggravated the condition. For example, the programs might have contributed to a welfare mentality, characterized by the feeling among the poor that the government has an obligation to provide them with food, shelter, and clothing and that this provision is a right they need not work for or otherwise earn.

Finally, you *evaluate* by determining which explanation for the government's failure is most reasonable in light of the evidence. Is it insufficient funding, poor program design, ineffective management, the counterproductive effect of increasing poor people's dependency, or some other explanation?[10]

At this point, the W.I.S.E. approach will have enabled you to reach an informed opinion about the *issue* of public welfare. Moreover, in the process of doing so, it will have identified several *problems*—the difficulty of improving housing management, eliminating drug trafficking in public housing, overcoming the welfare mentality. You might be content to leave those problems to others, but if you want to solve them, you again would use the W.I.S.E. approach. Of course, there would be no need to repeat the first step because your analysis of the issue would have provided the necessary perspective. Thus, you would begin by investigating the particular problem more deeply, then speculate about possible solutions, and finally evaluate the solutions and choose the best one.

In this example, addressing the issue with the W.I.S.E. approach led to identifying (and perhaps solving) related problems. In other cases, the procedure might be reversed—that is, addressing a problem with the W.I.S.E. approach might lead you to identify issues that need to be resolved.

A CAUTION ABOUT BIAS

When you evaluate an argument, the greatest obstacle to critical thinking is not the complexity of the issue or the variety of viewpoints to be considered. It is, instead, your own biases. Here is a fairly typical example of how bias can stifle critical thinking.

---

[10] The best explanation could be *a combination* of these deficiencies.

Let's say you just read an article pointing out the deficiencies of home-schooling. Most parents who homeschool, the author says, are not trained teachers, and some have not even graduated from college. In addition, the author points out that even if the parent is a certified teacher, he or she is not likely to be skilled in art, music, *and* foreign languages, and will be unable to provide lab experience at home. Finally, the author argues that children who are homeschooled are deprived of opportunities for socializing with peers. Thus, in his view, they are woefully unprepared to relate to people of other religions and cultures.

Now suppose that you know little about homeschooling other than what you just read. Suppose, too, that you have graduated from public school, believe your experience there was positive, and therefore support tradi-tional classroom education. Given these facts, your bias would be almost imperceptible—nothing more than a slight leaning. Not enough to put you on alert, yet enough to cause you to accept the author's assessment at face value *without bothering to investigate the opposing viewpoint*.

If even a slight, subtle bias can keep you from thinking critically, imag-ine what a more substantial bias will do.

Incidentally, in the homeschooling issue (as in all controversial issues), there *is* another side to be considered. Creative homeschoolers have discov-ered ways to overcome or compensate for the lack of laboratories and other limitations. Homeschooled students often score as well as, and in some cases better than, public and private school graduates and are as respectful of other people as traditional graduates are.

No one has yet formulated an antibias serum, so inoculation is not a choice. The best you can do is to recognize bias when it arises and develop ways of resisting it. The sections that follow present the most common types of bias and suggestions for dealing with them.

Bias toward what confirms your personal view

We all tend to be protective of our opinions. This is true whether we reason them out or borrow them from others. Whenever we encounter information that confirms one of our opinions, our automatic reaction is to accept it. Similarly, we tend to reject information that challenges our opinions. *Sugges-tion:* Keep in mind that we all make mistakes now and then. The sooner we find out we've made a mistake, the better off we are. And the best way to find a mistake early is to be open to ideas that challenge our own.

Bias toward familiar ideas

Suppose you walked into a cafeteria and had the choice of sitting with people you know or with strangers. Which would you choose? No doubt you would choose people you know because you'd feel more relaxed and comfortable with them. It's the same way with ideas. All of us tend to be more accepting of ideas we've heard before than we are of new ideas. *Suggestion:* Remember that familiarity has little significance—the order in which we hear ideas and the frequency of our hearing them are matters of chance. The fact that we've heard something repeated a dozen times doesn't mean it is any more reliable than something we are hearing for the first time.

Bias toward your likes and against your dislikes

We all have our personal preferences. There's nothing wrong with that. The problem arises only when we let them interfere with our judgment. If someone shares your taste in television programming, you may see her as a person of great wisdom and taste. In contrast, anyone who speaks critically of your favorite programming may seem unintelligent and perhaps intentionally offensive. *Suggestion:* Even strongly held views can be mistaken, so carry your preferences lightly and be ready to question them in light of new evidence.

EXERCISES

2.1. A classmate says to you, "I'm not too clear about the difference between a problem and an issue." Write a brief clarification for her.

2.2. Do this exercise in wondering over a period of hours or even a day. Be alert for problems and issues—not just those that affect you personally but those that you hear being discussed or reported in the news. (*Tip:* Problems are revealed in the annoyance or frustration you or others experience with things or situations; issues are revealed in clashing points of view.) Keep a list of your findings and have them ready to share with others in class.

2.3. The history of writing instruments includes many breakthrough ideas. Visit the following website: www.ringpen.com/history.html. Select five inventions, and express the "How can . . . ?" question that led to each.

2.4. Visit the following website, which gives timelines of great achievements in the twentieth century: www.greatachievements.org. Choose a subject—telephone or airplane, for example. Then look over the achievements and reconstruct the specific "How can . . . ?" question that would have led to that achievement.

2.5. Each of the following statements describes a problem. Think of as many "How can . . . ?" expressions as you can for each. (Remember that each expression opens a different line of thought, so the more you can think of, the more possible solutions will result.) Then list as many possible solutions as you can for each expression.

a) The downtown area of your city has become dangerous after dusk. The number of assaults and muggings has risen dramatically in recent years. Particularly vulnerable are people whose work requires them to be there in the evening.

b) The parking area at Progress College is too small to accommodate the cars of students, faculty, and staff. As a result, late arrival for class and for work has increased, morale has declined, and violations of parking rules have become common.

c) Driving under the influence of alcohol or drugs continues to cause serious injury and death despite many public and private initiatives to solve the problem.

d) Many people believe that the contributions they made to Social Security over the years are gathering interest in a safe fund and that the contributions of today's workers are sufficient to maintain the fund. In reality, since 1965 the money in the fund has been appropriated for other purposes, and the fund now contains only a pile of IOUs. Also, the ratio of Social Security contributors to retirees has dropped from 16 to 1 in 1940 to 4 to 1 in 2000. By 2030, it is projected to be just 2 to 1.[11]

2.6. Select one of the *problems* you listed in your response to Exercise 2.2. Apply the W.I.S.E. approach to solving it. Record your work for all four steps, and be prepared to give a short presentation in class.

2.7. Select one of the *issues* you listed in your response to Exercise 2.2. Apply the W.I.S.E. approach to resolving it. Record your work for all four steps, and be prepared to give a short presentation in class.

2.8. Figure 2.1 in this chapter presented arguments and counterarguments for three issues: self-esteem, spanking, and boxing. Select one of those issues, and then apply the W.I.S.E. approach to resolving it. Record your work for all four steps; be prepared to give a short presentation in class or to engage in debate with classmates who disagree with your view.

2.9. The following issues are the subject of current, often vigorous debate. Select one, then apply the W.I.S.E. approach to resolving it. Record your work for all four steps; be prepared to give a short presentation in class or to engage in debate with classmates who disagree with your view.

a) School voucher programs provide parents with state or federal dollars to pay for schooling at institutions of the parents' choosing. Many people favor such programs, but many others are strongly opposed to them.

b) In *Kelo* v. *City of New London*, the U.S. Supreme Court upheld the City of New London's use of "eminent domain" to seize private homes and thereby permit commercial development of the land. There is widespread disagreement over the wisdom of this decision.

c) The issue of whether illegal immigrants should be granted amnesty is so emotion-laden that it has sparked a separate controversy over the term "illegal immigrants," with some people arguing for the term "undocumented workers" instead. (You may choose either of these issues.)

---

[11] James M. Henslin, *Sociology: A Down-to-Earth Approach*, 7th ed. (New York: Pearson, 2005), 375.

d) Opinion is divided over whether it is appropriate for senators and members of Congress to be guided by their religious beliefs and values in performing the duties of public office.

e) Many commentators claim that the media employ a harsher, more judgmental standard in their treatment of Christianity than in their treatment of other religions, notably Islam. Others disagree.

f) The issue of segregated college housing has a confusing history. At one time it was standard practice, then it was rejected as illegal and immoral, and now many people regard it as a natural and wholesome expression of diversity. Others believe that any such segregation, whether along racial, ethnic, or religious lines, is inappropriate on college campuses.

g) The research of Alfred Kinsey on sexuality, which helped to launch the "sexual revolution," was long thought to be solidly scientific. Many people still believe it to be so. Others, however, have argued that its methodology was so biased and flawed that it is not scientific at all.

h) Some people claim that the best federal tax system would be what they call the "fair tax." Others argue for a "flat tax." Yet many are satisfied with the present progressive tax system.

i) In 2010 Arizona Governor Jan Brewer signed into law a measure known as SB1070, which permitted police to ask for proof of immigration status from anyone detained for another violation. In the ensuing controversy, critics of the legislation labeled it racist, whereas supporters claimed it merely follows existing federal provisions.

j) Psychologists disagree over whether "traumatic amnesia" is a genuine natural phenomenon. (The condition is also known as "repressed memory" and "dissociative amnesia.") Some say the phenomenon is a natural condition; others deny it exists; still others assert that though the condition may exist, it has been seriously overdiagnosed.

k) For a long time it was widely accepted that living together before marriage reduced the chance of divorce. Yet some researchers have found reason to question that idea.

l) People have long debated the comparative effectiveness of homeschooling. Proponents claim it achieves results superior to those of traditional classroom instruction in public or private schools. Others dispute that view.

2.10. Two main causes of divorce are carelessness in selecting a marriage partner and ignorance of the demands of marriage and parenthood. In many cases, the home, the school, and the church are not meeting the challenge of preparing young people for marriage. Treat this situation as a problem, apply the W.I.S.E. approach, and either write a composition presenting your view or be prepared to debate the issue in class.

2.11. In recent years there has been a growing trend for government agencies to ban certain things, and require others, for the public good. For example, New York City banned large soft drinks and trans fats in restaurant food; San Francisco banned toys from fast-food meals. Many municipalities have banned smoking in public places; some have even banned bake sales and lemonade stands. And the Department of Agriculture issued new requirements for school meals that included providing fruits and vegetables and "grain-rich foods," substituting low-fat or fat-free milk for whole milk, and "limiting calories based on the age of children." Use the W.I.S.E. approach to research this issue and decide whether you support having the government ban things. Either write a composition presenting your view or be prepared to debate the issue in class.

2.12. What lessons can you draw from the Good Thinking profiles of Frank and Lillian Gilbreth and Elizabeth Loftus presented in this chapter? Explain how you can use each of those lessons in your career or personal life.

QUIZ

1. What does the acronym W.I.S.E. stand for?

2. List two advantages of the W.I.S.E. approach.

3. Name four things that lead to wondering.

4. One reason to investigate a problem is to determine the reason for people's dissatisfaction. True or false?

5. Name five kinds of evidence.

6. One type of evidence is perfectly reliable in all circumstances. True or false?

7. An argument, as defined in the chapter, is a quarrel between two people. True or false?

8. The W.I.S.E. approach is used somewhat differently for problems than for issues. True or false?

9. Sometimes problems give rise to issues, and vice versa. True or false?

10. Name the three kinds of bias you should avoid in evaluating arguments.

Answers to this quiz are available at www.cengagebrain.com.

Improving Your Investigative Skills

3

Chapter 2 introduced the W.I.S.E. approach to thinking—Wonder, Investigate, Speculate, Evaluate. In this chapter, we will look more closely at the second step, Investigate, because it has several components, each with special strategies. But before doing that, let's address more basic considerations.

DECIDING WHAT TO INVESTIGATE

In Chapter 1 we discussed the case of a New York newspaper, the *Journal News*, publishing the names of legal gun owners living in surrounding counties. Their action caused a number of unintended consequences and led to widespread condemnation. Despite their good intentions, their action was a classic example of poor thinking. We mentioned seven questions which, if asked, would have led them to reconsider their plan and avoid the harm it caused.

Those questions should have been asked before finalizing the plan of action, but another set of questions should have occurred *much earlier*—before the investigating stage, when the editors were first wondering about the issue. The following are among the most important of those questions.

Is it possible that gun ownership is not the only, or even the main, problem? What other factors may have caused or contributed to the epidemic of mass shootings? These questions would have helped the editors avoid tunnel vision—that is, the narrow perspective that evidently blinded them to other perspectives and insights. It would also have opened a different and more meaningful line of investigation than "Who are the registered gun owners in our area?"

This different line of investigation would have identified at least two other possible causes or contributing factors of violence in society: violent entertainment (movies, TV, and video games) and the side effects of prescription drugs.

Is there any evidence that these possible causes or contributing factors might be as important as, or even more important than, the increase in the number of guns? Investigating this would have produced considerable data, including the following:

Violent entertainment. In *The Early Window* (1988), Robert Liebert and Joyce Sprafkin reviewed hundreds of research studies on the effects of TV violence. In addition they examined several other research reviews. One of those reviews pooled the findings of 67 separate studies conducted over a twenty-year period. Another examined 230 studies. These research reviews agreed in concluding that there is a clear and unmistakable "causal relationship" between the viewing of TV violence and antisocial behavior and attitudes.

In *Adolescents and the Media* (Sage, 1995, pp. 19, 20), Victor Strasburger identified "more than 1,000 studies and reviews in the literature [that] point to media violence as one *cause* of real-life violence," and noted that one researcher concluded that "long-term exposure to television is a causal factor in approximately half of all homicides in the United States; therefore, 10,000 homicides could be prevented annually if television were less violent."

Side effects of prescription drugs. In 2010, three researchers—Thomas J. Moore of the Institute for Safe Medication Practices, Joseph Glenmullen of Harvard University, and Curt Furberg of Wake Forest University—published a study titled "Prescription Drugs Associated with Reports of Violence Toward Others." (See http://www.plosone.org/article/info%3Adoi%2F10.1371%2Fjournal.pone.0015337, accessed 8/29/2013.) The study, conducted over a five-year period, identified 31 drugs with a "disproportionate association with violence." Many of those drugs are prescribed for common conditions such as tobacco addiction, depression, and attention deficit disorder. The researchers concluded that "[the] data provide new evidence that acts of violence toward others are a genuine and serious adverse drug event that is associated with a relatively small group of drugs." The report identifies the drugs by name and includes references to 22 related studies and scholarly articles.

If these questions had been asked in the wondering stage, as they should have been, the editors might have decided that legal gun ownership, if significant to the issue of mass shootings at all, is much less significant—and less newsworthy—than violent entertainment and the side effects of prescription drugs.

This case serves as a vivid reminder of the value of the wondering stage in the W.I.S.E. approach.

FUNDAMENTALS OF INVESTIGATING

Before turning to the kinds of investigation and the strategies associated with them, it is worthwhile to identify three key approaches that will increase your effectiveness in all of them.

Put aside your own views and opinions while reading or listening. This is seldom easy. And the greater the difference between what the writer or speaker is saying and what you believe, the harder it is. As soon as you encounter something you disagree with, you will naturally think, "Wait a minute. This is wrong. The right idea is . . . ," and you will be strongly tempted to think about how you can defend your idea. Giving in to that temptation means abandoning the task at hand—understanding what you are reading or hearing. If you do give in, then later, when the time arrives to refer to what you read or heard, you literally won't know what you are talking about! So resist that temptation and pay attention.

Identify the main point or points the person is making and the evidence offered in support of them. The structure of the expression will often help you answer these questions. For example, in the statement, "I believe that . . . for two reasons . . . ," what follows "believe that" is the main idea and what follows "reasons" is the evidence. The evidence may vary from a single simple item to a long and complex series of points, even entire chapters in the case of a book.

The words "believe" and "reason" are not always used, of course. The person may say "I propose . . . because . . ." instead. Sometimes no signal words are used. In such cases, you will have to get the sense of the passage and then answer these questions: What position or viewpoint is the person taking? Why does the person believe that view is preferable to other, competing views?

Be alert for two kinds of statements—those of fact and those of interpretation or opinion. Chapter 1 discussed both in some detail. Take note of both kinds of statements as you are reading or listening. Don't be surprised if some statements of fact seem mistaken or some interpretations or opinions seem flawed. That may prove to be the case. But do *not* evaluate them while you are reading/listening. Make evaluation a separate task performed after you fully understand the view you are reading or hearing.

CONDUCTING LIBRARY RESEARCH

Research is merely a matter of finding information, and all that is necessary in any given situation is to identify relevant sources of information and then consult them. Following are the most basic information sources. The best library source is the professional staff. Ask your campus librarian to help you identify the sources listed below and answer any other research questions.

For a broad overview of a subject: an encyclopedia. An encyclopedia is a compendium of information about a wide variety of topics and is therefore a good starting point for research. Each article is written by a person or persons with specific knowledge of that subject.

For statistical data and miscellaneous facts: an almanac. The best-known almanacs include *The World Almanac* and *Information Please Almanac*.

For newspaper reports: The New York Times Index. This index is the standard newspaper index for the United States. It covers all stories that appeared in that newspaper from 1851 to the present.

Najlah Feanny/Corbis

For general magazines and journals: Reader's Guide to Periodical Literature. The *Reader's Guide* is an index of articles published in popular magazines.

For specialized periodicals: an appropriate index. Specialized indexes provide information on articles in scholarly journals comparable to the information *Reader's Guide* provides about popular articles.

For government publications: a state or federal monthly catalog. State and federal governments publish more documents than any other publishing source.

For abstracts of scholarly works: an appropriate database or abstract service. These sources offer summaries of scholarly articles in various fields.

For library holdings: your library's computer catalog. This source is your key to the books, tapes, monographs, and other materials available in your library. If you are looking for a specific title that is not available in your library, your librarian will usually be able to obtain it from another library. You can also visit your college's official website.

GOOD THINKING!

The Richard Feynman Story

Could solving difficult math and physics problems be *fun*? It was for Richard P. Feynman. Born and raised in Far Rockaway, New York, he spent his childhood satisfying what he called his *puzzle drive* in activities such as building a motor, studying paramecia and bugs under the microscope, and devising experiments to learn how ants found their way back and forth from their nests and how a dog's sense of smell worked. Later, after taking every physics course offered at M.I.T., he completed his graduate studies at Princeton.

During World War II Feynman worked on the atomic bomb project at Los Alamos, New Mexico. His curiosity had earlier led him to learn how to pick locks and, wanting to show Los Alamos colleagues that their safes there were not secure, he would pick the lock, remove a report, and then hand it to the person who wrote it. Everyone was astounded. When better locks were installed, he went to work—or from his perspective, to *play*—to beat the designers. He soon gained a reputation as a safe cracker.

For a time Feynman became "disgust[ed]" with physics, but on reflection, he realized that he had lost his playful attitude, so he set about regaining it. At the time he was teaching at Cornell University and one day, while sitting in the cafeteria, he noticed a student tossing a plate in the air. Feynman watched it wobble, wondered what lesson that fact conveyed, and "went to work on the equations of wobbles." That playful pursuit eventually earned him the Nobel Prize in physics.

Years later, when a reporter asked him whether his discovery was worth the Nobel Prize, Feynman answered, "I don't understand what [the Nobel Prize is] all about or what's worth what," adding that, though he appreciated honors and prizes, for him the *real* prize was "the pleasure of finding the thing out, the kick in the discovery, the observation that others use [his work]—those are the real things, the honors are unreal to me."

For more information on Richard P. Feynman, see his books *Surely You're Joking, Mr. Feynman!* (New York: Bantam Books, 1985) and *The Pleasure of Finding Things Out* (Cambridge, MA: Perseus Publishing, 1999).

In conducting library research (or any other form of research), keep in mind that reading is much more than running your eyes across the page and recognizing words. It involves grasping the *meaning* of what is written and understanding the relationship of each sentence and paragraph to all the others. To get more from your reading, follow this approach:

1. Take a few minutes to **skim** the chapter or article. Pay particular attention to the first two paragraphs and the last paragraph; also pay attention to the headings.

2. Take another few minutes to **reflect** on what you found by skimming. Ask yourself: "Is the author's main purpose to inform or to persuade the reader?" "What is the central idea of the piece?" (This is usually stated in the first or second paragraph and echoed in the last.) "What are the secondary ideas?" (The headings should suggest them.)

3. Now **read** the chapter or article. Keep a reasonable pace, neither rushing nor dawdling. Don't underline or highlight anything yet.

4. Finally, **review** what you have read. At this point, you should be clear about what is important and what is not. Mark the piece accordingly.

Ed Fisher/The New Yorker Collection/Cartoon Bank.Com

"We think you may be suffering from information underload."

This approach will take you no more time than one laborious reading. It may, in fact, take less. But it will increase your understanding. (This is useful as a general approach and also has specific application in understanding complex arguments.)

CONDUCTING INTERNET RESEARCH

The Internet is a major research venue, largely because it can be accessed without leaving home. Many traditional library resources are also available online. Following are three tips for efficient and effective Internet research.

Use a search engine

The name "search engine" conjures up the image of a large machine, but a more appropriate image might be that of a person who assists you in finding information. A search engine is a "research assistant." (We'll call this assistant "it" because it is genderless.) You tell it your thoughts by writing in a blank box and then hit "Search." It searches the World Wide Web of information for you and, in the blink of an eye, provides a list of locations where you can find what you are looking for.

This assistant can do everything—except read your mind. It will look for exactly what you tell it, nothing more or less. Therefore, you must choose your terms with care and revise them if you don't get the information you want.

There are many search engines and even metasearch engines, which search other search engines. For a clear and thorough explanation of the difference and helpful suggestions, visit this University of California at Berkeley website: www.lib.berkeley.edu/TeachingLib/Guides/Internet/MetaSearch.html.

The site recommends www.google.com and also makes favorable mention of www.alltheweb.com and www.altavista.com. Make one of these your personal assistant, and you will ensure that your Internet searches are quick and effective.

GOOD THINKING!

The Story of Larry Page and Sergey Brin

This story could well be titled "From Research Project to Empire." It began when two young graduate students met at Stanford University. Larry Page, the son of a computer science professor, and Sergey Brin, the Russian-born son of a mathematics professor, didn't much care for each other at first. Eventually, they collaborated on a research paper with the daunting title

"The Anatomy of a Large-Scale Hypertextual Web-Search Engine." That effort led them to found one of the most successful companies in recent history, known around the world by the odd-sounding name "Google." (The term is a modification of "googol," a math term meaning 1 followed by 100 zeroes.)

When Google was founded in 1998, a number of competing "search engines" were in use, but, as Brin points out, they did not focus exclusively on information searching or the order in which the results were presented. Page and Brin gave special attention to these concerns; they also "developed a system that determines the best and most useful websites." In doing so, they faced a number of challenges, notably how to ensure that the search results were *relevant* to the search term and *objective*—presenting a full range of viewpoints on an issue.

Their cash investment in the fledging company matched their time investment. As Page recalls, "We had to use all of our credit cards and our friends' credit cards and our parents' credit cards." But Google has been well worth the effort. It is the number one search engine in the world, with an estimated 65 million daily users.

Brin sums up the company philosophy as follows: "Google is all about getting the right information to people quickly, easily, cheaply—and for free. We serve the world—all countries, at least 100 different languages. It's a powerful service that most people probably couldn't have dreamed of twenty years ago. It's available to the rich, the poor, street children in Cambodia, stock traders on Wall Street—basically everybody."

For more information on Larry Page and Sergey Brin, see www.kottke.org/plus/misc/google-playboy.html or do a Google search on each individual's name.

Develop a resource list

The first dozen or so times you do Internet research, you will probably have to go to your favorite search engine, type in the subject, and sample the results before you find helpful sites. In time, this approach will produce a resource list for specific subjects.

Following is a brief list of helpful websites to get you started; for more resources, go to the website for this text.

For reference materials, including dictionaries, encyclopedias, and more:
www.bartleby.com/reference
www.infoplease.com

For news:
www.foxnews.com
www.ap.org
www.cnn.com

For historical matters:
www.besthistorysites.net

For informed opinion:
www.townhall.com (Click on "Columnists" and then on any of the featured columns or on any person's name.)
www.jewishworldreview.com (Click on any of the names in the Insight column toward the bottom of the home page.)
www.prospect.org
www.frontpagemag.com
www.blueeagle.com (This site lists 700 columnists, many cartoonists, and links to political websites.)

For quotations:
www.toinspire.com
www.quotationspage.com/

For legal information:
www.legalengine.com
www.law.com
www.nolo.com/legal-encyclopedia/

For health and medicine:
www.merckhomeedition.com
www.webmd.com
www.cdc.gov
www.medlineplus.gov

For checking hoaxes, rumors, and general facts/fictions:
www.snopes.com
www.hoax-slayer.com
www.casewatch.org/index.html
www.truthorfiction.com
http://urbanlegends.about.com/od/internet/a/current_netlore.htm

Ask questions about the websites you visit

Don't expect to see the warning "Let the Browser Beware" on any website, but it is a good caution to keep in mind. The ideas you find on the Internet have not been screened by a board of standards for accuracy or reasonableness.

No logic police force patrols the Internet looking for violators. It is up to you to avoid being victimized. The critical thinking practiced throughout this book is your best protection. Here are the most important questions to ask whenever you use the Internet.

Whose site is this?   You will likely visit many different sites, including government (.gov), education (.edu), and commercial (.com) sites. Each site will most likely reflect the bias and agenda of the people who created and maintain it. Knowing whose site it is will help you evaluate the reliability of the information you find there.

What function does the site serve?   Every site has a specific purpose. Generally speaking, government and education sites are designed to provide the public with important or helpful information. In contrast, commercial sites are designed to sell products and services.

Expect the companies that have commercial websites to present their products and services favorably and to ignore shortcomings and flaws. Don't be surprised if they imply that their competitors' products and services are inferior. Be aware that such statements and implications may or may not be true and should be tested rather than taken at face value.

Which statements are fact and which are opinion?   A fact is a generally accepted reality, a matter that informed people agree about. An opinion, on the other hand, is a belief or a conclusion open to dispute. After we accept something as a fact, we are no longer inclined to think critically about it. That is why it is important not to confuse opinion with fact.

Such confusion is potentially greater on the Internet than in print or broadcast media because the dissemination of ideas is easier on the Internet. Anyone can say anything on the Internet and reach a worldwide audience. Not surprisingly, rumormongers, manipulators, and other mischief makers have flocked there.

To keep your critical thinking sharp, regard all statements as opinions unless you are certain they are universally endorsed.

Where can statements of fact be confirmed?   Statements that are offered as factual may in reality be false. (Even honest people make mistakes, and not everyone is honest.) Suppose you encounter the statement "The divorce rate has tripled in the past twenty years." This is clearly a *statement* of fact. But is it factual? In other words, is it accurate? Prudence suggests that you seek confirmation by looking in an almanac or other statistical record.

The nature of the statement will determine where you can find verification. To confirm the statement that a congressional candidate was once convicted of sexual harassment, for example, you would check appropriate court records or, at the least, determine what other sources, if any, support the claim. Endorsement of the statement by the candidate's opponents would mean little; admission by his or her political *allies* would be significant.

How widely shared is this opinion? What do authorities on the subject think of it?   Knowing whether an opinion is shared by a majority or a minority will not tell you how reasonable it is. Minority opinions are not necessarily inferior. Many great insights can be traced to a single individual's advancing an unpopular view. But for every minority view that eventually is proven right, several are proven wrong.

To put it simply, the odds favor the consensus views of informed people. Identify the full range of opinions on the issue by consulting other Internet websites that deal with the topic in question. (Also, consult print and broadcast media sources.) Hesitate to accept any opinion that is rejected by most informed people, as well as any opinion about which informed people are sharply divided.

Is the reasoning behind the opinion logical?   Chapter 5, "Recognizing Errors in Thinking," discusses the errors in logic that can occur. (Consult that chapter for details.)

> *Errors of perception:* "mine is better" thinking, selective perception, gullibility and skepticism, preconception, pretending to know, either/or thinking, and false tolerance.
>
> *Errors of judgment:* double standard, irrelevant criterion, overgeneralizing or stereotyping, hasty conclusion, unwarranted assumption, failure to make a distinction, and oversimplification.
>
> *Errors of expression:* contradiction, arguing in a circle, false analogy, and irrational appeal.
>
> *Errors of reaction:* explaining away, shifting the burden of proof, attacking the person, and straw man.

Does the evidence support the opinion?   In making this decision, consider all the evidence you have found. That includes the evidence offered in support of the opinion as well as the evidence you found searching the Internet and other information sources. Remember, too, that your own personal observation and experience, if relevant to the issue, count as evidence.

One problem in doing research on the Internet is that, unlike newspapers, magazines, and books, it is not subject to editorial scrutiny. Anyone can publish anything, and there is a greater risk of receiving erroneous information. To minimize that risk, consult www.wordtrack.com.au/web/internet/evaluating.html, which provides a number of evaluation tools; also see Janet E. Alexander and Marsha Ann Tate, *Web Wisdom: How to Evaluate and Create Information Quality on the Web* (Mahwah, NJ: Lawrence Erlbaum Associates, 1999).

A helpful tip: Some Internet searches will take you to sites that seem objective but really serve to sell you products and services. Such sites end in ".com," which stands for "commercial." (Note: The ending ".com" does not *necessarily* signify a lack of objectivity.) You can eliminate commercial websites from your Google searches by adding at the end of your search term the minus sign followed (without a space) by ".com." For example, if your search term were "vitamin therapy," you would type "vitamin therapy-.com" (without using the quotation marks).

CONDUCTING AN INTERVIEW

Your research needn't be limited to the library and the Internet. A number of instructors at your college may have expertise on your topic. If you decide to interview one or more, call to make an appointment and state what you want to interview them about and how long you will need. Here are some tips for conducting the interview.

1. Arrive on time, and don't overstay your welcome.
2. Ask for permission to tape the interview so the instructor will not have to wait while you take notes.
3. Avoid asking questions calling for a "yes" or "no" answer. Instead, ask "What do you think about . . .?" and "What is the basis for your thinking . . . ?"
4. Pay attention to the instructor's answers and ask follow-up questions where appropriate.

On the rare occasions when you can't find appropriate people with expertise at your college, use your ingenuity. For a medical issue, call the state public health department or the county medical association. The telephone directory will list the numbers of these agencies. Ask to be referred to an expert in your area.

AVOIDING PLAGIARISM[1]

After ideas are put into words and published, they become "intellectual property," and the author has the same rights over them as he or she has over a material possession such as a house or a car. The only difference is that intellectual property is purchased with mental effort rather than money. Anyone who has ever wracked his or her brain trying to solve a problem or

---

[1] This section is used with permission. Copyright © 2002, 2007 by MindPower, Inc.

trying to put an idea into clear and meaningful words can appreciate how difficult mental effort can be.

Plagiarism is passing off other people's ideas or words as one's own. It is doubly offensive in that it both steals and deceives. In the academic world, plagiarism is considered an ethical violation and is punished by a failing grade for a paper or a course, or even by dismissal from the institution. Outside the academy, it is a crime that can be prosecuted if the person to whom the material belongs wishes to bring charges. In the eyes of the law, stealing ideas and/or the words used to express them is as criminal as stealing the computer on which they were recorded.

Some cases of plagiarism are attributable to intentional dishonesty, others to carelessness. But many, perhaps most, are due to misunderstanding. The instructions "Base your paper on research rather than on your own unfounded opinions" and "Don't present other people's ideas as your own" seem contradictory and may confuse students, especially if no clarification is offered. Fortunately, there is a way to honor both instructions and, in the process, to avoid plagiarism.

Three steps to avoid plagiarism

Step 1   *When you are researching a topic, keep your sources' ideas separate from your own.* Begin by keeping a record of each source of information you consult. For an Internet source, record the website address, the author, title of the item, and the date you visited the site. For a book, record the author, title, place of publication, publisher, and date of publication. For a magazine or journal article, record the author, title, the name of the publication, and its date of issue. For a TV or radio broadcast, record the program title, station, and date of transmission.

Step 2   *As you consult each source, note the ideas you want to refer to in your writing.* If the author's words are unusually clear and concise, copy them *exactly* and put quotation marks around them. Otherwise, paraphrase—that is, restate the author's ideas in your words. In written material, write down the number(s) of the page(s) on which the author's passage appears.

If the author's idea triggers a response in your mind—such as a question, a connection between this idea and something else you've read, or an experience of your own that supports or challenges what the author says—write it down and put *brackets* [ ], not parentheses ( ), around it, so that you will be able to identify it as your own when you review your notes. Here is a sample research record illustrating these two steps:

> Adler, Mortimer J. *The Great Ideas: A Lexicon of Western Thought* (New York: Macmillan Publishing Co., 1992). Says that throughout the ages, from ancient Greece, philosophers have argued about whether various

ideas are true. Says it's remarkable that most renowned thinkers have agreed about what truth is—"a correspondence between thought and reality." 867 Also says that Freud saw this as the *scientific* view of truth. Quotes Freud: "This correspondence with the real external world we call truth. It is the aim of scientific work, even when the practical value of that work does not interest us." 869 [I say true statements fit the facts; false statements do not.]

Whenever you look back on this record, even a year from now, you will be able to tell at a glance which ideas and words are the author's and which are yours. The first three sentences are, with the exception of the directly quoted part, *paraphrases* of the author's ideas. The fourth is a direct quotation. The final sentence, in brackets, is your own idea.

Step 3   *When you compose your paper, work borrowed ideas and words into your writing by judicious use of quoting and paraphrasing.* In addition, give credit to the various authors. Your goal here is to eliminate all doubt about which ideas and words belong to whom. In formal presentations, this crediting is done in footnotes; in informal ones, it is done simply by mentioning the author's name.

Here is an example of how source material can be worked into a composition. The first paragraph contains the quoted and paraphrased material from Mortimer Adler. (You would insert a footnote or endnote number at the end of that paragraph, and the note would provide the necessary citation.) The second paragraph adds *your personal commentary* on the Adler material.

Mortimer J. Adler explains that throughout the ages, from the time of the ancient Greeks, philosophers have argued about whether various ideas are true. But to Adler the remarkable thing is that, even as they argued, most renowned thinkers have agreed about what truth is. They saw it as "a correspondence between thought and reality." Adler points out that Sigmund Freud believed this was also the scientific view of truth. He quotes Freud as follows: "This correspondence with the real external world we call truth. It is the aim of scientific work, even when the practical value of that work does not interest us."

This correspondence view of truth is consistent with the common-sense rule that a statement is true if it fits the facts and false if it does not. For example, the statement "The twin towers of New York's World Trade Center were destroyed on September 11, 2002" is false because they were destroyed the previous year. I may sincerely believe that it is true, but my believing in no way affects the truth of the matter. In much the same way, if an innocent man is convicted of a crime, neither the court's decision nor the world's acceptance of it will make him any less innocent. We may be free to think what we wish, but our thinking can't change reality.

How to correctly quote and paraphrase

Three problems commonly arise in quoting and paraphrasing. Here is an explanation of each, together with a practical way to solve it:

Problem 1: Deciding whether to quote or paraphrase   The general rule is to quote only when a statement is so well and concisely expressed that a paraphrase would add unnecessary length or lose the force of the original. Such instances are rare. Most passages can be stated as well—some can actually be improved—by being paraphrased.

Here are some examples of statements that should be quoted rather than paraphrased:

> No act of kindness, no matter how small, is ever wasted. —*Aesop*

> What we think, we become. —*Buddha*

> It is impossible for a man to learn what he thinks he already knows. —*Epictetus*

Here are some statements that should be paraphrased, with suggested paraphrasing:

> As a man thinketh in his heart, so is he. —*Proverbs 23:7*
> Paraphrase: As the Book of Proverbs reminds us, we are what we think.

> He does not believe who does not live according to his belief. —*Thomas Fuller*
> Paraphrase: Thomas Fuller thought that to be genuine, belief must be practiced.

Note that in each example, the source of the material is stated in the paraphrase so that appropriate credit is given for the idea.

Problem 2: Converting the author's words to your words   Constructing a paraphrase is mentally taxing because it involves thinking of alternative ways to express ideas. It is tempting to say "The way the author said it is the only way" and settle for a quotation. But if you do that, you'll find your paper covered in quotation marks. Not wanting to appear so obviously imitative, you may decide to leave the quotation marks off. Don't! You will be committing *plagiarism*!

To solve this problem, put forth a little effort and invest a little imagination to find alternative ways to express an idea. Here is an example of an effective paraphrase of a passage from Shelby Steele's book *White Guilt*. (For the purpose of this exercise, five passages that appear on different pages are joined together, with ellipses.)

Original Passage	Paraphrase
. . . This new black consciousness [of the 1960s] led blacks into a great mistake: to talk ourselves out of the individual freedom we had just won for no purpose whatsoever except to trigger white obligation. . . . The goal of the civil rights movement had escalated from a simple demand for equal rights to a demand for the redistribution of responsibility for black advancement from black to white America, from the "victims" to the "guilty." This marked a profound—and I believe tragic—turning point in the long struggle of black Americans for a better life. . . . Black militancy, then, was not inevitable in the late sixties. It came into existence *solely* to exploit white guilt as a pressure on white America to take more responsibility for black advancement. . . . Thus, since the sixties, black leaders have made one overriding argument: that blacks cannot achieve equality without white America taking primary responsibility for it. Black militancy became, in fact, a militant belief in white power and a correspondingly militant denial of black power. . . . But this sad symbiosis overlooks an important feature of human nature: human beings, individually or collectively, cannot transform themselves without taking *full* responsibility for doing so. This is a law of nature. Once full responsibility is accepted, others can assist as long as it is understood that they cannot be responsible. But no group in human history has been lifted into excellence or competitiveness by another group. —Shelby Steele, *White Guilt: How Blacks and Whites Together Destroyed the Promise of the Civil Rights Era* (New York: HarperCollins, 2006), 45, 58, 59, 60, 62.	Shelby Steele contends that blacks in America have allowed whites to overcome their guilt for the evils of slavery and discrimination by treating blacks as victims and taking over all responsibility for black people's advancement. This he regards as a serious error because "no group in human history has been lifted into excellence or competitiveness by another group." **Comments on the paraphrase:** (1) *The first four words make clear that the author is paraphrasing Steele.* (2) *Some individual key words that appear in the original, such as* advancement *and* responsibility, *also appear in the paraphrase. Such repetition is often unavoidable and does not constitute plagiarism.* (3) *The only group of words that is taken verbatim from Steele appears in quotation marks. To omit the quotation marks would have constituted plagiarism.* (4) *Although the paraphrase embraces the entire idea expressed in the original, it is more compressed. This is a typical feature of paraphrasing.*

Problem 3: Constructing ideas of your own to blend with paraphrased and quoted material   If the subject is unfamiliar or complex, you may wonder what you can possibly add to the words of the authors you consulted. Using the Shelby Steele passage as an example, here are ways you might solve this problem. After your paraphrase of his ideas, elaborate on Steele's views by mentioning some of the supporting evidence he offers. Give the views of other authors who *share* Steele's perspective and their supporting evidence. Discuss the views of authors who *disagree* with Steele on this issue and their supporting evidence. Make sure you exercise the same care in paraphrasing, quoting, and citing your sources. Present your evaluation of the issue, explaining which author(s) you agree with and which you disagree with, in each case presenting *your reasons* for your thinking.

Your evaluation makes the composition or research paper uniquely your own. It represents your thinking and your expression. The more carefully you approach it—explaining thoroughly, providing evidence, anticipating and answering objections—the better its quality will be.

EXERCISES

3.1. To use many of the information sources listed in this chapter you'll need your campus librarian's help. Select three information sources with which you are not familiar and ask your librarian for help in accessing them. Record the librarian's response.

3.2. Visit the Internet Public Library (IPL) at www.ipl.org and examine the available resources. Report the results of your investigation.

3.3. This exercise is designed to help you become familiar with search engines. Go to Google (www.google.com) and click, in turn, on each of the blue words on the home page. As you read each of the pages, click on key words to learn more about Google's offerings. List the features you find most useful.

3.4. Go to the Google home page again. In the search box, type the words "free online encyclopedia" and click the Search button. Then click on each of the first ten search results (more, if you wish) and decide which ones you find most helpful. Repeat this procedure with the phrases "free online almanac" and "government publications." Record your decisions and add the websites to your personal resource list.

3.5. Do an Internet search using the search term "community outreach [name of your city and state]"; for example, use "community outreach Boston MA." Examine the websites your search produces, noting programs that address problems that interest you. Then write a brief description of each of those problems and be prepared to present your findings in class.

3.6. Write an effective paraphrase of each of the following passages, using direct quotation only when the author's phrasing is unusually clear and concise. Then compare your paraphrase with that of a classmate. If you detect any suggestion of plagiarism in either paraphrase, work together to revise it. Be prepared to explain your evaluation in class.

PASSAGE 1

In the first part of this [the twentieth] century, we adopted the principle of mass-producing low-quality education to create a low-skilled work force for mass-production industry. Building on this principle, our education and business systems became very tightly linked, evolving into a single system that brilliantly capitalized on our advantages and enabled us to create the most powerful economy and the largest middle class the world had ever seen. The education system, modeled on industrial organization, was crafted to supply the work force that the industrial economy needed. America's systems of school organization and industrial organization were beautifully matched, each highly dependent on the other for its success, each the envy of the world.

But most of the competitive advantages enjoyed at the beginning of the century had faded away by midcentury, and advances in technology during and after the war slowly altered the structure of the domestic and world economy in ways that turned these principles of American business and school organization into liabilities rather than assets.

. . . Our country is locked in a time warp, wedded to a worldview and to strategies long since outmoded by events. . . . Though the top executives of our best firms are among the most ardent advocates of school reform, the vast majority of American employers do not want more than eighth-grade-level skills in the people that they hire for their front-line work force. —Ray Marshall and Marc Tucker, *Thinking for a Living: Education and the Wealth of Nations* (New York: Basic Books, 1992), xvi–xviii.

PASSAGE 2

. . . Any attempt to restore a man's inner strength in the [World War II Nazi concentration] camp had first to succeed in showing him some future goal. Nietzsche's words, "He who has a *why* to live for can bear with almost any *how*," could be the guiding motto for all psychotherapeutic and psycho-hygienic efforts regarding prisoners. Whenever there was an opportunity for it, one had to give them a why—an aim—for their lives, in order to strengthen them to bear the terrible *how* of their existence. Woe to him who saw no more sense in his life, no aim, no purpose, and therefore no point in carrying on. He was soon lost. The typical reply with which such a man rejected all encouraging arguments was, "I have nothing to expect from life any more." What sort of answer can one give to that?

What was really needed was a fundamental change in our attitude toward life. We had to learn ourselves and, furthermore, we had to teach the despairing men, that *it did not really matter what we expected from life, but rather what life expected from us.* We needed to stop asking about the meaning of life, and instead to think of ourselves as those who were being questioned by life—daily and hourly. Our answer must consist, not in talk and meditation, but in right action and in right conduct. Life ultimately means taking the responsibility to find the right answer to its problems and to fulfill the tasks which it constantly sets for each individual. —Viktor E. Frankl, *Man's Search for Meaning,* 3rd ed. (New York: Simon & Schuster, 1984), 84–86.

PASSAGE 3

[Note: In the book from which this passage is taken, the author argues that the contemporary diversity movement, which divides rather than unites people, is out of touch with Dr. Martin Luther King, Jr.'s vision of Americans united by values and principles despite injustice and discrimination. When he uses the italicized form *diversity*, he is referring to that movement.]

Diversity is big. It's everywhere. Schoolchildren are taught to celebrate it; high courts weigh and scrutinize it; corporate personnel offices assiduously seek it out; unions that once feared it now robustly champion it; artists offer searching introspections of diversity in their own lives; museums exhibit it; restaurants serve it; churches worship it; and tourists vacation in it. . . . Is *diversity* better suited to the pursuit of good character? Not if good character means putting aside stereotypes and treating individuals as individuals. Does *diversity* assist in the pragmatist's project of promoting many different kinds of excellence? It seems more closely associated with lower admissions standards, grade inflation, undemanding undergraduate majors, and a falling off in what we expect high schools to teach college-bound students. Does *diversity* play its part in passing on a valuable legacy to a new generation? Only if one considers the perpetuation of racialist categories a legacy worth having. Does *diversity* help the young on their way to making the world anew? It seems rather to insist that the future will be patterned on the divisions of the past—or on new divisions adopted in reaction to the old. —Peter Wood, *Diversity: The Invention of a Concept* (San Francisco: Encounter Books, 2003), 16, 136–137.

3.7. Meet with a group of two or three classmates and discuss whether each of the following passages would be better quoted or paraphrased. Where disagreements arise, have the person who argues for paraphrasing construct a paraphrase for the group's consideration.

Science without religion is lame, religion without science is blind.
—*Albert Einstein*

Opportunity is missed by most because it is dressed in overalls and looks like work.
—*Thomas Edison*

Nobody can make you feel inferior without your permission.
—*Eleanor Roosevelt*

A conclusion is the place where you got tired of thinking.
—*Steven Wright*

No man is free who is not master of himself.
—*Epictetus*

The deepest human defeat suffered by human beings is constituted by the difference between what one was capable of becoming and what one has in fact become.
—*Ashley Montagu*

3.8. Many campuses have adopted speech codes to ensure an atmosphere of respect and civility. However, these codes have given rise to controversy.

Some people see them as helpful and even necessary. Others regard them as an exercise in foolishness or, worse, a violation of their constitutional rights. Analyze this issue using the W.I.S.E. approach detailed in Chapter 2. Following are two opposing viewpoints on this issue to get you started:

CAMPUS SPEECH CODES ARE REASONABLE

By Priscilla Prentice

A generation ago, rage was an uncommon word. Today it is not only common—it comes in a number of varieties. We have road rage, in which drivers become furious at fellow motorists for real or imagined violations of the rules of the road. We have air rage, in which passengers on airplanes take out their frustrations on other passengers or flight attendants and have to be restrained. And we have sports-event rage, characterized by fans leaping onto the playing field and pummeling someone, usually a player or official or, in the case of little league competitions, the coach who didn't give little Johnny or Sally sufficient playing time.

We also have campus rage, which may be defined as the practice of intimidating and harassing students or faculty one doesn't like. Typically, the victim of this kind of rage is a member of a minority group—for example, homosexuals, African Americans, Latinos, or Muslims. Campus rage tends to be expressed in epithets and insults rather than in physical assaults, so the wounds it causes are invisible. But they are no less real or less lasting for that fact.

Campus speech codes are a sensitive and sensible response to campus rage. They make understandable to everyone at what point commentary on an idea or issue ends and attacks on individuals begin, marking the latter as impermissible. When such codes are well written, they also inform everyone exactly what the penalties will be for violations. The only people who *should* be against campus speech codes are irresponsible individuals who don't care about other people's feelings. I mean people who have something to fear from them—the kind of people who scrawl hate messages on buildings; use ugly, demeaning terms to describe other human beings; and spread stereotypes and vicious rumors.

To be fair, some honest people are against speech codes. But their arguments are flawed. The most significant of those arguments is that campus speech codes violate the right to free speech. There is an element of truth—albeit a small one—in that argument. Any regulation, rule, or law sets a limit on behavior. For example, a traffic light makes us stop when we want to continue going forward. The designation "one-way street" restricts our freedom to go the other way. Airport security requirements require us to submit to questions we would rather not answer and searches we would rather not submit to. But responsible people don't object to these restrictions because they understand that the restrictions serve a purpose that is higher and more important than any individual's convenience.

Campus speech codes should be viewed in the same light. They do limit our right to free speech in a minor way. Yet they do so in order to honor another, equally important right: the potential victim's right to the pursuit of happiness. The idea behind campus speech codes is simply this—just as no one is allowed to assault others physically, no one should be permitted to assault others verbally. Nothing could be more reasonable than that.

CAMPUS SPEECH CODES ARE INTOLERABLE

By Zachariah Brescia

Campus speech codes come wrapped in idealistic language. They supposedly aim to create an environment where fairness reigns, no one's feelings are ever hurt, and everyone feels comfortable. What could possibly be wrong with that? Plenty.

To begin with, campus speech codes are not about fairness at all but privilege. And they are not about soothing feelings but suppressing ideas that don't pass the test of Political Correctness. Anyone who takes the unpopular side of an issue is shouted down or assigned an ugly label. Those who speak against affirmative action are branded racists. Those who oppose gay marriage are called homophobes. Those who speak out against abortion are branded "antichoice." (So much for being concerned about people's feelings.)

On most campuses, it is permissible to say "all men are rapists," "George W. Bush is a war criminal," and "the United States deserved what happened on September 11, 2001," but not to challenge those ideas. Similarly, denouncing religion is acceptable, whereas praising or—GASP!—*professing* a religious belief is considered an outrage.

The punishment doesn't end with name calling and denunciation either. The Politically Correct crowd have also borrowed a tactic from their ideological mentors, the communists. The tactic is called "re-education," but its real meaning is brainwashing. For example, on many campuses people who challenge the liberal dogma of Diversity are required to undergo "diversity training," which consists of sitting silently and being "persuaded" of one's error.

An even more creative trick is to establish "free speech zones" on campus—that is, special places where people can go whenever they want and say whatever they want. At first thought, this sounds perfectly reasonable. Only when you ponder the idea for a while and ask pertinent questions do you realize what's happening. *Question: Where will these "free speech zones" be?* In front of the administration building? At the fountain in the center of campus? Behind the sewage treatment plant? *Question: Will the number and size of these zones ever change?* For example, if the people who use the zones vigorously question Politically Correct ideas, will the zones get fewer and fewer and smaller and smaller?

Questions such as these expose the nature of the game being played. Speech code advocates are pretending to *give* something to the campus community (free speech zones) when they are really taking something away (free speech). Listen carefully and you'll be able to hear the Founding Fathers turning over in their graves. (Incidentally, "Founding Fathers" is politically incorrect because it omits mothers.) When those wise men wrote the U.S. Constitution they were espousing the free expression of ideas, even ones that some people find offensive. They believed that the way to conquer bad ideas is not by suppression but by countering them with good ideas. If they were with us today, they would condemn campus speech codes. And so should we.

3.9. Analyze the following essay using the W.I.S.E approach detailed in Chapter 2. In conducting your research, be especially careful to find and examine viewpoints that differ from the one presented. Write a composition presenting your findings.

A DISSERVICE TO EVERYONE

By Bruce Malone

Talk-show TV often displays a mindlessness that's as amazing as it is appalling. One show, for example, featured teenagers who had decided to drop out of high school. The program began with the teens presenting their reasons for quitting, then proceeded to have their parents, a guest expert, and the host try to persuade them to stay in school. Finally, the teens were given a chance to answer the arguments of their elders.

If the show's host and producers thought they were helping solve the problem of high school dropouts, they were mistaken. Appearing on television is an honor few people receive, even if they have made significant contributions to society. Yet those teens received just that honor for threatening to drop out of school. Their foolishness was dignified and they were made to feel like celebrities. Worse, by being allowed to have the last word on the issue, they were given an advantage over the adults.

The chances that those teens changed their minds after the program are slim to none. They very likely had the show videotaped and ran the tape over and over, showing their friends how they held their own in the debate. They may even fantasize that a career in television awaits them. It's not hard to imagine them becoming the heroes of the neighborhood.

Such programs make the jobs of parents and teachers more difficult. Popular culture has already convinced many young people that they know more than their elders, that their opinions have special value, and that learning is a waste of time. Television shows that reinforce such nonsense are surely not a public service. If anything, they are a public disservice.

3.10. The public tends to take airline safety for granted. But when a serious accident or terrorist attack occurs anywhere in the world, people begin questioning how safe air travel is in this country. The issue has many facets, including the age and condition of aircraft, the quality of maintenance, and the adequacy of air traffic control procedures and equipment. Investigate this issue on the Internet. Then report the sites you consulted and what you found there. Finally, apply the critical thinking strategy you have been using throughout this book. State your conclusion and the reasoning that led you to it.

3.11. The issue of term limits concerns whether elected officials at the local, state, and national levels should be allowed to remain in office indefinitely or be limited to, say, two or three consecutive terms. Investigate this issue on the Internet, being careful to consider both pro and con arguments. Next, report the sites you consulted and what you found. Then finish applying the W.I.S.E. approach. State your conclusion and the reasoning that led you to it.

3.12. Although sex education has been a part of most elementary and secondary curriculums for many years, it remains controversial. There has been sharp division on a number of matters including these: Is sex education helping to solve the problem of teen pregnancy or aggravating it? Do the methods and materials used in sex education support or challenge community standards? Should parents be given a larger role in the development of sex education programs? Investigate these and related questions on the Internet, being careful to consider both pro and con arguments. Next, report the sites you consulted and what you found. Then finish applying the W.I.S.E. approach. State your conclusion and the reasoning that led you to it.

3.13. Imagine that you've decided to buy a new car and need to find the best terms on an auto loan. Search the Internet, identify a number of lenders, and compare the terms they offer. Summarize your findings. Then decide which lender would be the best one for you and explain your reasoning in a brief composition.

3.14. For years we've heard that multitasking is the way to become more productive and efficient. Then again, we often encounter news items that suggest that multitasking may not be as advantageous as we've been led to believe. For example, people have walked into walls, ponds, and off subway platforms while texting or talking on their cell phones—not to mention the drivers who have come to sad ends while being distracted with other tasks. Such reports make us wonder: Is multitasking ever a good idea? Use the W.I.S.E. approach to find out. (Note: Researchers who have done studies on multitasking include Rebecca Clay, Russell Poldrack, and Tamara Waters-Wheeler. It may be helpful to see what they say on the matter.)

3.15. What lessons can you draw from the Good Thinking profiles of Richard Feynman and of Larry Page and Sergey Brin in this chapter? Explain how you can use each of those lessons in your career and/or personal life.

QUIZ

1. What is the most important resource available in any library?

2. What does the chapter suggest as a good starting point for research?

3. Few, if any, traditional library resources are found online. True or false?

4. Define the term "search engine."

5. Ideas found on the Internet have been screened by a board of standards for accuracy. True or false?

6. The chapter describes a way to eliminate commercial websites from your Internet searches. True or false?

7. Questions calling for a simple yes or no answer are not the best ones to ask in an interview. True or false? Explain.

8. Define plagiarism.

9. Most cases of plagiarism are due to intentional dishonesty. True or false?

10. List the three steps you can take to avoid plagiarism.

Answers to this quiz are available at www.cengagebrain.com.

Strengthening Your Individuality 4

Chapter 2 introduced the W.I.S.E. approach to thinking and showed how each step works. Chapter 3 dealt with investigation. This chapter will explain how strengthening your individuality will help you apply the W.I.S.E. approach more effectively, with special emphasis on the third stage of the approach—Speculation.

AP Images/Terry Vine/Blend Images Inc.

WHAT IS INDIVIDUALITY?

The term *individuality* is easily defined: it is the quality or qualities that set one person apart from others. However, the question of when and how a person becomes an individual is more difficult to answer, and the way we answer has a significant effect on the way we approach critical thinking. The popular view is that individuality occurs at conception, and anything we think, say, or do expresses our individuality. The contrasting view is that individuality must be earned. Simple observation will reveal which view is more accurate.

If everyone were unique, imitation would be rare. Indeed, it might not exist at all. We'd find little similarity in dress, speech patterns, and mannerisms, let alone viewpoints. Yet even a casual glance at people reveals a different picture.

Count the number of young men's feet in unlaced high-top sneakers. Tally the number of designer labels on male or female jeans. Notice how

J.B. Handelsman/The New Yorker Collection/Cartoon Bank.Com

"Never mind what I did, Your Honor. I want to be judged for who I am, as an individual."

many businessmen wear suits, shirts, and ties in the current style. See how many businesswomen have hemlines precisely where this year's fashion experts declared they should be.

Note speech patterns, observe mannerisms, and listen to opinions on issues from abortion and capital punishment to taxation and welfare reform. You're likely to see much more sameness than difference.

Such observations suggest that the popular notion of individuality is shallow. People are not born with individuality but with the potential to develop it. Likewise, people's actions and words may not express individuality at all but mindless conformity. In short, strengthening individuality takes continuing effort.

INDIVIDUALITY AND THE W.I.S.E. APPROACH

Perhaps the most important characteristic of genuine individuality is intellectual independence—that is, thinking for yourself rather than mindlessly adopting other people's thinking. That does not, of course, mean going out of your way to disagree with others or being different merely for the sake of being different. Disagreeing does not prove your independence, nor does agreeing disprove it. The test for intellectual independence is how you reach your conclusions—and the right way is through your own thought processes. Never fear considering other people's views; just avoid using them as a substitute for your own thinking.

Independence of mind is vital at all four stages of the W.I.S.E. approach. But we will focus here on its importance at the third stage, Speculation. To do this we will return to the issue of what has caused the mass shootings that have plagued America. (Chapter 1 introduced this case, and Chapter 3 extended the discussion.)

We saw that if the newspaper editors had wondered whether other factors than gun ownership might be involved in the epidemic of mass shootings and then had investigated further, they would have found, among other data, that violence in the media and certain prescription drugs are also linked to actual violence. If they had proceeded to speculate about their findings to decide how to solve the problem, they would have identified a number of ideas worthy of consideration, including the following:

Gun ownership is a constitutional right.

Legal gun owners seldom become involved in criminal activity.

Tightening gun regulations will make it more difficult for both honest people and criminals to obtain guns.

Criminals generally get their guns illegally, so they are less affected by regulations than honest people are.

Publishing the names and addresses of legal gun owners is not likely to prevent criminals from getting guns. In fact, it could have the reverse effect by letting them know where to steal guns.

Research has shown a definite link between violence in entertainment—movies, TV shows, and video games—and actual violence.

Research has established that side effects of a number of prescription drugs, including some quite commonly used, include aggression, hostility, delusions, and/or violent actions.

Tightening gun control cannot solve violence caused by violent entertainment or the side effects of prescription drugs. Solutions in those cases can only come from voluntary action by the entertainment and pharmaceutical industries, or government regulations, or both.

Continuing their speculation, the editors would have compared these and other ideas—for example, the idea of lengthening sentences for those convicted of crimes involving guns. Then they would have decided which idea, or combination of ideas, offered the most promising way to end the epidemic of mass shootings. That way would have been the one they supported editorially. An exercise at the end of this chapter will give you an opportunity to decide for yourself what the most promising way was in this case.

ACKNOWLEDGING INFLUENCES

The first step in becoming an individual is to admit that other people have shaped you. There's no shame in this—it is an unavoidable consequence of living in society. When we were children, we learned by imitating other people. This happened first with our parents and relatives and later with our teachers and peers. The way we think and speak and act, even today, naturally reflects those childhood lessons. And though our imitation is less conscious and obvious in adulthood, it is no less real.

Another powerful influence is the popular culture disseminated by the communications and entertainment media, notably television. During our formative years, most of us saw thousands of hours of television. Small children have difficulty distinguishing between commercials and program content, so we no doubt gave the claims of used car salespeople the same trust we gave the weather reports. In time we learned that not everyone who appears on the screen is equally believable. Yet by then most of us had become accustomed to relaxing our minds while watching TV, so we remained—and remain—vulnerable to the influences of the people who control what we watch.

Over the years those influential people have numbered in the thousands. They included the screenwriters who created TV dramas and comedies, the actors who brought the scripts to life, the newscasters who reported the events, and the pundits and commentators who told us what it meant. Those people may have intended to do nothing more than entertain or inform us. But, whatever their intentions, they were also planting ideas and shaping our thinking and behavior in subtle but significant ways.

Suppose that you open today's newspaper and the headlines say that a well-known person led a protest march, a politician resigned in disgrace, and a snowstorm blanketed the Midwest. You may take it for granted that those stories represent the most important events that occurred in the past 24 hours. But stop and think about that. The editors who selected those stories have their own ideas of what is newsworthy, and their ideas may be debatable.

GOOD THINKING!

The Story of Viktor Frankl

Viktor Frankl (1905–1997), a renowned Viennese psychiatrist, was influenced by two older Viennese psychiatrists, Sigmund Freud and Alfred Adler. Freud believed the sex drive is the strongest psychological drive in human beings; Adler believed it is the drive for power.

But Frankl eventually formed a different view—that the strongest drive in human beings is the drive to find meaning in life. His evidence came not only from the psychiatrist's couch but also from his experiences as an inmate in Nazi concentration camps where his wife, father, mother, and brother perished.

The experience of camp life included near-starvation, lack of warm clothing, disease, hard labor, and unspeakable brutality. In such conditions, Frankl found, the sex drive and the drive for power were quickly suppressed. But the drive to find *meaning* in the suffering, a reason for living, remained strong.

Amid the horrors of the camps, many inmates put aside selfishness and displayed compassion and kindness toward their fellow inmates. Some even forgave their captors.

Frankl survived the camps, largely because of his determination to tell the stories of decency and nobility he witnessed and to teach others the lessons he learned about finding meaning in one's life, regardless of one's circumstances.

The best known of Viktor Frankl's books, *Man's Search for Meaning*, presents these stories and lessons. To date, more than 9 million copies are in print in numerous languages.

For more information on Viktor Frankl, see Viktor Frankl, *Man's Search for Meaning*, 3rd ed. (New York: Simon & Schuster, 1984), or do a Google search for "Viktor Frankl."

For example, many editors follow the principle "If it bleeds, it leads," which may not be the most responsible principle to follow. Consider, as well, that in choosing their stories, editors also chose to ignore many other stories.

Did you read about the historic conference in Washington, D.C., featuring a Catholic priest, a Protestant minister, a Black Muslim, a Hindu, a rabbi, and a Buddhist talking about their common spiritual and social values? (This event took place in November 2000.) Chances are you didn't hear about it because most editors around the country decided it wasn't newsworthy.

The same pattern exists in book and magazine publishing. Authors are free to take any view they want about any subject. But what editors select for publication is what they think the public should know or what will sell.

Given all these influences, it is almost certain that many of the ideas, attitudes, and values you consider your own actually came from other people. "Wait a minute," you may be saying. "How could I ever mistake other people's ideas for my own?" The following sequence of events illustrates how this happens.

You're watching your favorite TV series and one of the characters expresses an offhand opinion about a controversial issue, but you don't pay much attention because you have little interest in the issue and you are busy concentrating on the story line. A few days later, you are listening to a radio talk show while doing some chores, and you hear someone express the same opinion. It sounds familiar to you, but you are too involved in what you are doing to think further about it.

The following week you're sitting with a couple of friends, and the discussion turns to the same issue. Your friends disagree about it and then ask you where you stand. Not wanting to admit that you haven't really thought much about it, you say the first thing that comes to mind—the opinion you heard others express.

Once you express the opinion, of course, you stop thinking of it as *an* opinion—it becomes *your* opinion, the *right* opinion. And the more often you express it, the more convinced you will be of its soundness, and the more passionate you will be in defending it. *All this for an idea you never examined critically but merely heard others say!*

Acknowledging that you have been—and continue to be—influenced by other people will motivate you to be more critical of your own ideas and more willing to reject them when they prove unworthy. It will also help you to appreciate the wisdom in C. M. Ward's observation: "There are times when the greatest change needed is a change of my viewpoint."

UNDERSTANDING ATTITUDES

Attitudes are beliefs that are expressed indirectly. We are seldom as aware of our attitudes as we are of our other beliefs. Some people's tone of voice, mannerisms, or actions reveal that they believe they are more important than other people. They may never say to anyone, "I am more important than you," and perhaps they don't even think those words to themselves, but their attitude is expressed in the way they treat other people. For example, they may demand kindness, sensitivity, and loyalty from others but never reciprocate; they may break dates or change plans whenever they wish but resent their friends doing so; or they may expect apologies but never offer them.

Our attitudes are strongly influenced by our culture—that is, by the moral code, religious beliefs, political perspective, and social customs we were introduced to at home and in our community. There is nothing mystical about this influence. It can be explained by the fact that cultures differ in the behaviors they approve and disapprove and in the strength of their convictions about those behaviors.

It is well known that students in many Asian countries have a more respectful attitude toward parents and teachers than American students typically have. Some observers believe this attitude is responsible for the unusually high level of academic achievement among Asian students. Similarly, the Old Order Amish have a stricter moral and social code than most other Americans and, perhaps not coincidentally, a much lower incidence of crime.

Over the last half-century, a new kind of culture—*popular* culture—has emerged in a number of western countries, particularly in the United States. The entertainment and communications media disseminate this popular culture, and its values are very different from those of traditional culture. The result has been a "culture war" that popular culture seems to be winning.

Consider, for example, the changes in the public's attitude toward sex and violence in media. Traditionally, most people strongly opposed the use of vulgar language and graphic depictions of sex and violence. Audiences were offended when "damn" was used in *Gone with the Wind*. Navels had to be covered in shows such as *I Dream of Jeannie*. Depictions of two people in bed, even a married couple, were outlawed for decades.

Then filmmakers and television writers began to push limits by breaking one taboo after another. As such material became more common and familiar, the public's attitude changed. Today many people not only tolerate but expect—in some cases *crave*—a steady diet of the scandalous and the sensational. And not just from dramatic shows but also from the news! This change is but one indication of popular culture's powerful influence on our attitudes.

Evaluating your attitudes is an important step in becoming a critical thinker. Before you can decide whether your attitudes are responsible and beneficial, you must identify them. And doing so can be difficult if you are not aware that you have them. The following exercises are designed to help you identify your attitudes about some matters important in college, at work, and in personal relationships.

FOUR EMPOWERING ATTITUDES

We have discussed what attitudes are and how they are acquired, as well as how you can identify and evaluate your own attitudes. Now let's consider some specific attitudes that can help you become a critical thinker and make you more successful in your studies, your career, and your personal life.

Attitude 1: There's always room for improvement

For centuries most people believed that human beings are imperfect creatures and no matter how far they advance toward perfection, there will always be room for improvement. This belief was the foundation of the concept of self-improvement. But over the last few decades, something strange happened. Self-improvement books and tapes began to focus less on *improving* and more on *approving*. Self-acceptance became the dominant theme. Some authors even advised us to chant "I'm wonderful just as I am," "I'm perfect," even "I'm divine." They told us if we acknowledged our imperfections or faults, we'd suffer a fatal loss of self-esteem.

These authors overlooked a crucial fact of life—*people never strive to obtain what they believe they already have.* Only a foolish person would waste time fixing what isn't broken.

If you believe you are already filled with knowledge, understanding, and wisdom, you probably aren't enthusiastic about your studies. Similarly, if you believe you have no personal faults—rudeness, selfishness, or meanness, for example—you probably spend little time wondering whether you have acted inappropriately. Instead, you assume that if other people take offense at something you say or do in school, at work, or in your personal life, there must be something wrong with *them*.

The moment you admit to yourself that you haven't accomplished all you have the potential to accomplish, and that you aren't all you could be as a person, you'll become more open to improvement.

Attitude 2: Criticism, including self-criticism, has value

The same influential people who claim that we are already wonderful also advise us to reject criticism from other people and even from ourselves. Many of us follow this advice and assume that anyone who criticizes us is disrespecting (in popular parlance, "dissing") us. We expect total acceptance from other people—that is, unqualified agreement with what we say and praise for what we do. And if we don't get it, we are offended.

Such an attitude is unrealistic. Think of any learning situation you have been in—learning how to ride a bike, drive a car, play a team sport, write an essay, or perform a new procedure at work. In all of these cases, you probably had a parent, teacher, coach, or mentor saying, "No, that's not the way," and offering suggestions for doing it right. (Even if you learned by yourself, you told yourself something similar.)

If you rejected the criticism, you probably had difficulty learning. In fact, you may not have learned at all. Athletic coaches describe people in the latter category as "uncoachable" and often drop them from the team, even if they have significant athletic potential. On the other hand, if you put aside ego, accepted the criticism, and followed the advice, you probably learned faster and better.

Do some people criticize too much or do so in an inappropriate way? Yes they do, and the best way to deal with this is to accept only the valid part of the criticism and ignore the rest. Can *self*-criticism be carried too far, to the point that paralyzes effort? Yes again, but this consequence can be easily avoided. Just keep your self-criticism focused on the positive goal of doing better next time.

Attitude 3: Effort is the key to success

Many people have the attitude that success depends solely on talent. For example, when others get better grades in college, they think, "I wish I were that smart." When they see accomplished athletes perform, they say, "It must be nice to have such natural ability." When they read of people who have been successful in business, the professions, or the arts, they say, "I wish I had their gifts."

That attitude is mistaken. Talent is a factor in performance, but it is not the only factor. Two others are desire and effort. Moreover, these two are more important because *you can control them*. People with only modest talent who really want to learn something and are willing to work hard often surpass more talented people who lack their desire and initiative. And with achieving a hard-earned goal comes the exciting realization that their talent was greater than they imagined.

According to Thomas Edison, one of the greatest inventors of all time, "Genius is 1 percent inspiration and 99 percent perspiration." Making this your attitude will bring out the best that is in you and, in the process, produce the healthiest kind of self-esteem—*earned* self-esteem.

Attitude 4: Other people are as important as I am

Modern culture has conditioned us to be more concerned with rights than with responsibilities. Given this emphasis, it is understandable that many people who believe they should be treated well feel no obligation to treat others similarly.

In sharp contrast to this self-serving attitude is the attitude embodied in the traditional view of the "gentleman," as expressed in the following quotations from *A Gentleman's Code According to Confucius, Mencius, and Others.*

A gentleman daily examines his personal conduct on three points: In carrying out the duties entrusted to him by others, has he failed in conscientiousness? In dealing with his friends, has he failed in sincerity and faithfulness? In all his dealings, has he failed to pass on whatever he has learned which may assist others?

—*Confucius*

A true gentleman helps others to realize what is good in them; he does not help others to discover their weaknesses and failings.

—*Confucius*

A gentleman sets strict standards for himself, but makes allowances for others.

—*Confucius*

A gentleman tries to banish from his bearing all traces of violence and arrogance, to remove from his actions all insincerity, to purge from his speech all vulgarity and impropriety.

—*Confucius*

A gentleman is one who thinks more of other people's feelings than his own rights; and more of other people's rights than his own feelings.

—*Matthew Henry Buckham*

One of the marks of a gentleman is his refusal to make an issue out of every difference of opinion.

—*Arnold H. Glasgow*

This is the final test of a gentleman; his respect for those who can be of no possible service to him.

—*William Lyon Phelps*

It is almost a definition of a gentleman to say he is one who never inflicts pain.

—*John Henry, Cardinal Newman*

All these quotations embody the attitude that other people are as important as we are and therefore deserve the same level of respect we wish for ourselves. Far from being a mark of weakness, this attitude will gain you respect and admiration.

RECOGNIZING MANIPULATION

Manipulation is a form of influencing. What distinguishes it from other forms is that it uses *dishonest* means. Among the most common of those means are biased reporting, dishonest appeals to emotion, stacking the deck, suppressing dissent, and repetition. Let's look at each in turn.

Biased reporting

A number of books have been written on the subject of biased reporting, including *Bias* and *Arrogance* by Bernard Goldberg and William McGowan's *Coloring the News*. But the book that provides the most useful insights is Bob Kohn's *Journalistic Fraud*. Kohn focuses his analysis on a single newspaper, the *New York Times*, because it has long been regarded as the "journal of record" and because it is the single most influential news source in the western world. In this country alone, more than 650 other newspapers subscribe to the *Times*'s news service, and many broadcast news organizations lean heavily on its news reports.

As Kohn notes, codes of journalistic ethics used to require that opinion be confined to the editorial page. A 1923 code stated: "News reports should be free from opinion or bias of any kind." A journalism textbook written the same year taught that "a news article should tell what happened in the simplest, briefest, most attractive and accurate manner possible; it should draw no conclusions, make no gratuitous accusations, indulge in no speculation, give no opinions." For years, the *New York Times* endorsed that standard, promising to "give the news impartially, without fear or favor, regardless of party, sect or interests involved."

According to Kohn, the *Times* and many other news agencies no longer follow that standard. As a result, much of today's news unfairly favors the particular news agency's or individual reporter's point of view. Such bias can take a variety of forms, notably the following.

Biased headline   Let's say the Senate votes 93 to 7 in favor of a health care bill. A fair headline would be "Senate Passes Health Care Bill." A reporter or editor who disapproved of the vote might substitute this biased headline: "Opinion Divided on Health Care Bill."

Biased "lead"   The term *lead* refers to the opening sentence or sentences of a news story. A fair lead simply states who did what, as well as when and where the event occurred. An unfair lead injects opinion in an attempt to influence the reader's reaction to the news. For example, if a government commission issued a proposal and the reporter didn't like it, he or she might begin, "In a move sure to create controversy. . . ." The bias in this case is that instead of reporting, these words predict a future event which may or may not occur.

Biased reporting of polls   Fair reporting is evenhanded in presenting the results of polls. In contrast, biased news reporting is inconsistent. If the news agency agrees with the results, it puts the story on the front page. If it disagrees, it buries the story or, in extreme cases, omits it altogether. In some instances, a news organization will itself commission a poll or study and, when the results are disappointing, decline to publish it.

Biased handling of quotations   Readers have a right to expect that the quotations used in news stories will fairly depict the range of viewpoints on the subject. Unbiased reporters strive to meet that standard. However, biased reporters try to advance their own personal opinions. One way is to include numerous strong quotations on their side of the issue and only one or two, preferably weak, quotations on the other side. A more blatant approach is to include *no opposing quotations* at all and thus create the impression that no responsible person would take the opposing side of the issue. The most dishonest approach is to twist a quotation so that it seems to say something very different. For example, if the quotation were "I initially had some reservations about the program, but after examining it closely I believe it is excellent," a dishonest reporter might merely say that the person expressed "some reservations" about the program.

Even journalists who sincerely desire to report objectively are sometimes tricked into using biased material. As former activist Tammy Bruce explains in her book *The New Thought Police*, reporters get much of the information they use in their news accounts from "the press releases sent to them by publicists, activists, and politicians." According to Bruce, such people don't even call the propaganda they write "press releases" anymore. They call them "news releases" to make them sound like objective information.

Keep in mind that biased reporting is not limited to one political, religious, or philosophical perspective. It is no less manipulative if done by people on your side of the issue than if done by people on the other side.

Dishonest appeals to emotion

We react to language not only with our intellects but also with our emotions. Some words evoke emotion more than others. For example, we react more emotionally to "home" and "family" than to "state" or "government"; to "values" and "beliefs" more than to "concepts" or "ideas"; to "freedom" and "liberty" more than to "constitutional guarantees."

Emotional language has great value—it has the power to elevate our vision, reinforce important principles, and inspire responsible action. Virtually all of the great writers and speakers in history have used emotional language for such purposes, and we are fortunate for that. Without such language, communication would be mechanical, lifeless, dull, and ineffective.

Unfortunately, emotional language can also be used to manipulate us. Devious people would prefer to have others accept what they say uncritically and to act in conformity with their wishes. They choose language to elicit positive emotional responses to ideas and people they support and negative emotional responses to those they oppose. Such attempts at deception can be found in every area of life, but they are especially prominent in politics. Former White House advisor Dick Morris says that today's political speeches are like collections of "greatest hits"—the speakers do studies to find out what the public wants to hear and then say it.

It is not always easy to tell when an appeal to emotion is dishonest. However, you can be reasonably sure that it is dishonest when writers or speakers *routinely* use highly favorable terms to describe their side of the issue and highly unfavorable ones for the opposing side. Dishonest speakers will call people who agree with their position "moderate," "centrist," "progressive," or "pragmatic" and call people who disagree "radical," "extremist," "divisive," or "partisan." Deceptive writers will excuse serious mistakes by leaders they approve of while condemning minor mistakes in others. They will ascribe high intelligence and noble motives to those who agree with them and low intelligence and devious motives to those who disagree.

Stacking the deck

The term *stacking the deck* derives from card games in which the dealer arranges the cards to cheat one or more of the players. This form of manipulation often occurs on TV talk shows about controversial issues.

A typical format features a host and two guests with different views of an issue. Fairness demands that the host remain neutral and give each guest an equal opportunity to present his or her case. Sometimes, however, the host will become a participant in the discussion, thus creating a two-against-one situation. Even more unfair is the practice of choosing guests of unequal stature and ability—in other words, inviting a well-known, highly accomplished person to represent the favored view and a relative unknown to represent the unfavored view. If, by chance, the relative unknown seems to be getting the better of the discussion, the host will give him or her less time to speak.

Suppressing dissent

For all its deviousness, stacking the deck at least acknowledges that there is an opposing view. Suppressing dissent, on the other hand, creates the impression that *there is no opposing view*. A good illustration of the effectiveness of this technique is a personal experience Tammy Bruce describes in *The New Thought Police.*

Bruce is a gay feminist who was once the president of the Los Angeles chapter of the National Organization for Women (NOW). In her ten years as an activist, she had no difficulty getting her essays published in the *Los Angeles Times*. Whatever she submitted was always accepted.

Then Bruce became disturbed at what she perceived to be the unfair treatment of Dr. Laura Schlessinger by other gay activists. She composed a short commentary expressing that view. The *Times* held it for three weeks and when she called to ask what was happening, she found an editor had decided not to publish it, essentially because it was on the "wrong" side of the issue. Next, Bruce submitted the commentary to the *New York Times*, where she got an enthusiastic reception. However, they edited it in such a way that it was against Dr. Schlessinger rather than for her. She refused to accept the changes, so the commentary was never published.

The newspapers' refusal to publish Bruce's commentary as she wrote it amounted to a suppression of dissent. As a result, readers of those newspapers were led to believe, erroneously, that no one in the gay community supported Dr. Schlessinger.

Repetition

One of the simplest and most effective techniques of manipulation is simple repetition. The more familiar an idea is, the more people tend to believe it. Realizing this, spinmeisters and hucksters repeat their lies and distortions over and over to trick us into accepting them. Of course, honest people also repeat what they believe to be true. In either case, we have to decide whether what is repeated is true.

For example, during the election campaign of 2004, Senator John Kerry's opponents kept repeating, "It's impossible to tell where he stands because he takes *both* sides of every issue." And during the election campaign of 2012, President Obama's supporters repeated that as a rich person, Mitt Romney was out of touch with the needs and aspirations of the average voter. In both cases, the people who made these statements were trying to persuade others. The public had to decide whether the statements represented honest persuasion or manipulation.

RESISTING MANIPULATION

Given the number of individuals and groups eager to manipulate you and the many means at their disposal, it is important to have an active strategy for resisting their efforts. The following strategies are especially helpful.

Step 1: Be prepared

Manipulation does the greatest harm when you are unaware it is occurring. Therefore, the surest way to avoid its influence is to *expect to encounter it* whenever you read a book, magazine, or newspaper, whenever you see a movie or TV show, and whenever you listen to the radio, visit the Internet, or engage in a discussion. This doesn't mean you need to be suspicious of everyone, just be aware that misinformation and lies can be spread in much the same way that computer viruses are spread—by honest people who have themselves been fooled.

Being prepared means remaining alert for signs of manipulation. For example, when you read or watch the news, look for biased reporting. When you watch a talk show (or even a drama or sitcom), look for dishonest appeals to emotion, stacking the deck, and repetition. Suppression of dissent is hardest to detect. Instead of looking for what is present, you must look for what is absent—that is, what has been purposely *omitted*. Keep in mind that there are two (or more) sides to every controversy. Whenever you are presented with only *one* side, you may reasonably conclude that the other has been suppressed.

Step 2: Ask questions

We all start out life with abundant curiosity. Because everything is new to us, we are filled with wonder and constantly asking questions, especially "What is that?" "Why is it that way?" and "What does it mean?" Unfortunately, our parents and teachers get tired of answering, so we stop asking, and our curiosity eventually shrivels.

Happily, curiosity can be reactivated. Begin by forcing yourself to ask probing questions about what you see and hear. Do so with everyday matters as well as with controversial situations. In time, wondering will become a habit. Here are some sample situations and kinds of questions you might ask.

SITUATION 1. You are sitting with some friends in the campus cafeteria. One of your friends is expressing dissatisfaction. She says: "I'm disappointed with the instructors at this college—they seem content to offer uninteresting courses. For example, they stand at the lectern and lecture all period without enthusiasm for their material. On the rare occasions when they open discussion to the class, they call on the same few students. The rest of us have to sit squirming, waiting for the boring ordeal to be over."

QUESTIONS: As she is speaking, ask yourself these questions: How likely is it that your friend knows all or most of the instructors at this university? How likely is it that all or most of the instructors teach strictly by lecture and without enthusiasm? Why are the same few students always called on (assuming this claim is accurate)? Do these students raise their hands and show an interest in the lecture? Do other students, including your friend, ever volunteer a comment or question? Are all but a few students at this college really so bored, or is your friend projecting her reaction on them? Is it possible that the students who squirm have overly negative attitudes? Is it the instructor's responsibility to make a class interesting? Do the students bear any responsibility?

SITUATION 2. While driving through a rather rundown neighborhood, you pass a house with a sign advertising psychic services. It reads: "Madam X. Palm readings, tarot cards, your future foretold!"

QUESTIONS: As you drive by, ask yourself: What could a psychic accomplish if she used her powers to better herself? Wouldn't she be able to make a fortune at the racetrack or in the stock market or the lottery and afford to live in the most exclusive section of town? So why isn't she living in a better section of town? Could it be that she has too much integrity to use her powers for her own advantage? Might she instead be a charlatan?

SITUATION 3. While reading the newspaper, you notice this advertisement: "Good news! Due to the unprecedented success of our giant end-of-year furniture sale, we have extended it for ten days."

QUESTIONS: Pause in your reading and ask yourself: How would the store have looked after a successful sale? Would the stock be noticeably depleted? Would the store be empty of furniture? If they did sell most of the furniture, why do they need to extend the sale? And where are they getting the furniture for the extended period? Was the sale, instead, such a flop that they were left with a store full of merchandise and they have to extend the sale to get rid of it? If so, why didn't the furniture sell? Were the prices too high? Is the quality too low? How do competitors' prices compare?

SITUATION 4. You are reading a magazine article about the violence that sometimes occurs at heavy metal rock concerts. The author says that it's unfair to blame the violence on the musicians or the music, and then asserts that human beings are naturally violent.

QUESTIONS: Ask yourself: What other kinds of musical events might be compared with heavy metal rock concerts? Square dances, polka or bluegrass festivals, operatic performances? Have I ever seen a newspaper headline such as "Riot Mars Pavarotti Performance" or "Rowdy Polka Contestants Attack Bystanders"? If violence is due to human nature, then shouldn't it be found in all societies and all groups within a society? How common are incidents of group violence in Europe, Asia, or Africa? For that matter, how common is violence among Amish groups in the United States?

Step 3: Be imaginative

Two ways to be imaginative were illustrated in Step 2. One was creating a mental picture of how the store would look after a successful sale. The other was producing relevant examples—the examples of the racetrack, stock market, and lottery in one situation, and musical events, newspaper headlines, and comparisons with Europe, Asia, Africa, and the Amish in the other situation.

Another way to be imaginative is to **create realistic scenarios**. Suppose the issue in question is whether or not television has had a harmful effect on communication in families. Here are three realistic scenarios you might imagine:

1. It's dinnertime and the family is gathered at the dining room table. The television set is positioned so that everyone can see. All eyes are glued to the set. The only sounds that can be heard, other than those coming

from the TV, are occasional comments such as "Pass the potatoes" or "Is there any more meat in the kitchen?" At one point someone says, "Guess what happened to me today?" And everyone else says in unison, "*Sshhhh.*"

2. It's dinnertime and the family is gathered in the living room, each behind a TV tray. No one looks at or speaks to the others.

3. Dinner is over, the dirty plates are in the dishwasher, and each member of the family has headed to a different corner of the house and his or her own TV set.

These scenarios suggest questions and insights about the effect of television on communication in families.

A fourth way to be imaginative is to **construct a new viewpoint**. This approach works well in situations in which you are being pressured to adopt one of two positions on an issue, neither of which is completely satisfactory. For example, let's look at the issue of whether the Ten Commandments should be displayed in public school classrooms.

The "pro" viewpoint: The Ten Commandments should be displayed because they are honored in two of the world's great religions, Judaism and Christianity; they express the religious and moral sentiments of the vast majority of Americans; and they provide an ethical dimension that many think has been sadly lacking in recent decades.

The "con" viewpoint: The Ten Commandments should not be displayed because they are not honored by people of other faiths and those of no faith; their presence in the classroom would give favored status to Judaism and Christianity, status the Constitution forbids; and the ethical dimension the Ten Commandments provide is necessarily a form of religious doctrine.

By being imaginative, you could construct a view that may be more reasonable than either the "pro" or the "con" view.

The Ten Commandments should be displayed, along with any similar codes from other religious or philosophical traditions, including agnostic or atheistic, because knowledge of the principles that have guided human conduct in various times and places is as valuable as knowledge of diverse cultures and customs and because the display of many codes would favor none.

Step 4: Check sources

Did you hear about the high school student from India who proved Albert Einstein wrong and is being considered for a Nobel Prize in physics? Have you read about the recently discovered 1895 eighth-grade examination proving that students back then were far superior academically to today's students? Both these stories, and many others that may be waiting right now in your email inbox, are *false rumors* or *hoaxes*. They often come to you from people you know, sometimes from individuals who are usually alert but from time to time fail to check before passing a story on.

Whenever you encounter an interesting story or a startling claim, try to determine where it came from. If you encounter it in your reading, look for source citations such as footnotes or endnotes. In magazines and newspapers, the sources are often mentioned in the article itself. Be wary when no sources are mentioned or they are identified only as "knowledgeable people" or "individuals who prefer to remain anonymous."

If people you know tell you the story or make the claim, ask where they encountered it. If they read it somewhere, ask where; if they heard it from someone, ask whom. Don't be surprised if they can't say—they may have assumed it was true and never checked it.

If the source is provided, check it. If no source is given, check with an appropriate source. For example, check a health claim with a medical organization and a story about pending federal legislation with your congressional representative's office. The following websites are especially helpful for checking rumors and hoaxes:

Hoaxbusters: http://hoaxbusters.ciac.org

About.Com: Urban Legends: http://urbanlegends.about.com

Truth or Fiction: www.truthorfiction.com

STRATEGIES FOR DEVELOPING INDIVIDUALITY

At the beginning of this chapter, we noted that we are not born with individuality but, instead, with the potential to develop it. We then discussed a number of ways for you to develop that potential—by acknowledging how other people influence you, by adopting positive and constructive attitudes, and by recognizing and resisting manipulation.

This section explains an additional way to develop your individuality—by cultivating the strategies associated with critical thinking, the most important of which are described here.

Strive for humility

In recent decades the emphasis has been on bolstering self-esteem. We are advised to tell ourselves that we are knowledgeable, talented, and wonderful in every way. That emphasis doesn't leave much room for humility. That is unfortunate because humility is fundamental to critical thinking. To put it simply, thinking we know everything prevents us from learning anything.

The ancient Greek philosopher Socrates frequently reminded himself of how little he knew, and that strategy helped him to become one of the greatest thinkers in history.

Be wary of first impressions

A taxicab driver who prided himself on his ability to spot (and avoid) suspicious people related this experience. While passing a posh hotel, he noticed someone waving for his attention. The man was dressed in a suit, an expensive-looking topcoat, and a fedora, and he carried a leather briefcase. The driver's impression couldn't have been more positive, so he stopped and picked him up. A few minutes later, the man opened his briefcase, took out a pistol, and said, "Give me all your money."

Not all first impressions are mistaken, but many are. The person who seems self-absorbed and rude may turn out to be exactly the opposite when you get to know her. The person you take an instant dislike to may, in time, become your best friend. On the other hand, the one you react to most positively to at first may eventually disappoint you. Sadly, many "love at first sight" relationships have ended in divorce court.

The problem does not lie in forming first impressions. (We couldn't avoid doing so even if we wanted to.) It is, instead, in trusting them so much that you close your mind to later perceptions. This habit increases your vulnerability to manipulation and the pressure to conform.

The solution to this problem is to give as much consideration to subsequent impressions and to be willing to change your mind when experience warrants your doing so.

GOOD THINKING!

The Story of Stephanie Kwolek

Many a police officer's and soldier's life has been spared because of a bullet-stopping Kevlar vest. Kevlar has also proved useful for bridge cables, auto brakes, boats, parachutes, truck and bicycle tires, skis, gloves, and spacecraft—in all, about 200 specific applications. The credit for this remarkable material goes to a woman who took a job as a chemist in DuPont's research laboratory in order to earn money for medical school—Stephanie L. Kwolek.

Kwolek's interest in science was nurtured by her father, who encouraged her to explore the wooded areas near their Pennsylvania home. In growing up, she had many other interests, notably fashion design and teaching math to neighborhood children. When she finished college with a chemistry degree, she joined DuPont and began working in the Pioneering Research Library, attempting to find "new ways of making polymers." The result was "hundreds of thousands of polymers that could not be made by the old methods," including Orlon and Lycra.

One particular project involving "high-performance fibers" was offered to a number of researchers, but they all declined. Kwolek, however, accepted and began a variety of experiments. In each case, she sent the resulting material to the laboratory for testing. One material produced such amazing results that she sent it back to the lab several times to be sure they were not in error. That product was Kevlar.

Stephanie Kwolek never did make it to medical school, but the patent Stephanie Kwolek received for Kevlar, as well as those for sixteen other inventions, won her entry into the National Inventors Hall of Fame in 1995. Some time later, an interviewer asked Kwolek to explain what qualities made her so successful. She cited her love of chemistry and her dogged refusal to give up when faced with a challenge.

For more on Stephanie Kwolek, see http://web.mit.edu/invent/a-winners/a-kwolek.html.

Be honest with yourself

One of the most memorable lines in philosophy is the directive "Know thyself." The key to following this wise advice is to be completely honest with yourself. This is not as easy as it sounds. It means facing a number of unpleasant truths, notably the following:

Much that we blame on others is really our own fault.

When we deny our mistakes, we compound them.

Others can usually see our faults better than we can.

Most of us tend to be too concerned about our rights and not concerned enough about our responsibilities.

Much that we think we know, we really only guess or assume.

The first step in self-improvement is admitting the need for it.

Fight confusion

Like everyone else, critical thinkers are sometimes confused. What sets critical thinkers apart is that they respond actively to confusion. For example, if the meaning of a sentence escapes them, instead of just accepting confusion, they consider a number of *possible* meanings and then choose the most likely one. If a question arises and they don't know the answer, they look in a reference book or check with an authority to find it.

How might you apply this approach? Suppose you are somewhat puzzled by this proverb: "The girl who can't dance says the band can't play." You might wonder if the reference here is just to dancing or to other situations as well. Just how broad is its meaning? Then you would consider how the proverb might apply to other situations, such as a small boy having trouble catching a ball and blaming the thrower or a student having trouble with a course and blaming the teacher. Finally, you would conclude that the proverb refers to any situation in which people tend to blame others for their own shortcomings.

Produce many ideas

Many people are idea-poor. When confronted by a challenge, they embrace the first response that pops into their minds, often one that they have seen in print or heard on television. With that approach, the odds of their producing insightful ideas are slender.

Consider this example. When the price of a postage stamp was increased by three cents, people needed to combine older stamps with three-cent stamps for the correct postage. The lines at post offices in some areas were unusually long, and the demand for three-cent stamps quickly exceeded the supply. One reason was that some people bought many more stamps than they needed. For example, people who needed 10 three-cent stamps bought 50 or 100. (Perhaps they believed the stamps would increase in value.)

It got even sillier. One man entering a post office saw the sign "Sorry, we're temporarily out of three-cent stamps." He grumbled in displeasure and said as he walked away, "I've driven to four post offices and they're all out of stamps. Now I've got to try a fifth." Apparently he never considered other options. He could have walked up to the window, bought some four-cent stamps—plenty were available—and mailed his letters.

To avoid such embarrassing mistakes, produce lots of ideas before embracing any specific one. Extend your effort to identify possibilities. A helpful technique is *springboarding*. Here's how it works: Think of an idea and write it down. Don't worry about writing complete sentences; a word or short phrase will do. Resist the urge to dwell on details. Use one idea to propel you to others. To keep the process going, end each item in your list with the word *and*.

Let's say that the subject you are addressing is students' attitudes in class. Your list of ideas might be as shown in the box on this page. The cue questions are in boldface. Note how asking questions helps you to continue springboarding.

What attitudes?
Disinterest in class and hostility to the teacher *and . . .*

Are there more?
Disapproval of students who speak and uncooperativeness in class discussion and disrespect for other students *and . . .*

How are attitudes revealed?
Smirking and whispering while others are talking and arriving late for class and making rude remarks and doing unrelated things like cleaning nails *and . . .*

Why do students do these things?
To maintain a "tough" image and to hide fear of failing and to make teachers uncomfortable *and . . .*

What are some favorable attitudes?
Cooperativeness and willingness to listen to others' viewpoints and patience when the discussion gets complex *and . . .*

How are these attitudes revealed?
Looking at the person speaking and waiting for her to finish before you speak and refraining from side discussions and emphasizing the positive *and . . .*

   This list could be continued. You could think about how some students develop positive attitudes and others develop negative ones. Or you might explore how teachers can effectively deal with students who have negative attitudes.

   Here is an additional tip: Be open to ideas at all times. You may find that insights occur to you when you don't expect them—while you shower, walk from class to class, or fall asleep at night. Perhaps you said to yourself on some of these occasions, "I've got to remember this idea," and found later that you had forgotten it.

   Keep a pen and paper or a micro-tape recorder handy to record ideas as they come to you. Send yourself a text message on your cell phone. Chances are you'll be rewarded with many more ideas.

Acknowledge complexity

In controversial issues the truth is often complex. Unfortunately, those are the very issues in which we are tempted to oversimplify. For example, when the issue of the integrity of politicians arises, we may immediately think, "They're all crooks and hypocrites." Actually, this thought is inaccurate and irresponsible. Some politicians may be dishonest and hypocritical, but many, arguably most, aren't. Moreover, the challenge of balancing the needs of different constituencies may create the appearance of dishonesty where it does not exist. Fairness demands that each politician be judged individually and on the basis of careful analysis, not preconceived notions.

Before you judge any issue, consider whether it may be more complex than it appears. And if it is, make your judgment reflect that complexity.

Look for connections among subjects

Over the centuries, educators found it convenient to divide human knowledge into various subject areas and to assign each to a separate academic department. There are English departments, history departments, chemistry departments, and so on. An unfortunate and unintended consequence of such division is the tendency to consider each subject area as totally unrelated to other subject areas.

In reality, the principles, concepts, and strategies learned in one subject often apply to other subjects as well. Moreover, most serious problems touch many subject areas. AIDS, for example, creates not only medical challenges but psychological, legal, and moral challenges as well. The more open you are to the relationships that exist among subjects, the more you will be rewarded with new insights.

Consider other viewpoints

To many people, intellectual independence means ignoring other people's views. This perspective hinders learning. Life is too short for learning solely through your limited experiences. By adding other people's ideas and experiences to your own, you will be able to broaden and deepen your knowledge, and in many cases gain valuable insights. This will happen precisely because you avoided the tunnel vision and hasty conclusion that we saw in the journalists' response to the epidemic of mass shootings in the United States. (Incidentally, the journalists of the *Journal News* were not the only ones who made this mistake. Many elected officials at both the state and federal levels committed the same mistake.) And keep in mind that considering other viewpoints is not the same as embracing them; it only means thinking about them and deciding whether they *deserve* your support.

Could openness to other people's viewpoints cause you to lose your intellectual independence? Yes, but only if you accept their views uncritically. As long as you test their ideas before accepting them, you will have nothing to fear. Recall the example of Carol Tavris presented in Chapter 2. She began her work by considering the widespread belief that expressing anger openly makes us feel less angry. But she didn't stop there. She also considered dissenting views and thought critically about all her findings. Her conclusion that expressing anger tends to reinforce and even intensify it was the result of openness to all viewpoints plus critical thinking!

GOOD THINKING!

The Story of Stanton Samenow

Stanton Samenow's first job as a clinical psychologist was working with young criminals in a hospital psychiatric unit. He brought to the job a conviction that criminals were victims of early traumatic experiences, poverty, and family instability. His treatment was based on that viewpoint. The only problem was, the treatment didn't work.

Eventually a family friend, Dr. Samuel Yochelson, issued Samenow an invitation and a promise: If Samenow would join Yochelson in the latter's work with criminals, he would learn a new and much more successful treatment theory and approach. Samenow accepted the invitation and, in time, achieved what was promised.

Samenow discovered that his assumptions about criminals had been seriously mistaken. He learned, in his words, "that criminals choose to commit crimes. Crime resides within the person and is 'caused' by the way he thinks, not by his environment. Criminals think differently from responsible people. What must change is how the offender views himself and the world. Focusing on forces outside the criminal is futile."

The approach consisted of having criminals keep meticulous journals, in which they wrote down the thoughts they entertained day-to-day. Then they met in small groups and learned ways to change their thinking patterns. Stanton himself has worked with many hundreds of criminals, Yochelson with many more, and their success rate has been impressive. Samenow details his experiences with the program in his book *Inside the Criminal Mind.*

The obvious lesson in Samenow's story concerns his discoveries that the problem of crime is that "we are as we think" and that people who are in the habit of thinking irresponsible, harmful thoughts can change that habit. But there is another, broader lesson in his story, one that reflects Samenow's own behavior. When his original theory proved mistaken, he set it aside, rethought the matter, and developed a more reasonable theory. In short, he dared to change his mind.

For more information on Stanton Samenow, see Stanton Samenow, *Inside the Criminal Mind* (New York: Times Books, 1984).

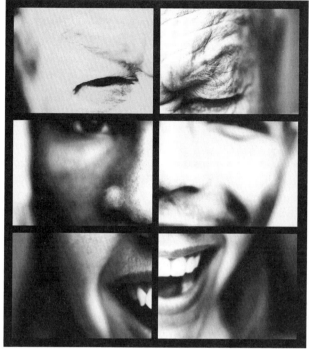

Bruce Gardner

Dare to change your mind

Some people believe that changing one's mind signals a lack of conviction. This belief allows them to think critically about other people's ideas but not about their own. To maintain this double standard, they are forced to ignore unpleasant facts, defend unworthy views, and value ego more highly than truth.

It is easy to identify people who harbor this belief. They treat all their opinions as if they were convictions and all their convictions as unquestionable. They are quick to disagree with views that differ from theirs but take offense when anyone disagrees with them. And they refuse to acknowledge the insights of individuals on the other side of an issue.

Let's be honest. Changing our minds is seldom, if ever, enjoyable. We can't help being a little embarrassed, even if the change occurs privately rather than publicly. Although we gain more than we lose when we exchange a weak idea for a strong one, we may feel the loss more acutely. That is understandable because we bond with opinions in much the same way that, as children, we bonded with our favorite blanket and stuffed animal. Familiar opinions provide a sense of security.

Nevertheless, changing our minds in response to evidence does not signal a lack of conviction. On the contrary, it signals courage and integrity. The key to developing this habit is to remember that *many of the ideas in our minds aren't even our own.*

All day long we receive ideas from the people around us, as well as from TV, radio, newspapers, magazines, and books. Unless we are very vigilant—and most of us aren't—false notions can take up residence in our minds. After they have been there for a while, we may be deceived into thinking they resulted from careful thinking on our part.

But what about opinions you are certain are your own? Should you be willing to change those too? Absolutely. The reason is simple: *Your opinions and convictions do not own you; you own them.* Any time you find an opinion to be lacking in quality, you have a right to discard it. If you think carefully and well, of course, many of your opinions will pass the most rigorous examination. When that happens, you can congratulate yourself. But you should be prepared to change your mind whenever new evidence is discovered.

Let's see how this process of changing one's mind works in an actual situation. For many years Jennifer considered astrology a good guide to everyday living. Her reasons were that numerous newspapers, magazines, and television treated it seriously and that many well-known, educated people used it as a guide to their decision making. But then she was involved in a discussion with someone she respected. That person asserted that astrology is not only unscientific but also illogical. Jennifer left that discussion wondering whether her view of astrology was reasonable.

Seeking more evidence, Jennifer visited the library and found a number of books and articles, some supporting astrology and others rejecting it. She also checked the Internet, and interviewed a professor of psychology and a professor of comparative religion. Finally, she consulted the Yellow Pages and called a local astrologer.

After evaluating her reading and discussion, Jennifer changed her initial view. Her revised view and her supporting reasons are as follows:

> Many well-known, educated people believe in astrology. Even so, I think it's an ineffective guide to everyday living. One reason is that astrology is based on superstitions of a primitive time. For example, because the planet Mars appears red, it has been associated with blood and aggression. Another reason is that astrology continues to say that planets influence us at the moment of birth even though the science of genetics has shown beyond question that the moment of conception is a more influential time. A third reason is that astrologers offer no answer to this question: If the planets Uranus, Neptune, and Pluto were discovered after 1780, weren't all horoscopes before that time necessarily wrong?

By having the courage to change her mind when the evidence called for it, Jennifer was able to adopt a more realistic view of astrology.

Base your judgments on evidence

The real measure of any viewpoint is how well it fits reality, and that is determined by the amount and the quality of the evidence. Unfortunately, many people ignore the need for evidence. They typically form judgments first and seek support for them later. The support they end up with is often nothing more than wishful thinking or foolish excuses. For example, some people say, "I smoke because science hasn't conclusively proved that it is harmful," "I don't use sunscreen because I'm not susceptible to skin cancer," or "I don't wear seatbelts because I don't want to be trapped in case I get in an accident." All three statements conveniently ignore the considerable evidence supporting the *opposite* view.

We humans are a proud species. Once we form a judgment, even a careless one, we are reluctant to change it because doing so means admitting a mistake. The best way to prevent pride from blocking insight is to keep your judgment tentative until you have examined the evidence.

Use your own ideas and your own words

Chapter 3 dealt in some detail with the problem of plagiarism. The emphasis there was on the fact that it is dishonest and therefore can carry serious consequences if discovered. But there is another important reason to avoid plagiarism. It robs you of your independence. Passing off someone else's ideas or words as your own is acknowledging, "I'm not bright enough to have ideas or phrasing of my own, so I have to steal other people's." It's hard to feel good about yourself with that admission in mind.

Temptations to plagiarize are plentiful. When you research any subject, you are bound to find many well-reasoned and well-expressed essays, and just as many excuses for stealing them: "I'll save a lot of time taking this." "I couldn't say it as well if I stayed up all night." "Chances are, nobody will find out." Maintaining your individuality is all about avoiding those temptations. Why limit yourself to dependence on others when you can think and speak for yourself?

Here's a thought: the next time you face such a temptation, look back at Chapter 4 and remind yourself how easy it is to be independent.

EXERCISES

4.1. Make a list of the people who have most influenced you and the specific effects of their influence (example: "My mother's warnings made me suspicious of strangers"). Aim to identify less obvious influences, including some that you have never recognized before (example: your imitation of the dress and manner of a celebrity).

4.2. Record your first thought about each of the following subjects. Respond directly and honestly. *Don't screen out any ideas or change them to fit what you think others might want you to say.*

Keeping promises

Being on time

Manners

Personal appearance

Success in life

Parents, teachers, employers

Free speech

Discipline

Apologizing

Excellence

Now evaluate what you recorded. In each case, decide whether your reaction is positive, constructive, and beneficial. If it is not, explain what reaction would be better.

4.3. Have you ever made, or heard others make, any of the following statements? If so, describe the occasion. Then identify and evaluate the attitude each statement suggests.

"This course doesn't matter because it's not required for my major."

"This instructor is assigning too much work."

"It's only fair for the instructor to put something on the test if she said we were responsible for knowing it."

"If the class gets too tough, I'll drop it."

"The reason I'm doing poorly is that the teacher doesn't like me."

"Students who take part in class discussions are just trying to impress the teacher."

4.4. Describe your reactions to the following situations—that is, what you would typically think, say, and do. Then identify the attitude underlying that response.

You express a point of view in a conversation and a friend disagrees with you.

You're in a large class and the teacher calls on you.

You're doing a homework assignment and are unsure how to proceed.

You're listening to someone you don't like. He's talking to a group of your friends, and they seem interested in what he's saying.

You begin reading a book or an article on a subject you feel strongly about. Then you realize the author's view strongly opposes yours.

4.5. While reading an essay, you encounter this statement: "Each individual creates his or her own morality. The moment a person decides that a behavior is acceptable, it becomes acceptable for that person, and no one else has any business criticizing the behavior." Create several realistic scenarios that could help you decide whether this viewpoint is reasonable. Then decide what those scenarios suggest about the viewpoint.

4.6. Using the approaches you learned in this and previous chapters, evaluate each of the following passages. State and briefly support your conclusion.

"I'm fascinated with the future because the future is where we're going to spend the rest of our lives."

A television commercial for a used car sales agency says, "We'll cosign your loan even if you've had a bankruptcy. That's because we take the trouble to handpick and inspect these cars before you even see them. . . . We guarantee financing because we only sell quality cars."

A guest on a self-help radio program says, "In my counseling practice, I advise my clients to replace all their negative thoughts with positive ones. In other words, if they think 'I'm impatient,' they should say, 'No, I'm patient.' 'I'm clumsy' becomes 'I'm graceful,' and 'I'm a poor athlete' becomes 'I'm an excellent athlete.' I tell them that whatever they believe themselves to be, they will be."

4.7. When Budweiser Dry beer was introduced, a series of television commercials appeared with the tagline "Why ask why? Try Bud Dry." The ad raised a few questions, such as "The Mona Lisa has no eyebrows. Why?" and "Chickens have no lips. Why?" and then recited the slogan, "Why ask why? Try Bud Dry." Was this advertisement manipulative? If so, in what way? What harmful effect, if any, might it have had?

4.8. Express a *tentative* opinion about each of the following issues. Then ask pertinent questions about what you have written, apply the techniques of imagination (see pages 86–87), and check the sources of your information. If your information is inadequate, do further research on the Internet or in the library. Finally, revise your view, as necessary, to make it reasonable.

Can animals think?

Should gambling be legalized?

Should teachers be allowed to spank elementary school children who misbehave in school?

Do smokers tend to discount the evidence that smoking can kill them?

Should the government assume control of the Internet, deciding who can have access and under what conditions?

Is it wrong to criticize another person's view of a controversial issue?

Is it acceptable to subject animals to painful experiments in order to find cures for diseases?

Is it possible for atheists to be as moral as religious believers?

4.9. State your present opinion on one of the following issues and your reason(s) for that opinion. Next, consider alternative views—by going to the library, conducting interviews, or doing Internet research—and keep a record of your sources. Then decide how reasonable your view is. If it is not as reasonable as it could be, revise it.

1. Should athletes be required to meet the same entrance standards as other students?

2. Should the federal government pass laws to prohibit pornography on the Internet?

3. Should schools or companies have policies limiting use of the Internet to school- or work-related activities?

4.10. In recent years health experts have become concerned about the increasing numbers of Americans who are significantly overweight or obese. By publicizing their concerns, the experts sparked a national debate about finding the cause(s) of this phenomenon. The following essays express very different views. Read each carefully. Then apply the W.I.S.E. approach and determine which view is more reasonable. Write a brief composition stating and supporting your decision.

SHAME ON FAST-FOOD MERCHANTS

By Elena Rodriguez

Obesity is no joke. It has been linked to heart conditions, high blood pressure, sleep apnea, diabetes, and respiratory problems. And one in five Americans qualifies as obese—that is, 30 percent heavier than the normal weight for one's height. The increase in obesity among children over the last decade or so is especially alarming.

Who is to blame for this increase? To some extent, the people themselves for eating fattening foods and not getting enough exercise. In the case of children, parents share some responsibility for allowing kids to snack continuously. But a good share of the blame must go to the fast-food industry, particularly to restaurants such as McDonald's, Burger King, and Wendy's.

The fast-food industry rejects that argument, and that comes as no surprise. If the courts were to uphold it, the dollar settlements would be huge (no pun intended). Their position would be believable if they just sat between the golden arches or whatever and waited for people to walk in and place an order. But they don't do that. They *advertise*. Translation: they use all kinds of slogans and gimmicks to entice people in, especially young people.

Think of all the scenes of good times and friendship you have seen in fast-food ads, with trim, athletic people chattering happily or singing jingles and dancing. (Not a bulging size 3X in sight!) Think, too, of the mouthwatering pictures of burgers and fish fillets, steam rising, ketchup oozing, and the accompanying invitation to "supersize" your order. (Never a reference to mega-milligrams of salt, mounds of sugar, or artery-clogging fat!)

When you've got all those images firmly in mind, you'll realize why the fast-food industry bears the main responsibility for the current obesity problem—because their ads deceive the public.

MCD'S FAULT? GIVE ME A BREAK

By Shandon Jackson

Time was when people were held accountable for their behavior. Now no one is. Rude, obnoxious people blame their parents for their offenses. Semiliterate ignoramuses blame their teachers. Incompetent workers blame their employers. People who destroy their lungs by smoking blame cigarette manufacturers. Given this "blame someone else" mentality, it was predictable that sooner or later overweight people would blame fast-food vendors.

The lawsuits that have been filed against fast-food restaurants are pure frivolity, totally without merit. Anyone with a smidgeon of common sense knows that fast food is fattening and lacking in nutritional value. Restaurants shouldn't have to post signs announcing the fact, any more than stove manufacturers should have to warn buyers that hot surfaces burn.

Do fast-food advertisements make our mouths water? Of course. Ads for diamonds and Porsche convertibles tempt us, too, but so what? Sales pitches are *meant* to sell us things we may not need or may not be good for us, and they do so by exaggerating.

The Romans invented a wonderful rule to cover such cases. It's called *caveat emptor*, "let the buyer beware." That's a polite way of saying, "If someone snookered you, take a good look in the mirror, say 'shame on you' to the person who looks back, and then get on with your life." That's still good advice.

If we don't put a stop to frivolous lawsuits, before long short people will be suing their parents for depriving them of "tall genes," chocoholics will be suing Hershey for causing their skin to break out, couch potatoes will be suing sofa manufacturers for enlarging their butts, and defeated politicians will be suing the voters for frustrating their ambitions. Enough is enough.

4.11. In light of what you learned in this chapter, what do you believe is the greatest obstacle to individuality facing young people today? Meet with a group of two or three classmates and discuss your individual answers to this question and the reasoning that underlies those answers. During this meeting make a special effort to apply the strategy for group discussion.

4.12. Party line voters vote for the candidates of their party automatically, without considering the merits of the opposing candidates. Such voters reason that the candidates their party selects are much more likely to share their views and values than opposing candidates. In contrast, issue voters are not much concerned about party affiliation. They give equal consideration to Democratic and Republican candidates and choose the ones who share their views, if not on every issue, then at least on the issues they consider most important. Use the W.I.S.E. approach and decide which approach to voting is more responsible. Write a brief essay supporting your decision.

4.13. Some time ago, according to news reports, a 36-year-old North Dakota woman married *herself*! There was a ceremony attended by her friends, and even an exchange of rings with her "inner husband." The whole affair was not a gimmick, the bride/groom explained, but instead a celebration of herself. Some would consider such an event absurd, but others would regard it as a perfectly reasonable extension of the idea of marriage, and even a creative expression of individuality. Using the W.I.S.E. approach, examine the issue, identifying the pros and cons and deciding what view is more supportable. Either write a composition presenting your view or be prepared to debate the issue in class.

4.14. Earlier in this chapter (see page 73) we saw how Step 3 of the W.I.S.E. approach would have led the editors of the *Journal News* to a number of ideas about the causes of mass shootings. We ended that discussion by noting that the editors would have compared those (and other) ideas and decided which one(s) offered the most promising way to end the epidemic of mass shootings. Review those ideas (and whatever others you find) and decide what way you believe is most promising.

4.15. What lessons can you draw from the Good Thinking profiles of Viktor Frankl, Stephanie Kwolek, and Stanton Samenow presented in this chapter? Explain how you can use each of those lessons in your career and/or personal life.

QUIZ

1. What is the first step in becoming an individual as explained in this chapter?

2. Most of us were, and still are, vulnerable to the influences of other people. True or false? Explain your answer.

3. What is an "attitude"?

4. The chapter uses the term "culture war." Define that term and identify the parties to the conflict.

5. State the four "empowering attitudes" discussed in the chapter.

6. How does manipulation differ from other influences?

7. Name two forms of manipulation and explain why we should resist them.

8. Identify the steps suggested for resisting manipulation.

9. List three strategies for individuality and explain why each is important.

10. Changing your mind undermines your individuality. True or false?

Answers to this quiz are available at www.cengagebrain.com.

Avoiding Errors in Thinking 5

The final step in the W.I.S.E. approach is evaluating. This means examining the points of view you have found in your investigation and the ones you have formed in your speculation, and then deciding which view is best. Your goal will be to identify the point of view that offers the most practical and effective solution to the problem or the most reasonable and defensible response to the issue.

In some cases, one view will be clearly superior to the others in most, if not all, respects and will therefore need no modifications at all, or only minor ones. In other cases, several competing views will have sufficient merit that the challenge will be to find a way to combine them. How you accomplish this will depend on the problem or issue, but it will generally involve accepting parts of each competing view and rejecting other parts.

The key question, of course, is *how exactly will you do the accepting and rejecting*? The answer is, by determining which ideas reveal errors in thinking. Over the centuries scholars have identified more than 100 such errors. By streamlining our list and grouping the errors by kind, we can make the job of analysis much easier.

FOUR KINDS OF ERRORS

> Most often people seek in life occasions for persisting in their opinions rather than for educating themselves. Each of us looks for justification in the event. The rest, which runs counter to that opinion, is overlooked. . . . It seems as if the mind enjoys nothing more than sinking deeper into error.
>
> **—André Gide**

Perhaps Gide overstated the problem in suggesting that we *enjoy* error. But he was wise in noting our difficulty in dealing with issues objectively and logically. To overcome that difficulty, we need to understand the kinds of errors that can entrap us and the steps we can take to avoid them.

Four broad types of errors are common: errors of perception, errors of judgment, errors of expression, and errors of reaction. By understanding not just the errors themselves, but when they occur, we are better able to recognize and correct them.

ERRORS OF PERCEPTION

Errors of perception are not blunders made while examining issues. They are faulty ways of seeing reality, preventing us from being open-minded *even before we begin* to apply our critical thinking. The following are especially serious.

"Mine is better" thinking

As small children we may have said, "My mommy is prettier than any other mommy" or "My daddy is bigger and stronger." Perhaps we had similar thoughts about our houses, toys, and finger paintings.

Now that we've gotten older, we probably don't express "mine is better" thinking. Yet we may still indulge in it. Such thinking often occurs in matters that are important to us, such as our race, religion, ethnic group, social class, political party, or philosophy of life.

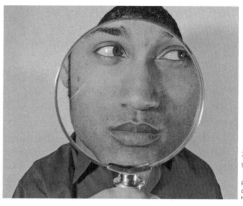

This habit is not always obvious. In fact, "mine is better" thinking can be subtle. We may be uninterested in a person until we find out she is Irish, like us. Suddenly we feel a sense of kinship. We may think a person is rather dense until he says something that matches our view. Then we decide he's really quite bright after all.

"Mine is better" thinking is natural and often harmless. Even so, this kind of thinking creates distance between people through a win–lose mentality, which can easily create an obstacle to learning from others. To prevent this from happening, remember that opening your mind to ideas from other people can broaden your perspective and lead to fresh insights. Give every idea a fair hearing—even an idea that challenges your own.

Selective perception

In one sense, we see selectively most of the time. Let's say you and two friends, a horticulture major and an art major, walk through a shopping mall. You want to buy a pair of shoes; the others are just taking a break from studying. The same reality exists for each of you: stores, potted plants, and people passing by. Still, each of you focuses on different things. While you are looking for shoe stores, one friend notices plants. The other friend studies faces for interesting features.

Later, one of you says, "Hey, did you see the big new store in the mall?" The others say no. Though the store was before all of your eyes, two of you screened it out.

That kind of selective perception is often harmless. Another kind of selective perception takes place when we focus on things that support our current ideas and reject anything that challenges them. Suppose someone thinks that a particular ethnic group is stupid, violent, cheap, or lazy. Then "stupid" behaviors will capture that person's attention. And if his bias is strong enough, he will completely miss intelligent behaviors from members of that group. He'll see only evidence that supports his prejudice.

You can break the habit of selective perception by looking and listening for details you haven't seen before. Also press yourself to balance your perception. If you find yourself focusing on negative details, look for positive ones, and vice versa.

Gullibility and skepticism

Philosopher Alfred Korzybski observed, "there are two ways to slide easily through life: to believe everything or to doubt everything—both ways save us from thinking." To believe everything we are told is to be gullible. To doubt everything is to be skeptical.

An alternative to gullibility and skepticism is questioning. This means greeting all ideas with curiosity and wonder, judging none of them in advance, and being equally prepared to find wisdom, foolishness, or some combination of the two.

GOOD THINKING!

The Story of Sylvia Earle

To say that Sylvia Earle loves her work would be an understatement. After 6,000 hours underwater and 50 oceanographic expeditions, she wrote, "And I can still feel that leap of enthusiasm, and real joy, at the prospect of finally getting out to the beach, and running around." Her fascination with nature began as a small child when she lived near the New Jersey shore and continued when her family moved to Florida. Blessed with affectionate parents who themselves loved nature, she had always wanted to work with plants and animals. For a time she thought she'd become a veterinarian, but she preferred wild creatures and eventually decided on marine science.

At first she was in awe of the tremendous knowledge contained in the thousands of books on her subject, so she studied diligently at Florida State and Duke universities, earning her Ph.D. at the latter. But then she came to realize "there is so much that we do not know. Each of those books represents a door that can lead you to hundreds, thousands of questions. . . . It could take ten lifetimes [to answer them]." She took special pleasure in wrestling with problems, putting one fact with another, and achieving "a flash of light in the brain." She calls that experience "sheer joy."

Earle's love of nature and fascination with its challenges led her to a remarkable professional career. She led the first team of female aquanauts, living underwater for two weeks, and founded her own ocean exploration company. She has written more than 100 scientific articles and books and taken part in science programs in more than 60 countries. She has served as chief scientist of the National Oceanographic and Atmospheric Administration. Today, as explorer-in-residence at the National Geographic Society, she continues her cause of protecting the planet's seas.

For more on Sylvia Earle, see www.greatwomen.org/component/fabrik/details/2/53 and www.achievement.org/autodoc/page/ear0int-1.

Preconceptions

A preconception about the majority or the minority   Preconception tends to follow our affections. If we feel more comfortable with the majority on our side, we may take for granted that the majority view is correct. If we identify with the underdog and love the challenge of confronting superior numbers, we may make the same assumption about the minority view.

Each of these choices can occur with little or no awareness that we are making up our minds in advance. And in each case we put feelings of comfort and personal preference above the evidence. Critical thinking means deciding issues on their merits rather than on the number or the celebrity status of the people on the opposing sides.

A preconceived view of change   According to an old joke, conservatives have never met a new idea they liked, and liberals have never met a new idea they didn't like. Each observation contains an element of truth.

Some people find even small changes, like returning home from school and finding the furniture rearranged, upsetting. Major changes, like moving across the country, can be even more disturbing.

New ideas can have a similar effect on such people. Old beliefs provide a sense of comfort and security. When those beliefs are challenged, people may feel that reality has been pulled out from under them. That's probably why ancient rulers killed the bearers of bad news. It's also one reason why persuading others can be difficult.

Unfavorable preconceptions about change may be older and more common than favorable ones. Yet the latter seem to be increasing today, perhaps because technology is advancing so rapidly. Some people think that old ideas, old beliefs, and old values are of little use today. For them, new is always better.

Neither perspective is consistent with critical thinking. Some new ideas are clearly better than those they replace. Progress has in fact occurred in every area of life, including science, technology, education, and government. Yet this reality has another, less beneficial side. New ideas can contain serious flaws that go unnoticed at first. Time and experience can prove that the supposed great leap forward was actually several steps backward.

To avoid preconceptions about change, know your own mental habits. Also resist the temptation to accept first impressions.

Pretending to know

Some people believe that confessing ignorance makes them look ineffective, so they pretend to know things. After a while, pretending becomes a habit that hinders critical thinking. Suppose someone says on several occasions, "I've read quite a few books on psychology." Also suppose the truth is different, and he's never read a book on the subject. The idea will become so familiar that he might take it for the truth. What's more, he'll begin to confuse his guesses about psychology with real knowledge. Practice staying aware of your statements and remaining alert for pretense. Whenever you find it, acknowledge the truth, and resolve not to lie to yourself or others again.

Of course, your pretense may not be conscious but instead unconscious. This can happen easily when the subject is very much in the news. During a political campaign, for example, you may hear unsupported charges against a candidate repeated so often that you regard them as unquestionably true. The way to combat this mistake is to be more curious about whatever you hear repeated by others. Ask yourself what motive the speakers might have to mislead you, and what evidence (if any) supports their claims. Keep in mind, too, the possibility that those speakers may not have *intended* to mislead you but were simply not curious enough about what they heard repeated by others.

Either/or thinking

This error of perception means taking only extreme positions on issues when other positions are possible. For example, one person thinks that accepting evolution means rejecting the idea of creation. Another person thinks that being Republican means taking a conservative stance on every issue.

Yet it's possible to believe in evolution and creation. You could believe that God created the universe and planned for it to evolve over millions of years. (You could also be a Republican without always taking a conservative stand.)

Either/or thinking hampers critical thinking. This error prompts us to take extreme, unreasonable views. To avoid either/or thinking, look for times when there seem to be only two possible views. Ask yourself, "Are these the only possibilities? Could another view be more reasonable—perhaps one that includes elements of both?"

An example is the debate over crime prevention. Some elected officials argue for banning assault weapons and registering handguns. The National Rifle Association argues for getting criminals off the street. You might ask, "Why not take both actions and add others, such as building more prisons, as well?"

False tolerance

Tolerance is an important concept. Unfortunately, a number of misconceptions have arisen about it. For example, you may have the impression that to be tolerant, you must affirm that all ideas and behaviors are equal and refuse to judge other people's opinions, beliefs, or actions. That notion is both mistaken and mischievous.

If you examined the history of any academic subject, you would find the same general situation—ideas and beliefs in conflict. Whether the subject is science or math, social science or humanities, business or technology, practitioners devote their lives to deepening their understanding and discovering the truth about the subject. And the process is the same in all subjects, at least among conscientious individuals—careful testing of ideas and beliefs to determine whether they can be improved.

It is no exaggeration to say that throughout history a distinguishing quality of such individuals has been their *intolerance* of shallow, shabby, or otherwise inferior ideas and beliefs. The subject of critical thinking is important precisely because it helps students develop the same habits of careful investigation, evaluation, and judgment exhibited by noteworthy contributors to human knowledge.

The reference to intolerance in the previous paragraph may seem to deny the importance of tolerance. In fact, it does not. Tolerance is something we owe to *people*, not to ideas. By virtue of being human, people have an inherent dignity and from that dignity flow certain "inalienable" rights, including the right to form their own opinions and beliefs. To be tolerant means to respect other people and affirm their rights, even when their opinions and beliefs differ from ours. By extension, it also means giving those who disagree with us the benefit of the doubt whenever possible—for example, by assuming that they formed their views honestly.

However, tolerance in no way requires that we endorse other people's *ideas*. To begin with, as human beings we too have the right to form and express our views, including our assessments of other people's opinions and beliefs. Of course, the way we form and express our views should never be disrespectful of other people or their rights. In other words, we should (1) take the time necessary to understand other people's opinions before criticizing them, (2) base our criticisms on evidence rather than personal preference, and (3) speak and act courteously and with sensitivity to other people's feelings.

ERRORS OF JUDGMENT

Errors of judgment occur in the process of sorting out and assessing evidence. They prevent us from reaching the most reasonable conclusion. The following errors of judgment are among the most common.

Double standard

This error consists of using one standard of judgment for our ideas and an entirely different, more demanding standard for ideas that conflict with ours.

People who employ a double standard ignore inconsistencies, contradictions, and outrageous overstatements in arguments they agree with. Yet they nitpick their opponents' arguments. They even use different vocabularies. Allies are described as "imaginative," "forceful," and "brutally honest." Opponents with the same qualities are labeled "utopian," "belligerent," or "mean-spirited."

Critical thinking demands a single standard of judgment for both those who agree and those who disagree with us.

Irrelevant criterion

This error consists of criticizing an idea because it fails to do what it wasn't intended to do. Say that a chief executive proposes a new reward program for employees' cost-saving ideas in his company. Supervisors argue against the program because it doesn't increase the percentage of women and minorities in the company. In this case, the supervisors are invoking an irrelevant criterion.

The point is not that fairness to women and minorities is unimportant. Rather, fairness is a different issue and should not be made the measure of the reward program.

You can avoid the mistake of using irrelevant criteria. When you evaluate an idea, set aside all separate issues and agendas, no matter how important they are or how committed you feel about them.

Overgeneralizing or stereotyping

Generalizations are judgments about a class of people or things. Political pollsters are generalizing when they say, "Most voters don't care much about either presidential candidate." Though such a statement covers tens of millions of people, it's a fair one if based on a representative sample of those people.

Generalizations don't have to be based on a scientific sampling in order to be fair. They need only be based on a reasonable number of contacts with a reasonable number of people in the group. For example, your instructor might say, "My present students are more willing to participate in class than my students were last year." Or you could say, "The people in my neighborhood are friendly."

Overgeneralizations are unfair generalizations. They exceed what's appropriate to conclude from our experiences. Suppose a professor teaches only advanced French literature and sees only a small, unique group of students. If she says something about "the students at this college" based solely on her experience, she is thinking uncritically. Or consider a first-semester student who has contact with only five instructors. This person would be overgeneralizing if he judged "the faculty at this school."

Stereotypes are overgeneralizations that harden into convictions shared by many people. There are stereotypes of people: fundamentalists, politicians, feminists, psychiatrists, and rock musicians. And there are stereotypes of places and things: New York City and San Francisco, marriage and farming.

Overgeneralizations and stereotypes hinder critical thinking by blinding us to important differences among individual people, places, and things.

GOOD THINKING!

The Story of Martin Seligman

One day when Martin Seligman was a young graduate student working in the experimental psychology lab at the University of Pennsylvania, the laboratory dogs were behaving strangely. Instead of responding to the stimuli as they had previously done, they were lying still. Pondering the situation, Seligman decided they must have inadvertently been taught to be helpless. Since there was no historical data that could be used to solve the problem, Seligman's professor suggested that Seligman and his partner Steve Maier undertake their own research.

Seligman and Maier's research revealed the phenomenon now known as "learned helplessness." By illustrating how animals or people become emotionally paralyzed when they believe that their efforts in a particular situation are futile, this and subsequent studies revealed the error of the reigning stimulus–response theory. They also presented a formidable challenge to behaviorism's mechanistic view of the mind.

Meanwhile, a much larger challenge was taking shape in the field of psychology—academic psychologists were being outnumbered by clinical psychologists. Seligman noted that psychology was fast becoming "almost synonymous with mental illness," and the National Institute of Mental Health (NIMH) was becoming concerned "exclusively about mental disorders, rather than health." Seligman realized that learning about mental and emotional problems was necessary and useful, but believed that this emphasis had done harm as well. As he observed, "People want more than just to correct their weaknesses. They want lives imbued with meaning. . . . The time has finally arrived for a science that seeks to understand positive emotion, build strength and virtue, and provide guideposts for finding what Aristotle called the 'good life.'"

Seligman began studying the science of how people could add meaning to their lives. He developed a discipline he called "Positive Psychology"; this is arguably his greatest contribution to his profession.

For more information on Martin Seligman, see his *Learned Optimism* (New York: Free Press, 1990) and *Authentic Happiness* (New York: Free Press, 2002).

Hasty conclusion

Hasty conclusions are drawn without enough evidence. Consider this case: A student often leaves the door to his room open, and many people have access to the room. One day he discovers an expensive pen is missing from his desk. He concludes that his roommate took it. This is a hasty conclusion. It's possible that his roommate stole the pen. It's also possible that someone else stole it. Or perhaps he lost or misplaced the pen.

In many cases, two or more conclusions are possible. Critical thinking means having a good reason for choosing one over the others. If no such reason exists, suspend judgment and seek more evidence.

Unwarranted assumption

Assumptions are ideas we take for granted. They differ from conclusions in an important way: Assumptions are *implied* rather than expressed. In many cases we make them unconsciously. Consider this exchange:

SALLY: You say that discrimination against women is a thing of the past. That's just not true.

RALPH: It certainly is true. I read it in a magazine.

Ralph may not be aware of it, but he is assuming that whatever appears in a magazine is necessarily true. This assumption takes too much for granted, so it is unwarranted.

There's nothing necessarily wrong with assumptions. Making them allows us to conduct our daily activities efficiently. When you got up this morning, you assumed there would be enough hot water to take a shower. If you drove to school, you probably assumed that your car would start and your instructors would hold classes. Unless there was a good reason not to make these assumptions—for example, if you knew your water heater was broken—they would be valid.

The assumptions that hinder critical thinking are unwarranted assumptions. They prevent us from asking useful questions and exploring possibilities. For example, if a student assumes that it is the teacher's job to make class interesting, she is unlikely to ask herself, "What responsibility do my fellow students and I have to make class interesting?" Here are some common unwarranted assumptions.

Unwarranted Assumption	Why Unwarranted
People's senses are always trustworthy.	Senses are imperfect and can mislead us.
Having reasons proves that one has reasoned carefully.	Some reasons are not thought out at all but simply borrowed from others.
Conviction constitutes proof.	It is possible to be passionately committed to a mistaken idea.

Unwarranted Assumption	Why Unwarranted
Familiar ideas are more valid than unfamiliar ideas.	If we hear a false statement often enough, it becomes familiar and we naturally regard it as true.
If one event occurs soon after another, it must have been caused by the other.	Sometimes the closeness in time is merely coincidental.
The way things are is the way they are supposed to be.	Because we humans are an imperfect species, what we invent or establish is almost always subject to improvement.
Whatever hasn't been done is impossible to do.	According to Edward Karsner and James Newman, "the first steam vessel to cross the Atlantic carried, as part of its cargo, a book which 'proved' that it was impossible for a steam vessel to cross anything, much less the Atlantic" (Larrabee, 91). The author of that book obviously assumed that what hadn't yet been done couldn't be done.
If an idea is in one's mind, it must have originated there.	All day long, every day of our lives, we read and hear other people's ideas. Those we hear only once may be quickly forgotten, but those we hear many times are reinforced, especially when we repeat them in our own words. In time we may mistakenly regard them as uniquely ours.
Widely accepted ideas must be true.	Nations and cultures can be as easily mistaken as individuals. History is filled with examples, such as the popular notion that high self-esteem is correlated with success and low self-esteem with failure. Harold Stevenson and James Stigler tested this idea in a study of elementary students from Japan, Taiwan, China, and the United States. All the Asian students outperformed the Americans academically yet scored lower in self-esteem. Moreover, in 1990 a group of scholars, many of them favorably disposed to the self-esteem theory, reviewed the research on self-esteem and found, in the words of sociologist Neil Smelser, "the associations between self-esteem and its expected consequences are mixed, insignificant, or absent" (Kohn, 274).

Because assumptions are unstated and often unconscious, they are difficult to detect. When you look for assumptions in your own thinking and writing, go beyond what you consciously thought or wrote. Ask yourself, "What am I not expressing but merely taking for granted?"

Failure to make a distinction

Distinctions are subtle differences among things. Care in making distinctions can help you overcome confusion and deal effectively with complex issues. Following are some important distinctions to recognize.

The Distinction	Why Necessary
The distinction between the person and the idea	Critical thinkers judge an idea on its own merits—not on the celebrity status or expertise of the person expressing it. Though experts usually have more informed views than novices, experts can be wrong and novices can have genuine insights.
The distinction between assertion and evidence	Some people pile assertion upon assertion without evidence. If these people are articulate, the casual thinker may be persuaded. Critical thinkers judge ideas on how well supported—and supportable—they are. This is more important than how well the idea is expressed.
The distinction between familiarity and validity	We're naturally attracted to the familiar. It's easy to believe that reasoning is valid merely because we've heard it many times. Critical thinkers, however, are not swayed by familiarity.
The distinction between categorizing the person and evaluating the argument	Uncritical thinkers tend to think that once they have determined a person's philosophical, political, or religious perspective, they need not consider the merits of the person's argument. Such thinkers are fond of saying "I've got her pegged—she's a liberal" (or "a Democrat" or "a Republican") and then closing their minds to the person's ideas. Critical thinkers know that an argument deserves to be considered on its merits, regardless of who advances it.
The distinction between often *and always,* seldom *and* never.	Uncritical thinkers tend to ignore these distinctions. They might say something "always" occurs when the evidence supports only "often," or they might say it "never" occurs when the evidence supports only "seldom." Critical thinkers are careful to make the distinction.

Oversimplification

There's nothing wrong with simplifying. In elementary school especially, teachers simplify their subjects. Professionals such as engineers and chemists simplify to communicate with people untrained in their fields.

"If I work hard, I'll get good grades. If I get good grades, I'll go to a top college. If I go to a top college, I'll get a great job. If I get a great job, I'll make a lot of money. If I make a lot of money, everyone will hate me. That's why I didn't do my homework."

Randy Glasbergen/glasbergen.com

Oversimplification differs from simplification. It goes beyond making complex matters more understandable and distorts reality. Consider this idea: "High school teachers have it made. They're through at three o'clock every day and work only nine months of the year." Though there is some truth to this statement, it's inaccurate. Teachers often prepare four or five classes a day, grade homework, keep records, chaperone activities, and advise organizations. These activities often occur outside the normal eight-hour day. In addition, teachers are often required to take summer courses.

ERRORS OF EXPRESSION

Errors of expression occur when we are communicating our thoughts. The most common of these errors are the following.

Contradicting oneself

In Chapter 1 we discussed the principle of contradiction, which states that a statement can't be both true and false at the same time and in the same way. Consider, for example, the statement "British Petroleum was *solely responsible* for the devastating oil spill in the Gulf of Mexico in 2010." We may not know now—indeed, we may never know with certainty—whether that statement is true or false. However, we can be certain that it is not *both* true and false.

Most of our discussion in Chapter 1 concerned situations in which the points of view of two individuals are irreconcilably opposed. Here we are speaking of the error of contradicting *ourselves*. It can happen quite easily. For example, at the beginning of a composition, you may say that capital punishment is never morally justifiable and then in a later paragraph speak approvingly of the death penalty for child molesters. Or you say that obesity is a serious problem among high school students, but then explain that the media have greatly exaggerated the problem.

Your remarks on the death penalty are clearly contradictory; so the only way to correct the error is to decide which point of view you believe and be consistent in your presentation. Your remarks on obesity *appear to be* contradictory, so you should clarify your view. For example, you might say that obesity is a serious problem despite the fact that the media have overstated its seriousness.

Arguing in a circle

Arguing in a circle occurs when we set out to explain something complex or difficult and end up where we started, without having accomplished our stated intention. Here are some examples.

Statement: The reason that many college graduates lack basic communication skills is that they lack the ability to put their thoughts into words.

Comment: This says, in effect, many graduates can't communicate well because they can't communicate well.

Statement: The reason the federal deficit has spiraled out of control is that our expenditures have been greater than our revenues.

Comment: A deficit is, by definition, a result of spending more than is taken in, so this apparent explanation explains nothing. (Such statements are popular among politicians because they create the illusion of defending a position without actually doing so.)

To avoid the error of arguing in a circle, make sure that your explanations provide an explanation and not just a restatement of your point.

False analogy

Analogy is the use of something familiar to explain something unfamiliar. It says, in effect, "this is *like* that." The strength of analogy is its ability to make complex things clear, often in a vivid way. However, analogies are necessarily imperfect because things that are analogous rather than identical will always differ in some respects.

Acceptable analogies point to the similarities without oversimplifying reality or misleading us about the dissimilarities. False analogies oversimplify or mislead. In the worst case, they assert a similarity where none exists. Let's first consider some acceptable analogies.

A corporation is like a human body—its health depends on each constituent part performing its function properly.

Before John's body was cold, his relatives had descended like vultures to pick his estate clean.

The universe is like a safe to which there is a combination. But the combination is locked up in the safe. —*Peter De Vries*

Harrison Ford is like one of those sports cars that advertise acceleration from 0 to 60 mph in three or four seconds. —*Richard Schickel* (referring to Ford's ability to respond to the emotions inherent in scenes)

Now consider these false analogies.

Analogy: Voters are like little children—they need to be told what to think and do for their own good.

Comment: Voters may in some ways be childlike—aren't we all?—but not in this sense of needing to be controlled or manipulated.

Analogy: "You can't make an omelet without breaking eggs."

Comment: This infamous analogy was made by Vladimir Lenin to justify killing those who opposed the Russian Revolution. It ignored the more significant fact that, unlike eggs, people have inherent dignity.

Irrational appeal

The term *appeal*, as we are using it, means a reference to something respected that is employed to persuade others. An appeal is rational if it is reasonable and irrational if it substitutes emotion for critical thinking. Here are the most common types of irrational appeals.

Irrational appeal to tradition ignores the question of whether the tradition deserves allegiance in the present situation. Circumstances can render a tradition invalid, so it is important to react thoughtfully rather than emotionally.

Irrational appeal to moderation encourages compromise on an issue without considering whether compromise will mean abandoning a core belief. In some cases, it will.

Irrational appeal to authority comes in several forms, as David Hackett Fischer has pointed out. One is "I'm an expert, you're not; therefore, I'm right and you're wrong." Another is the use of pedantic words, concerning which he quotes Bertrand Russell: "In Chicago I had a large seminar, where I continued to lecture on the same subject as at Oxford, namely, 'Words and Facts.' But I was told that Americans would not respect my lectures if I used monosyllables, so I altered the title to something like 'The Correlation between Oral and Somatic Motor Habits.' Under this title, or something of the sort, the seminar was approved." A third form of irrational appeal is using many quotations merely for the sake of appearing scholarly. A fourth form is multiplying the number of words to substitute bulk for substance. A fifth form is the appeal to the authority of the printed page, as in "I read it so it must be true."[1]

Irrational appeal to loyalty encourages putting loyalty to an ideal or institution above other, arguably more important factors, notably ethical standards or legal requirements.

Irrational appeal to fear plays on people's insecurities rather than identifying specific dangers to be concerned about or to avoid. Often these irrational appeals do not specify the danger but keep it vague, as in "I wouldn't do that; you can't tell what could happen if you do."

ERRORS OF REACTION

Errors of reaction occur when we express a viewpoint and someone reacts negatively. They are defensive reactions that preserve our self-image and provide an excuse to maintain our view. The following errors of reaction are the most common.

Explaining away

Ron has been a marijuana smoker for several years. He maintains that marijuana is harmless. Last night he and a group of friends were talking, and one of them mentioned that his health instructor had distributed an article from the *Journal of the American Medical Association*.

That article reported the results of a clinical study of marijuana use. It concluded that "contrary to what is frequently reported, we have found the effect of marijuana to be not merely that of a mild intoxicant which causes a slight exaggeration of usual adolescent behavior, but a specific and separate clinical syndrome." The main effects the study noted were "disturbed awareness of the self, apathy, confusion and poor reality testing."

Ron's reply was heated. "Those articles are written by a bunch of guys who never smoked a joint. They're guessing, fantasizing, or worse, making up scare stories for parents to feed their kiddies. I've smoked pot for years, and I can tell you it's had no effect on me."

Ron found the prospect of being wrong about marijuana and the possibility of injuring himself too unpleasant to consider. This is understandable. Still, critical thinking would suggest that he at least read the article and examine the evidence. Instead, he resorted to a tactic long used in uncritical thinking: explaining it away.

When people explain away challenges to their ideas, they don't change reality. They just postpone dealing with it. The longer they postpone, the

---

[1] Fischer, *Historians' Fallacies*, 283 f.

more painful the experience. If you wish to avoid such results, face unpleasant ideas directly and honestly.

Shifting the burden of proof

Accepting the burden of proof means supporting our assertions. The more the assertions challenge accepted wisdom, the greater the burden. What's more, this burden falls on the person who makes the assertion. Here's how this concept applies in an actual case. Two students are discussing greatness in boxing:

ZEKE: Mike Tyson was the greatest heavyweight boxer of all time.

BRAD: Wait a minute. There have been a lot of great heavyweights over the years. I doubt Tyson was better than all of them.

ZEKE: I stand by my position. Prove me wrong if you can.

There would be nothing wrong with Zeke's asking Brad why he doubts Tyson's greatness. But when Zeke says "Prove me wrong," he's shifting the burden of proof. Since Zeke made the original statement, he should be prepared to defend it.

When you make an assertion, you might be called on to defend it. And if you find that you can't defend the assertion, avoid shifting your burden of proof. Instead, withdraw the assertion.

Attacking the person

In uncritical thinking there's a common way of reacting to challenges: attack the challenger. Here's a common scenario.

Melissa argues that it makes no sense for students to vote while they're away at college. The process of obtaining an absentee ballot is time-consuming, she says. And with so many people voting, a student's vote isn't that important.

Agnes challenges Melissa's view. "I voted by absentee ballot last year," she says, "and the process was simple." Agnes adds that some elections are close enough to be decided by a few thousand votes. What's more, hundreds of thousands of college students are eligible to vote.

Now Melissa is embarrassed. The weakness of her view has been exposed in front of other students. She launches an attack on Agnes. "You have no business lecturing me about right and wrong. Just last week you cut Friday's classes so you could go home early, and then you lied to your instructors about being sick. Stop being a hypocrite, Agnes."

Even if this attack on Agnes is true, it has nothing to do with the issue of college students voting. It's merely a way for Melissa to save face.

How would Melissa respond if she practiced critical thinking? She would focus on Agnes's idea rather than on Agnes as a person. And since the idea seems reasonable, Melissa would probe it further before dismissing it. She could say, "Perhaps I'm mistaken. What steps are needed to vote by absentee ballot?" Then if Agnes's answer showed that the process was simple, Melissa could respond, "I guess you're right."

By acting this way, Melissa would not lose face. In fact, the other students might be impressed at her flexibility and willingness to admit a mistake.

Straw man

This error involves make-believe. Specifically, the error means pretending others have made statements that they didn't make, and then denouncing them for making the statements.

Imagine this situation: Someone has proposed that your school's attendance policy be revised to permit unlimited absences from class without penalty. You argue against the proposal, claiming that students who attend class sporadically slow the pace of learning for others and degrade the quality of class discussion.

Then someone responds to your argument as follows: "I take exception to your view. You say that adults should be treated as children, that students must leave their constitutional rights at the college gate, and that individuals whose work obligations sometimes force them to miss class are inferior creatures deserving of punishment."

Those stirring words, which bear no relation to reality, constitute the error of straw man. They attribute to you something you did not say. To avoid the error of straw man, listen to or read others' arguments carefully. Focus your criticism on what was actually said or clearly implied.

In all these errors of reaction, ego gets in the way of critical thinking. It's in your long-term interest to acknowledge error and learn from it. Doing so promotes knowledge and wisdom.

ERRORS CAN MULTIPLY

Errors would be costly enough if they occurred singly and separately. Yet in many cases one error invites another, and that leads to several more. It's natural for us to want knowledge and wisdom. (Have you ever met anyone who *wanted* to be ignorant and foolish?) And it's easy to go from wanting it to pretending we have it and then to seeing the world in a way that reinforces our pretense.

Such a chain of perception errors paves the way for errors of judgment. For example, it can lead to assuming too much, ignoring important distinctions, and jumping to conclusions that flatter our viewpoint. And once we embrace errors of judgment, express them to others, and hear them criticized, we may be tempted to commit errors of reaction to save face.

Remembering the ways in which errors tend to multiply can keep you motivated to think critically.

EXERCISES

5.1 Consider each of the following situations, being alert for errors of perception. Such errors are often implied rather than stated directly, so you are likely to find hints rather than clear-cut evidence of error. Identify whatever hints you find, and explain why you believe they point to an error of perception.

a) In April 2007, NFL quarterback Michael Vick pleaded guilty to charges related to his involvement in an illegal dog fighting operation. He also admitted he personally helped kill a number of dogs after they lost their fights. When Vick was first charged, Marvin and Oscar were discussing the news reports. Marvin took the position that if Vick was guilty of the charges, he should receive the maximum penalty provided by law. Oscar questioned the news reports, arguing that star athletes—especially black star athletes—are often falsely accused.

b) In a classroom discussion on the subject of terrorism, Ethel claimed that moderate Muslims around the world are not speaking out forcefully enough against Muslim terrorists. "I know that if acts of terrorism were committed by Jews or Christians, the Jewish and Christian communities around the world would loudly denounce their actions," she said. "The fact that Muslims remain silent is a scandal."

c) Claude believes that efforts to improve the health care system in the United States are completely misguided. He supports this belief with statistics showing serious problems in the health care systems of Canada, England, France, Sweden, and Cuba.

5.2 Think of a time when you've committed each of the following errors of perception and describe the situation. Explain how you reacted and what events followed. Then decide how you might have avoided each error and how the consequences might have been different. (If you can't think of an error of your own, identify one you encountered through reading or observation.)

"Mine is better" thinking
Selective perception
Gullibility and skepticism
Preconception
Pretending to know
Either/or thinking
False tolerance

5.3 Think of a time when you've committed each of the following errors of judgment and describe the situation. Explain how you reacted and what events followed. Then decide how you might have avoided each error and how the consequences might have been different. (If you can't think of an error of your own, identify one you encountered through reading or observation.)

Double standard
Irrelevant criterion
Overgeneralizing or stereotyping

Hasty conclusion
Unwarranted assumption
Failure to make a distinction
Oversimplification

5.4 Read each of the following passages carefully, looking for errors of judgment. Remember that such errors are sometimes implied rather than stated directly. Explain your findings.

a) SUE: My English instructor makes us rewrite any composition that contains more than three errors in grammar or usage. And she's always demanding that we do better in our writing. I think she dislikes us.

ELLEN: I know what you mean. The professors at this college seem to think it's Harvard.

b) MORRIS: Did you notice all the people using food stamps in the grocery store this morning?

OLAF: Yeah. It seems everybody has them these days. It's the fashionable thing to plead poverty.

MORRIS: One woman was dressed well. I'll bet her lazy husband was waiting for her outside in a big fancy car.

OLAF: It makes me sick, people like that leeching on society. Darwin had the right idea: survival of the fittest. If people can't survive on their own, let them suffer.

c) Times change, and values in one age are different from values in another. Parents fail to realize this. That's why they keep harping about avoiding alcohol and drugs and postponing sexual involvement. They think that what was right for them is right for us.

d) BORIS: Can you believe the price of textbooks? The average amount I spent for a book this semester was $80, and a good half of my books are paperbacks.

ELAINE: Everybody's complaining about it. When the cost of books keeps going up and up, there's only one explanation: The authors and publishers are getting greedy.

BORIS: Yeah, and you know one of my instructors has the nerve to make us buy a book he wrote. And get this: He teaches Ethics!

ELAINE: Wow.

e) ZEB: Did you read the latest about Senator Fosdick? The candidate running against him claimed he knowingly received illegal campaign contributions.

CLARISSA: How ironic. Senator Fosdick has been talking about campaign reform for years. Now it turns out he's as big a crook as the rest of them. What a hypocrite.

f) CYNTHIA: A study has shown that as the speed limit has been raised, there's been an increase in traffic fatalities.

MARK: Speed limits don't cause traffic fatalities. Careless drivers do.

g) ABDUL: Any athlete who physically attacks his coach shouldn't just receive a fine. He should be arrested and charged with assault.

SIMON: I disagree. No player attacks a coach without good reason. Besides, coaches are too negative, telling players what to do and yelling at them when they make mistakes. That behavior invites physical attack.

h) SAUL: Hey, Paul, why so glum?

PAUL: I can't believe it. I got a D on that paper after I spent four hours on it. The instructor must really have it in for me.

i) JUWAN: Ever since I arrived on campus last month, I've been appalled by the manners of the students here. They're unbelievably boorish.

SAMANTHA: Right. And the townspeople are so unfriendly. I don't know why I ever picked this college.

JUWAN: Oh, I'm not sorry I came. The professors are helpful and encouraging. They go out of their way to explain things.

5.5 Think of a time when you committed each of the following errors of expression and describe the situation. Explain how you reacted and what consequences followed. Then decide how you might have avoided each error and how the consequences might have been different. (If you can't think of an error of your own, identify one you encountered through reading or observation.)

Contradiction

Arguing in a circle

False analogy

Irrational appeal

5.6 Read each of the following passages carefully, looking for errors of expression. Explain your findings.

a) The Obama administration did not act promptly to contain the British Petroleum oil spill because the response took a longer time than anyone in the administration anticipated.

b) Given the imminent threat of global warming to our planet, you owe it to your fellow human beings to trade in your gas guzzling SUV and buy a hybrid. Every moment you wait compounds your offense against them.

c) While expressing his views in a debate, Charles says, "Everyone who is taken into custody for any offense has the right to face his accusers in open court." Then, a few minutes later, in response to a classmate's comment, he says, "Undercover agents should not be required to testify in open court against the people they have accused because to do so would blow their cover."

d) A talk show host criticizing government officials is like someone shouting "Fire" in a crowded theater. Such criticism should therefore be made a criminal offense.

5.7 Consider each of the following situations, being alert for errors of reaction. Such errors are often implied rather than stated directly, so you are likely to find hints rather than clear-cut evidence of error. Identify whatever hints you find, and explain why you believe they point to an error of reaction.

a) A woman named Elvira Arellano was deported to Mexico, leaving her young son behind. Unlike her, he is a citizen because he was born in the United States. In discussing this case, Rowena stated her belief that the law should be changed so that only individuals born to parents who are legally in the United States should receive automatic citizenship. Raoul responded, "You are saying that Elvira's son and thousands of others like him are lacking in dignity and unworthy of basic human rights. That is a shameful view to hold."

b) One of the many proposals for tax reform is the "flat tax," which would do away with many of the present categories of deduction and tax everyone's income at the same rate—for example, 10 percent. Thus, someone who earned $25,000 a year would pay $2,500 in taxes, and someone who paid $250,000 would pay $25,000. In a campaign debate, one candidate for the U.S. Senate endorsed the flat tax, and his opponent immediately accused him of being an elitist who was more concerned with the interests of the wealthy than the interests of common working people.

c) In a classroom discussion about the situation in the Mideast, Bertrand made the following statement: "Recent history has proven that the United States is too quick to reject diplomacy and wage war. The world would be safer and more peaceful today if our leaders had resisted the urge to attack Iraq and, instead, sat down with Saddam and with the leaders of Iran and Syria and given trust and reason a chance. I challenge those who disagree with me to disprove the wisdom of this approach to international relations."

5.8 Consider each of the four errors of reaction. Think of a time when you committed each and describe the situation. Explain how you reacted and what consequences followed. Then decide how you might have avoided each error and how the consequences might have been different. (If you can't think of an error of your own, identify one you encountered through reading or observation.)

Explaining away
Shifting the burden of proof
Attacking the person
Straw man

5.9 According to Thomas Gilovich, "A large majority of the general public thinks that they are more intelligent, more fair-minded, [and] less prejudiced . . . than the average person." He cites, among other evidence, a survey of 1 million high school students in which 70 percent rated themselves above average in leadership ability and only 2 percent rated themselves below average. In addition, 100 percent rated themselves above average in ability to get along with others, with 60 percent claiming to be in the top 10 percent, and 25 percent claiming to be in the top 1 percent. Another study found that 94 percent of university professors thought themselves better at their jobs than their colleagues.[2] A similar study of British motorists found that 95 percent rated themselves better drivers than the average person.[3] Review the list of errors discussed in this chapter and decide which, if any, were committed by the people in these studies. Explain your answer.

---

[2] Thomas Gilovich, *How We Know What Isn't So: The Fallibility of Reason in Everyday Life* (New York: Free Press, 1991), 77.

[3] Stuart Sutherland, *Irrationality: Why We Don't Think Straight!* (New Brunswick, NJ: Rutgers University Press, 1994), 240.

5.10 Many logicians use the traditional term "logical fallacies" to refer to the errors in thinking discussed in this chapter. In some cases, they also use different terms for the specific errors discussed here. Because others may use those terms in discussing issues with you, it is helpful to be familiar with them. Do a Google search using the search term "logical fallacies." From the results of your search, select at least five websites, taking note of the terms and descriptions of specific fallacies they list. Then compare those terms and descriptions with those used in this chapter, noting similarities and differences. Finally, meet with a group of two or three classmates, compare your findings, and prepare a group report to the class.

5.11 Following is a difference of opinion that has had a significant effect in psychology and in education. Apply the W.I.S.E. approach to this controversy. Then either write a composition detailing your findings or be prepared to debate the issue in class, as your instructor specifies.

> Psychologist Abraham Maslow explained the hierarchy of human needs by using the figure of a pyramid (see illustration). The lower needs, he believed, must be met before the higher needs are pursued. At the bottom of his pyramid are physiological needs (food, clothing, shelter). Then comes the need for belongingness and love. Above that comes self-esteem, then aesthetic and intellectual needs. At the top, representing the highest need, is self-actualization.

> Austrian psychiatrist Viktor Frankl challenged this order. He argued that self-transcendence—forgetting about self and seeking challenging tasks to add meaning to one's existence—is the highest human need. He also believed that self-actualization cannot be pursued but comes only by achieving self-transcendence. Several decades have passed since these two views were first presented, and in the United States Maslow's has been more influential.

5.12 Many Americans in both political parties are troubled by what they perceive as a decline of leadership in government. Among the examples they cite are the

U.S. Senate ignoring its obligation to create an annual budget for more than three years; Congress pressuring banks to make highly risky loans and then blaming the banks when financial disaster occurred; the recurring attempts to solve the nation's debt crisis by *increasing* the debt; legislators passing major legislation without reading it first. Using the W.I.S.E. approach, examine this issue and decide (a) what factors have caused the decline in leadership and (b) what can be done to remedy it. Write a brief explanation of your conclusions.

5.13 Should "illegal aliens" be accorded the same rights as U.S. citizens? The debate over this issue has become intense since the 9/11 attack on the World Trade Center. Analyze this issue using the W.I.S.E. approach. Following are two opposing viewpoints on this issue to get you started.

LAWS ARE MEANT TO BE OBSERVED

By Kareem Ali

An alien in a country is a person who lives there but whose home is in another country. An illegal alien is one who entered the country where he is living without having gone through the established legal process for doing so. Substituting the term *undocumented worker* is an exercise in linguistic sleight-of-hand, the equivalent of calling a shoplifter "a non-paying customer." To paraphrase Shakespeare, you can call a rose by another name but it remains a rose.

Illegal is not a pretty word, but it accurately defines a situation in which law is broken. Entering a country without fulfilling the requirements set by that country is as illegal as taking an item from a store without paying for it.

The law makes provision for people to come to this country and become citizens or, if they wish, simply to work or study for a time and then to return home. The process is orderly and fair. Of course, time and paperwork are involved but that is unavoidable. It is certainly not an excuse for people to flout the law.

The number of illegal aliens in the United States is estimated at between eight and thirteen million individuals. To be sure, most simply wish to pursue a better life. But some are criminals or terrorists who pose a threat to our citizens and our way of life.

A movement has arisen in this country to ignore or even approve illegal immigration. Supporters of that movement believe that people here illegally should be granted the same rights as those who honored the immigration laws and even the rights of citizenship, including voting rights. Some even would approve in-state tuition preferences. This would mean that an illegal immigrant in California would pay significantly less to attend college there than a U.S.-born citizen of Nevada or Oregon!

Despite their good intentions, people who approve illegal immigration are undermining our legal system, supporting the individuals engaged in smuggling in immigrants (many of whom are also drug smugglers), creating a burden on the American taxpayer, and threatening homeland security. Their efforts should be strongly opposed.

SEND ME YOUR POOR

By Maria Maloney

To begin with, the term illegal alien is abhorrent. Illegal suggests that the person's existence is somehow suspect. And calling human beings "aliens" puts them in the same category as imaginary beings from another planet. That's offensive!

Let's be clear about this. This issue concerns flesh and blood people like you and me who have fled poverty or oppression in search of a better life. True, they didn't fill out all the forms required by the immigration bureaucracy and get the required visa, but that's not reason enough to imprison or deport them.

The vast majority of undocumented individuals in the United States are hardworking people. Not only are they willing to perform menial work that others won't do—many companies are eager to employ them. And here's another dirty secret: some of the politicians who shout the loudest about securing our borders conveniently ignore the immigration status of the nannies, maids, and gardeners they hire.

Debate about undocumented individuals often focuses on whether they are entitled to the rights enjoyed by U.S. citizens. Some writers have argued for denying them driver's licenses, voting rights, access to health care facilities, and education. That position is exclusionary, vindictive, and inhumane.

What makes a country great is not the size of its military arsenal, the extent of its natural resources, or the monetary wealth of its citizens. No, what makes a country great is the depth of its compassion towards the poor and needy. If America wishes to merit the title "great," it must accept all who reside within its borders regardless of how they happen to have arrived.

All Americans would do well to remember the words inscribed on our Statue of Liberty: "Give me your tired, your poor,/ Your huddled masses yearning to breathe free,/ The wretched refuse of your teeming shore./ Send these, the homeless, tempest-tossed to me,/ I lift my lamp beside the golden door!"

5.14 Each of the following brief essays presents one side of a controversial issue. Choose one of these issues and, using the essay as a starting point, apply the W.I.S.E. approach. In conducting your research, be especially careful to look for errors in thinking and examine viewpoints that differ from the one presented. Then either write a composition detailing your findings or be prepared to debate the issue in class, as your instructor specifies.

ARGUMENT A

DISPLAY THE TEN COMMANDMENTS

Let me make it clear at the outset that I am not insensitive to the feelings of religious minorities. My great-grandparents came to this country from Ireland as young children in the 1890s. They attended public schools in

New York City. Their teachers often read from the King James (Protestant) Bible and even led the children in the recitation of the Protestant version of the Lord's Prayer. If Catholics (like my grandparents) or Jews objected, they were told to "get used to it." That wasn't acceptable then and it's not now.

Nevertheless, I am in favor of posting the Ten Commandments in every public school classroom in this country. Is this a contradiction? Not at all, because I favor posting other religious/moral codes alongside the Ten Commandments. Does that mean the Muslim, Buddhist, Hindu, and Native American equivalents of the Ten Commandments? Absolutely. The codes of atheistic or agnostic groups, such as Secular Humanists, too? Of course.

If this approach were taken, no students or parents would have reason to be offended. No one's beliefs would be excluded. No one would be given prominence. Some would argue that having no religious or moral codes on the wall is better than having many of them there. I say that the very purpose of the school is to lead students out of ignorance and into knowledge. Banishing all codes dignifies ignorance.

Religion has been among the most powerful forces in human history. So have moral codes. Putting reminders of both in prominent places in institutions of learning may not be a panacea. But if students happen to look at them, they might notice how similar most of them are. A few students might even get around to thinking about the connection between morality, law, and a safe society. I can think of worse things.

ARGUMENT B

THE HIGH COST OF POLICING THE WORLD

No sensible person would deny that the U.S.-led attack on Iraq has benefited the people of that country. Saddam and his brutal followers were a cancer that needed to be excised. Unfortunately, the success of that operation is likely to embolden the militaristic-minded to see it as the model for dealing with problems in other countries, in other words, for the United States to become the police force of the world. Here are four good reasons for such thinking to be rejected.

First, for the United States to take on the role of the world's police force would divert attention from domestic problems. These include needed improvements in public education, poverty, and joblessness in the inner city; homelessness and substance abuse; the destruction of the environment; and the limitations of present health insurance coverage.

Second, the use of U.S. troops in foreign policing operations would put them in harm's way. The nature of such operations puts restrictions on a soldier's ability to defend himself or herself. Whereas in military actions they can attack the enemy, in police actions they can only react, and even then may use only minimal force. Moreover, if members of the armed services are suitable in the role of police officers (a debatable matter), the place to use them is not in foreign lands but in the United States for the protection of our northern and southern borders.

Third, for the United States to police the world would place an immense financial burden on taxpayers. It is expensive enough to deploy troops in a single foreign campaign. The cost of doing so in many places at the same time would be prohibitive.

Fourth, if the United States assumed the role of police force to the world, the world's reaction would be to hate us even more than at present. The only thing worse than a meddler in other's affairs is an *armed* meddler. And that is just what we would be.

ARGUMENT C

HOW THE MEDIA DISTORT REALITY

TV and movie apologists are forever telling us that we have no business criticizing them because they are only holding a mirror up to reality. Many people buy that explanation, but they shouldn't.

It would be more accurate to say the media hold a magnifying glass to carefully selected realities—namely, the most outrageous and sensational events of the day, such as the tragic deaths of John F. Kennedy Jr. and Princess Diana, or the trials of celebrities such as O. J. Simpson, Kobe Bryant, and Michael Jackson.

Consider how this happens. The first platoon of media people report the latest sensational story as it unfolds, squeezing each new development for all the airtime or newsprint it will yield. Meanwhile, agents and attorneys are negotiating the sale of movie and TV rights to the story. The sleazier the story, the greater the payoff. After the movie is produced, every situation comedy, detective show, and western drama builds an episode around the successful theme.

In this way a single despicable, disgusting act—real or imagined—can generate months of sensational media fare.

In short, the media exploit our social problems for ratings, feed us a steady diet of debasing material, celebrate irresponsible behavior, and then have the audacity to blame parents and teachers for the social problems that result.

5.15 What lessons can you draw from the Good Thinking profiles of Sylvia Earle and Martin Seligman presented in this chapter? Explain how you can use each of those lessons in your career or personal life.

QUIZ

1. Explain each of the following terms and describe how errors in the category affect the thinking process:

Errors of perception

Errors of judgment

Errors of expression

Errors of reaction

2. Define each of the following errors, and explain when it occurs in the thought process:

Double standard

Irrational appeal

Shifting the burden of proof

Unwarranted assumption

"Mine is better" thinking

Gullibility and skepticism

Irrelevant criterion

Pretending to know

Attacking the person

Oversimplification

Preconception for or against change

Straw man

Explaining away

Contradiction

Selective perception

Hasty conclusion

False tolerance

Overgeneralizing or stereotyping

Failure to make a distinction

Preconception

Arguing in a circle

Either/or thinking

False analogy

Answers to this quiz are available at www.cengagebrain.com.

Persuading Others 6

Previous chapters have focused on strategies for improving your thinking skills. This chapter concerns how to express your thoughts more confidently and effectively. The two activities—developing sound ideas and communicating them to others—are essential to academic, business, and personal success. There are four broad kinds of communication: description, narration (telling a story), exposition (reporting facts), and persuasion. We will limit our discussion to the last one because it is most relevant to solving problems and resolving issues.

WHAT IS PERSUASION?

Many people define persuasion as convincing others. Let's examine that view. Have you ever had someone say, in the middle of a disagreement with you, "You're so right. I see the issue clearly now. I don't know how I could have reached such a silly conclusion. Thanks for helping me see my error." You probably haven't. People don't abandon their beliefs that easily.

131

Randy Glasbergen/glasbergen.com

"You did a great job describing my house in the Real Estate Ads. It sounds so appealing, I've decided to keep it!"

That's why it's a mistake to think of persuasion as convincing other people that your view is right and theirs is wrong.

Here's a more realistic definition: *Persuasion is the art of getting people to give a fair hearing to ideas that differ from their own.*

Opportunities to be persuasive arise every day in the classroom, in the workplace, in the community, and in relationships with other people.

Opportunities in the classroom

Some students consider examinations the educational equivalent of a medical checkup in which instructors examine the contents of each student's mind and make a diagnosis: "Your geography 'count' is excellent" or "You are seriously deficient in sociology."

But examinations can be considered opportunities for persuasion. From this perspective, your role is active rather than passive. You have the power to shape the conclusions your instructors reach about you. In this sense, you are the teacher, and they are the learners. This is especially true of essay examinations, which require more than merely circling the right answer.

Suppose you encountered the following question on a history exam: *Identify three factors that played a role in the outbreak of the Civil War. Which, in your judgment, is the most significant?* This is an opportunity to persuade your instructor that you understand the significant factors about the Civil War and that you have formed a reasonable opinion about them.

Class discussions provide additional opportunities to be persuasive. Let's say your sociology class is discussing the possible relationship between divorce and juvenile delinquency. The discussion will focus not only on what the textbook author says but also on what you and the other students *think* about what the author says. Your chance to speak represents an opportunity to persuade your classmates and instructor that your view has merit.

Opportunities in the workplace

The opportunity to be persuasive in the workplace begins when you compose your résumé and continues during the job interview. The question in every interviewer's mind is "Why should I hire this person?" Your challenge is to persuade the interviewer that you are the right person for the job.

Once you are on the job, opportunities to be persuasive can occur daily, or in some cases, hourly. At this very moment, these events are happening:

- A car salesperson is finalizing a deal with a customer.
- A stockbroker is explaining to a client why a change in investment strategy is advisable.
- A customer service representative is citing reasons why an irate customer should continue doing business with the company despite an unpleasant experience.
- A telemarketer is on the phone urging someone to switch long-distance providers.
- An inventor is trying to sell her latest invention.
- A corporate official is telling stockholders why the annual report is more encouraging than it appears.
- A junior executive is presenting her idea for a new product line to her superiors.
- A supervisor is appealing to his staff for more cooperation and teamwork in the office.
- The owner of a small business is attempting to secure a business loan.
- Thousands of people are sitting face to face with their bosses and explaining why they deserve a promotion or a pay raise.

GOOD THINKING!

The Story of Dorothea Dix

Many famous people identified their goals early in life—in some cases, before puberty. However, Dorothea Dix did not find hers until she was 39 years old. The occasion was a visit to a women's detention center, where she had volunteered to give a Sunday school lesson. There she saw prostitutes, alcoholics, criminals, and individuals suffering from retardation and mental illness, all living in unimaginable deprivation and filth. When she questioned the conditions, she was told that such people neither required nor deserved better treatment. At that time (1841), this was the prevailing view.

Dorothea was unprepared for this experience. She had, to be sure, experienced hardship herself. Having grown up in a household with an ill mother and an abusive father, she had spent most of her own childhood caring for her younger brothers. At age 15 she had taken on the responsibility of running a school for young girls. Later she was a tutor and a writer of children's books, but at age 34 she contracted tuberculosis and spent most of the next five years recuperating.

Then came her visit to the prison, which so outraged her that she made the reform of prisons and poorhouses her life's cause. She visited other facilities around the state of Massachusetts, took copious notes, and presented her findings to the legislature, where she eventually won support for the cause. Not satisfied with that success, she ignored her own continuing poor health, and extended her crusade to every state east of the Mississippi and to the U.S. Congress. Then she visited thirteen European countries and fought for similar reforms.

Dix's dedication to the cause of the mentally ill and other social outcasts led to the founding of many mental hospitals, schools for the mentally disabled and the blind, and nursing programs. She has been called "the most effective advocate of humanitarian reform in American mental institutions during the nineteenth century." Yet she remained humble about her achievements, refusing to put her name on her publications and shunning the spotlight. Dorothea Dix died in 1887 in one of the hospitals she helped to found.

For more about Dorothea Dix, see www.webster.edu/~woolflm/dorotheadix.html and http://en.wikipedia.org/wiki/Dorothea_Dix.

Opportunities in the community

Opportunities to persuade others also occur in your neighborhood, town, or city in roles such as Little League coach, den mother, hospital volunteer, Big Brother or Big Sister, or member of a service organization or church council.

In any of these roles, you are bound to encounter disagreement. Even issues of seemingly slight significance can stir passions and generate spirited debate. Should Little Leaguers buy T-shirts with logos or complete uniforms? Would Saturday afternoon or Sunday morning be the best time for a sale?

Community, in the larger sense, goes beyond neighborhood and municipality. As a citizen of a state, a nation, and the world, you probably have views on current social, economic, and political issues, and every day brings opportunities to express your views to other people.

Opportunities in relationships

Relationships with family, friends, and coworkers offer numerous opportunities for persuasion. For example, a close friend may be considering dropping out of school after receiving a disappointing grade, or a business associate may be angry with you for a perceived offense. Perhaps someone in your family is in the habit of drinking and driving. A young child may be inconsiderate of his friends and playmates.

HOW IS PERSUASION ACHIEVED?

When using persuasion, you are trying to get people to consider a viewpoint that they have not previously considered or that they have examined and rejected. The presentation has to be forceful enough to demonstrate the viewpoint's merits, but not so forceful as to give offense. The solution to this dilemma is to be so honest and fair-minded that the audience is open to receiving your message. Faking these qualities is not good enough—you must demonstrate that you possess them. Here is how to do so.

Respect your audience

People never respond favorably to those who disrespect them. One important way of showing respect is to give others the benefit of the doubt. Unless you have clear evidence to the contrary, assume that people who disagree with you are as honest and well-intentioned as you are.

Understand your audience's viewpoint(s)

It is not enough to be clear about your position on an issue. You must also understand the view(s) of the people you want to persuade. If you are trying to persuade one individual, you can simply ask. In the case of the friend who wants to quit school because she received a disappointing grade, ask: Is the course required or elective? Is this the first bad grade you've received in the course? Was it an exam grade or a project grade? Did you talk to your instructor about the possibility of retaking the exam or redoing the project? Have you explored other alternatives to quitting school, such as getting a tutor for the course?

Your friend's answers would reveal not only the facts of the situation but her reasoning about them, and put you in a better position to persuade her not to act rashly.

When your audience is a group of people, as is often the case in classroom discussions, understanding their viewpoints is more challenging. You may not be able to question them directly. In such cases, identify the various views that have been publicly expressed and, equally important, *the reasons offered* in support of those views.

Begin on a point of agreement

Beginning your presentation on a point of agreement establishes an atmosphere of mutual respect and puts your audience at ease. In such an atmosphere, they will be more inclined to give your viewpoint a fair hearing. In contrast, beginning on a point of disagreement can make your audience defensive and reluctant to consider your ideas.

Acknowledge unpleasant facts and make appropriate concessions

Your first inclination may be to fill your presentation with facts that support your view and to omit facts that challenge it. Similarly, you may be inclined to portray the opposing view as totally without merit. The first inclination is intellectually dishonest; the second is foolish. Giving in to either is likely to make your presentation less effective. Whenever you try to persuade others, be sure to acknowledge *all* the facts and insights from the various viewpoints, and do so graciously and generously.

GOOD THINKING!

The Story of Dale Carnegie

Dale Carnegie became one of the best-selling authors of all time, but he didn't start out with that goal in mind. When he graduated from college, he went to New York City in the hope of becoming an actor. To support himself, he began teaching a communications course for adults.

Carnegie quickly determined that his students' greatest needs were in "the ability to express ideas, to assume leadership, and to arouse enthusiasm among people." To help his students develop these abilities, he studied the lives of successful people, identified the principles and strategies they followed, and used their stories as teaching materials.

Over the years, Carnegie expanded and refined these teaching materials. Eventually he assembled them into a book, which he titled *How to Win*

Friends and Influence People. An instant success, it has sold tens of millions of copies in 38 languages.

The principles of positive relationships and successful living that Carnegie taught are surprising in their simplicity. Here is a small sampling in his own words:

Don't criticize, condemn or complain.
Become genuinely interested in other people.
Make the other person feel important—and do it sincerely.
If you are wrong, admit it quickly and emphatically.
Try honestly to see things from the other person's point of view.
Let the other person save face.

For more information on Dale Carnegie, see Dale Carnegie, *How to Win Friends and Influence People* (New York: Pocket Books, 1990).

Apply the Golden Rule

This ancient rule, "Do unto others as you would have them do unto you," can be applied to persuasion in the following five ways:

1. If you expect your views to be given a fair hearing, give others' views a fair hearing.
2. If you expect others to provide evidence for their views, provide evidence for yours.
3. If you dislike being forced to agree, don't force others.
4. If you resent others misrepresenting your ideas, don't misrepresent theirs.
5. If you expect civility, practice civility.

Keep your expectations modest

If you expect others to change their minds immediately on reading or hearing your ideas, you are bound to be disappointed. It takes time for people to change their minds, so expect days, weeks, or even months to pass before your attempts at persuasion bear fruit. Learn to settle for presenting your ideas as well as you can and hope that they will spur the other person to further reflection on the issue.

STRATEGY FOR PERSUASIVE WRITING

So far we have defined persuasion and identified the factors that make communication persuasive. Let's now consider a complete strategy for composing a persuasive presentation. This section will focus on persuasive *writing*. (Persuasive speaking will be covered in a subsequent section.)

The five-step strategy that follows is to be used *after* you have completed the W.I.S.E. approach and decided on a solution to the problem or a resolution to the issue.

Step 1: *State what you think why*

What you think about the issue will be the main idea of your paper; *why* you think it will be the supporting material. Amateur writers sometimes consider it a waste of time to write these ideas down: "I know what I think and why I think it, so why bother stating it?" they ask. The answer is that our thoughts are often less clear and precise, and our reasons less substantial, than we imagine. Writing them down brings our thoughts into focus and gives us a chance to refine them, if necessary. It also provides a visual reminder of our purpose in writing and keeps our attention on what we are writing.

Use this format for your statement: "I think ___ because ___." The following examples illustrate this format. (The views expressed in these examples may or may not be reasonable, and the reasons may or may not be valid and sufficient.)

> I think *the penalties for "white collar" crime should be stiffened* because *such crime does more harm to more people than "street crime"* and because *individuals with wealth and status should be treated no differently than ordinary people.*
>
> I think *an international effort is needed to protect the world's rainforests* because *many nations lack the power to resist logging conglomerates* and because *the depletion of the rainforests threatens to have worldwide climatic effects.*

In some cases, of course, there may be only a single reason; in others, many reasons. Be sure to express all important reasons in your statement.

Step 2: *Consider how those who disagree might react to your view*

Don't assume your view is so insightful that all reactions to your view will be positive. Those who disagree are sure to raise some objections. To identify your readers' objections, put yourself in their place and ask how they would react to your main idea and to each of your reasons. Write each objection and decide whether it has merit. If it doesn't, explain why. If it does, revise your view to eliminate the objection. (If you have analyzed the issue carefully, such revisions will usually be minor.)

In performing this step, keep in mind that if your response to a challenge is inadequate, it may prompt another objection, as the following example illustrates. Some years ago the U.S. Justice Department filed an antitrust action against Microsoft. The charge was that by bundling its Internet

Explorer with Windows 98, Microsoft had gained an unfair advantage over its competitors. To prevent Microsoft from having a monopoly and to protect the public interest, the government demanded that Microsoft either remove Internet Explorer from Windows 98 or add its competitor Netscape Communications' browser.

Microsoft Chairman Bill Gates reportedly responded that the government's demand was like "requiring Coca-Cola to include three cans of Pepsi in every six-pack." That response seemed adequate. But then the government's chief antitrust agent, Joel Klein, turned the analogy back on Gates. He said that the government's demand was like asking Coca-Cola to relinquish a little space on the grocery shelves so that Pepsi, too, could be sold there.

Step 3: Arrange your ideas and write a draft of your presentation

The simplest arrangement for writing a persuasive presentation is as follows:

- Begin with a noncontroversial statement, such as an objective summary of the issue, a brief description of a specific situation or case that illustrates the issue, or a statement of undisputed, relevant facts.

- Clearly state your main idea—your view of the issue—in a sentence or two. If you have applied critical thinking to the issue carefully, this step will not be difficult. (You may, however, want to experiment with different statements of your view to be sure you are expressing it accurately.)

- Present, in turn, each of your reasons for thinking as you do. Complete one reason before moving on to the next, and put your best reason last because that is the place of greatest emphasis. Don't *assume* that others will consider your reasons good—provide supporting evidence such as research results, statistics, and expert testimony. Because this step has the greatest potential to persuade your reader, you should give it the most attention and assign it the most space in your paper.

- Conclude your paper. The most obvious technique for concluding is to restate your idea. That technique is effective if your paper is long or complex enough that the readers may have forgotten your main idea. In a short paper, however, restatement may be insulting to your readers. Other, equally effective techniques of concluding include using a relevant quotation or presenting a brief anecdote. These techniques reinforce your main idea without restating it.

Follow these steps and prepare a rough draft. Do this at a single sitting without worrying about style, grammar, spelling, or punctuation. Generally, your paragraphs should be a modified version of the arrangement shown here, with the introduction and the main idea statement in one paragraph and each of the reasons and the conclusion in a separate paragraph.

Step 4: Check your draft for style

Read your draft critically to see where your writing style can be improved. If you read aloud rather than silently, you will be able to identify flaws you might otherwise miss.

If any of your sentences are *vague* or *confusing*, revise them to be simple and direct. If any of your sentences are too *wordy*, rephrase them. For example, change "in the area of" to "in," "in connection with" to "about," "judging on the basis of" to "judging by," "there are many cases in which" to "often," and "made inquiry regarding" to "inquired."

If your sentences are almost equal in length, create some variety. For example, combine several short sentences into a longer one. Let's say you wrote: "I entered the discussion sure of my view. Then I listened to the other students' ideas. As a result, my view changed." You could consider this revision: "Although I entered the discussion sure of my view, when I listened to the other students' ideas, my view changed."

GOOD THINKING!

The Story of George Orwell

George Orwell was the pen name of the English author Eric Blair. Born in Burma (now known as Myanmar), he went to college in England, then returned to Burma and worked as a police officer. Later he fought in the Spanish Civil War.

Orwell, one of finest prose writers of the twentieth century, is best known for his novels *Animal Farm* and *Nineteen Eighty-Four*. In "Politics and the English Language," his most famous essay, he showed how bloated, lifeless expression numbs the mind and leaves us vulnerable to manipulation. He also offered these timeless rules for avoiding such language:

Never use a metaphor, simile, or other figure of speech which you are used to seeing in print.

Never use a long word where a short word will do.

If it is possible to cut a word out, always cut it out.

Never use the passive where you can use the active.

Never use a foreign phrase, a scientific word or a jargon word if you can think of an everyday English equivalent.

Break any of these rules sooner than say anything outright barbarous.

For more information on George Orwell, see http://www.biography.com/people/george-orwell-9429833.

You can also add variety by changing the order of phrases and clauses, being careful not to create an awkward word pattern. For example, instead of writing "I did well in the course even though I lacked the background for it," you could write, "Even though I lacked the background for the course, I did well."

Step 5: Check your draft for grammar, usage, punctuation, and spelling

Some computer programs check for spelling and grammar errors, but even the best will miss some errors, especially the use of an incorrect sound-alike word—for example, using *principle* in place of *principal* or *preserve* instead of *persevere*. Use your spell-checking program, but do your own proofreading as well.

Before leaving this topic, let's address a rather obvious question: What connection do errors in grammar, usage, punctuation, and spelling have with the subject of persuasion or the larger subject of critical thinking? Your immediate answer may be that such errors have no connection at all; in other words, they are merely annoyances and distractions that readers (or listeners) will overlook when they become engrossed in your ideas. This is incorrect.

Persuasion, as we have defined it, is the art of getting people to give a fair hearing to ideas that differ from their own. The challenge of persuading others lies in the fact that they seldom want to give such a hearing to opposing ideas. In fact, their first impulse may be to find an excuse for *dismissing* such ideas. Errors in grammar, usage, punctuation, or spelling provide that excuse. They *invite* your reader to think, "If this person is careless about the relatively simple matter of writing and spelling correctly, then his or her *ideas* are not likely to have much value." Is that assessment fair or logical? No. But it is a huge obstacle to persuasion. Overcoming that obstacle is an important step in writing and speaking persuasively.

An example of persuasive writing

While driving to work, Maria couldn't help noticing the woman in the car in the lane next to her. She was talking on a cell phone as she drove and wandering from one side of her lane to the other. When traffic slowed, she sipped coffee. When it stopped at a light, she brushed her hair, put on makeup, and forced the drivers behind her to honk at her when the light changed. Maria shook her head and said to herself, "Now that's multitasking!"

Maria's spontaneous remark set her wondering: "Multitasking is the big rage today. Books and tapes claim it makes people more productive, efficient, and successful. But is that assessment accurate? Could there be a negative side to multitasking?" She made a mental note to investigate.

That evening, Maria searched the Internet, beginning with the search terms "multitasking" and "human multitasking." What she found made her curious about the role of concentration in achievement, so she added the term "concentration and success." Continuing with the W.I.S.E. approach, she speculated about the pros and cons of multitasking—that is, the arguments for and against it—and considered various scenarios to test the opposing arguments. Finally, she evaluated her findings and reached her conclusion—that multitasking has merit if used judiciously but is counterproductive if used carelessly.

Wishing to share her findings, Maria wrote a brief article to persuade others that the popular view of multitasking is largely mistaken.

MULTITASK WITH CARE

By Maria Sanchez

Millions of people find it difficult to keep up with the demands of modern living. That is why multitasking—doing two or more tasks at the same time in order to save time—has become so popular. But I recently had an experience that made me wonder just how beneficial multitasking is.

While driving to work, I noticed a multitasker in the car in the lane next to me. As she drove, she talked on her cell phone; when traffic slowed, she drank her coffee; and when the traffic lights turned red, she brushed her hair and applied makeup. She was certainly getting a lot done, yet her driving left something to be desired. She wandered from one side of her lane to the other. And when the light turned green, she continued to look in the mirror, forcing those behind her to lean on their horns.

My curiosity aroused, I sought to learn more about multitasking. I found that the contrary to the belief central to multitasking, the brain cannot do two things at once. The best it can do is alternate between two (or more) things, shifting attention back and forth from one to the other. Researchers have found that such alter-

John McKenna/Alamy

nating *increases* the time on task and the chance for error, so multitasking is both less efficient and less effective than dealing with one task at a time.[1]

Even more surprising were the findings of a study of multitasking conducted by Eyal Ophir of Stanford University with a group of 262 undergraduates. Ophir found that those who multitasked most scored *worst* on the skills of remembering, shifting between tasks, and maintaining their focus.[2]

Does this mean that multitasking should be avoided? No. As a number of authors have pointed out, the research simply cautions us to realize the limitations of multitasking and to use it sensibly.[3] The following guidelines reflect that caution:

- If an activity requires close attention and concentration to be done well, do not attempt any other activity at the same time. Driving a car is such an activity, as is doing an important assignment at work. Incidentally, in conducting my search I discovered a fascinating old (1910) *New York Times* article that presented numerous cases illustrating the role of concentration in the success of great achievers.[4]

- If an activity does *not* require close attention and concentration to be done well, feel free to combine it with one or more similarly undemanding activities. You could, for example, fold or iron clothes while watching television, or wash dishes while chatting on the phone with a friend, or browse your e-mail while being kept on "hold" when calling a government agency.

It is certainly disappointing to realize that the latest fashion for effective living doesn't measure up to the hype. At such times, laughter helps. At the height of the speed-reading craze of the 1960s, Woody Allen saw the humor in the situation and said, "I took a speed-reading course and read *War and Peace* [a novel of 1300 pages] in twenty minutes. It involves. Russia." The next time I see a multitasker on the highway, I'm going to have a good laugh . . . and stay out of her way.

---

[1] http://en.wikipedia.org/wiki/Human_multitasking, accessed 7/12/10.
[2] http://www.cbsnews.com/stories/2009/08/25/tech/main5264503.shtml?source=related_story&tag=related. Also, http://seattletimes.nwsource.com/html/nationworld/2012049123_webmultitask07.html, both accessed 7/12/10.
[3] See, for example, http://www.ideamarketers.com/?The_Pros_and_Cons_of_Multitasking&articleid=15493&from=PROFILE and http://www.oxfordlearning.com/letstalk/2008/07/25/multitask-or-not/, both accessed 7/12/10.
[4] http://query.nytimes.com/mem/archive-free/pdf?_r=1&res=9D0CE0DE1339E433A25753C2A9679D946196D6CF, accessed 7/12/10. (Note: To view this article, you must sign up for free membership.)

STRATEGY FOR PERSUASIVE SPEAKING

In several ways, persuasion is more difficult in spoken than in written communication. Printed words can be studied again and again; spoken words, once uttered, are gone. Also, speaking is usually less formal and precise and therefore more easily misunderstood. Moreover, in spoken presentations the audience sees, as well as hears, the speaker and is therefore more easily distracted.

A speech has the same basic structure as a composition and, in most cases, is organized on paper before being delivered. For this reason, the first three steps in the strategy for persuasive speaking are the same as those for persuasive writing: (1) State what you think about the issue and why you think it. (2) Consider how those who disagree might react to your view. (3) Arrange your ideas and write a draft of your presentation. (See the earlier section for details.) The remaining steps for persuasive speaking are discussed here.

Step 4: Create note cards

Why speak from note cards rather than from a completely prepared speech? Because it is almost impossible for an inexperienced speaker to *read* a presentation without seeming lifeless and mechanical. If you don't have the text of the speech in front of you, you can't succumb to the temptation of reading it.

In creating your note cards, use key words rather than sentences so that you won't be tempted to read. Write large and limit the number of points per card so that you can move from point to point without lowering your head and squinting. (If you will be using visual aids, such as overhead slides or PowerPoint, be sure to add appropriate cues in your notes.)

Step 5: Rehearse using a tape recorder or a camcorder

Deliver your speech into a tape recorder—or, even better, into a digital camcorder that can be attached to your computer—and then play it back, evaluating and taking notes. Repeat this as many times as necessary to achieve the following objectives:

Avoid distracting verbal mannerisms. Such mannerisms include punctuating every sentence or two with meaningless expressions (e.g., uh, like, and you know) and raising or lowering your voice in the same way at the end of every sentence.

Avoid distracting physical mannerisms. Such mannerisms include looking at the ceiling or at your notes instead of at your audience, shifting from foot to foot, or using the same gesture over and over. (To evaluate physical mannerisms, of course, you will need to *watch* your presentation rather than just listen to it.)

Finish each sentence before starting the next. It is bad enough to hear one speaker interrupt another, but it is even more frustrating to hear speakers interrupting themselves. This happens much more frequently than you might imagine. Fear is a common cause; eager to finish, the speaker tries to say several things at once. The solution is to discipline yourself to give each sentence the attention it deserves.

Speak loudly enough to be heard, and separate your words. The most meaningful material becomes meaningless if the speaker cannot be heard or if he or she runs words together in a way that makes people in the audience turn to one another and ask what was said.

Maintain a moderate pace. Pace is the speed at which you speak. Most people have a tendency to speak fast when they become nervous, so you may have to speak at a pace that seems too slow in order to have it be just right. By practicing, you will be able to develop a sense of what is appropriate.

Achieve vocal variety. What bores an audience most? Sameness, which suggests lifelessness. This effect occurs when the speaker's volume, pitch, pace, and inflection never change. To achieve variety, make your voice rise and fall in volume and pitch, and deliver key lines a little more deliberately, lingering over the most important words. Where appropriate, pause for dramatic effect and give your audience a chance to process what you have said. These techniques are never artificial when they match the real emotion you feel for your topic.

When you make your actual presentation, stand up straight and maintain eye contact with your audience rather than fixing your gaze at the ceiling, floor, or back wall. (Yes, they can tell the difference.) Don't stare at any one person, of course; look from person to person. And above all, forget about yourself, and focus on your message.

STRATEGY FOR GROUP DISCUSSION[1]

Some people view discussion as competition, with one winner and many losers. As a result, they approach it combatively. They interrupt, shout, and browbeat others into submission. Others view discussion as serial monologue, with every person taking a turn at speaking but no one listening to anyone else. Neither perspective enhances discussion.

At its best, group discussion is an opportunity to share, test ideas, and generate insight. But this opportunity is possible only in a context of cooperation. In this context, participants approach discussion eager to listen as well as to speak, and they are prepared to explore all views vigorously yet fairly without anger or resentment. Persuasion becomes possible precisely because everyone is as open to being persuaded as to persuading others.

The following guidelines will help you become a valued participant in discussion.

Prepare in advance   If the discussion is scheduled in advance, spend some time planning for it. Study the lesson or meeting agenda, considering each point to be discussed. Apply your thinking skills to problems and issues, and be prepared to share your thoughts.

Anticipate disputes   When people of different backgrounds and perspectives address issues, disputes often arise. These can be beneficial to the group, as long as they are approached constructively. The key is to detach your ego from your ideas. Be energetic in presenting your views but not arrogant. Expect others to disagree with you and criticize your views. Refuse to take such criticism personally.

Leave private agendas outside   From time to time you may find yourself working in a group with someone you don't care for. You may have had trouble with the person in a past meeting, or your personalities may just clash.

---

[1] The section "Strategy for Group Discussion" is reprinted with the permission of the copyright holder, MindPower, Inc.

Dislike for the person may tempt you to be disagreeable and even sarcastic. Such reactions hinder the group's efforts and make meetings unpleasant for everyone. You have an obligation to the group to give your best, so refuse to let your feelings toward anyone influence your behavior or your response to his or her ideas.

Cooperate with the leader   Keep in mind that the group leader has special obligations such as maintaining order, keeping discussion positive, and ensuring that all members are heard and all perspectives considered. When the leader attempts to meet those obligations, be understanding and cooperative.

Listen to others   It is impossible to respond meaningfully to what others say in a discussion unless you first understand what they say, and the only way to understand is to listen attentively. To that end, whenever another group member has the floor, look at that person and be attentive, whether you agree or disagree. Don't permit yourself to be distracted by other people or your own thoughts. And avoid doing anything that causes others to be inattentive.

Understand before judging   If you are uncertain whether you understand a particular view, ask the person who expressed it. For example, say, "Ann, I'm not sure I heard you correctly. Are you saying that . . .?" Then listen carefully to her answer. Base your evaluation on what she said, rather than on careless assumptions about what she meant.

Be balanced   Many of the views expressed in discussion are of mixed quality. That is, they are partly valid and partly invalid, somewhat wise and somewhat foolish. Thus, the most reasonable response will often be to agree in part rather than to agree completely or disagree completely. To be sure your evaluation is fair, take special care to find the flaws in views you agree with and the merits of views you disagree with.

Be courteous   When views clash and discussions grow heated, it's easy to forget the rules of civility. Whenever that happens, bad feelings usually follow, and group accomplishments are threatened. To avoid such outcomes, make it your habit to give no offense to others and to be slow to take offense yourself.

Monitor your contributions   Be aware of how often you contribute to the discussion. If you tend to speak a lot, make an effort to limit your contributions to matters you regard as important. On the other hand, if you seldom say anything, start contributing more often. (If others express your ideas before you get a chance, you can always express agreement and explain your reasons.) Also monitor the *kinds* of contributions that you make to discussions. Ideally, you will propose ideas of your own *and* offer constructive criticism of other people's ideas. If all your contributions are criticisms, you will be a hindrance rather than a help to the group.

Be alert for insights   When knowledgeable people exchange ideas, they often stimulate one another's thinking and produce new insights.

Unfortunately, insights are often so mixed with ordinary ideas that they go unnoticed. You will be better able to find insights if you actively look for them in all contributions, other people's as well as your own.

EXERCISES

6.1. Describe three recent opportunities to be persuasive. Comment on whether you were successful in getting a fair hearing for your ideas and, if so, why.

6.2. Describe a situation in which a speaker's or writer's being honest and fair-minded helped to persuade you or someone you know. Explain how the person demonstrated those qualities.

6.3. Describe a situation in which one or more of the qualities of persuasion mentioned previously were *lacking*. Explain what happened as a result.

6.4. Reread Maria Sanchez' essay on multitasking (pages 142–143) and note the ways in which she applies the chapter's suggestions for achieving persuasion.

6.5. The fact that many elementary and secondary school students have learning deficiencies has prompted a search for remedies. Some people believe the problem lies with poor teaching and propose that elementary and secondary school-teachers' salaries be based on their students' performance on standardized tests. Other people strongly object to this proposal and reject the idea it is based on. The following essays take opposing views on the issue. Read each essay carefully. Then apply the W.I.S.E. approach and either write a composition detailing your findings or be prepared to debate the issue in class, as your instructor specifies.

IF THE STUDENT HASN'T LEARNED, THE TEACHER HASN'T TAUGHT

By Greta Von Hoffman

Compared to their counterparts in other countries, U.S. students are mediocre academically. That's not pleasant to acknowledge, but it's been documented in international competitions for years. To cite but one example, thirty-four nations participated in the 1999 Trends in International Math and Science Study (TIMSS) competition. U.S. students scored nineteenth in math, behind Singapore, Korea, Japan, Canada, and even behind Slovenia, Bulgaria, and Latvia. And they did only slightly better in science, scoring eighteenth.

The problem is not confined to math and science. The deficiencies of U.S. students in geography and English—their native language!—are legendary. What could cause such embarrassing deficiencies? Not a lack of funding—the United States invests more money per pupil than almost any other nation. Not a lack of technology—there are more computers in U.S. schools than in any other schools in the world, with the possible exception of Japan. Surely not a national genetic deficiency.

What, then? To say it bluntly, half-hearted or downright incompetent teaching. The old saying, "If the student hasn't learned, the teacher hasn't taught," isn't just a clever slogan—it's a profound truth.

Many teachers are more concerned with collecting a paycheck than in expanding students' knowledge. Others are "hanging in" until they are eligible for retirement. Unfortunately for their students, their retirement is still ten or more years away. A considerable number of teachers have had more education courses than content courses. What good is it to know how to teach math or history or biology if you have only a nodding acquaintance with the subject of math or history or biology? It's like having a non-athlete coach a sport, or someone who can't drive a car teach driver education. Watch out world.

To reform a system with such fundamental problems will not be easy. No single solution can possibly do it. That said, one small but important step would be to base teacher's pay on their performance. Teachers whose students perform exceptionally well should receive a generous pay increase. Those whose students perform poorly should receive nothing except a warning—"Produce better results or look for another job." And then—this is most important—the schools should make good on the warning.

Such a regime will encourage the good teachers, weed out the poor ones, send a message to colleges to prepare their students better, and invite talented people to enter the field. As I said, this isn't the entire solution, but it would be a wonderful first step.

LET'S NOT SCAPEGOAT TEACHERS

By Pyadhammo Bikkhu

Given this country's resources, our education system should be the finest in the world. And our students' performance should be unquestionably superior to other industrialized nations. The fact that the system is badly flawed and our students are, to put it mildly, less than superior is a scandal of major proportions. No reasonable person would deny this fact.

The blame for this situation is usually placed on teachers and the standard solution is to hit them in the pocketbook as a punishment. Chief among the ideas proposed is to pay teachers according to the results they achieve—that is, the grades their students receive on national or international tests of competency.

At first thought, this all sounds very reasonable. However, it is not reasonable at all but the shabbiest kind of scapegoating. Moreover, it would be counterproductive. To begin with, students' academic deficiencies are not clearly the fault of teachers. Other candidates for blame include the school administrators, media, parents, and students themselves. Let's look at each of these groups.

Administrators have more control over what is taught and the way it is taught than most people realize. They usually have a major say in curriculum development, classroom schedules, textbook selection, and grading. Teachers are often required to spend valuable time on self-esteem, values clarification, sex education, environmentalism, and other politically correct topics, and this sharply diminishes the time they have to spend on academic subjects. Also, administrators often create bureaucratic busy work that further erodes instructional time. And, as if that weren't enough, when teachers attempt to maintain control of their classrooms, they get little or no support from principals and superintendents.

The media deserve a large share of the blame for student deficiencies because they have created a mass culture in which feeling good ranks above obtaining knowledge and learning self-discipline. The media also ridicule virtually every value that conscientious teachers and parents try to instill in students. Not every parent is conscientious, of course, and those that aren't tend to approve and even model the harmful attitudes that block students from learning.

Finally, and every bit as important, there are the students themselves. The most admirable parents, enlightened school administrators, and dedicated teachers cannot make students learn if the students choose not to do so. And many students make that choice.

In light of these considerations, the idea of punishing teachers by taking away their salary raises is grossly unfair. Teachers' pay is already the lowest among the professions, as little as $29,000 to start in some states. That's after four years of hard work and $75,000 or so of education loans to be repaid. To expect teachers to work for such wages and have their salary advancement tied to factors over which they have no control is absurd.

For all these reasons, the idea of paying teachers according to students' performance should be tossed in the wastebasket where it belongs.

6.6. In the previous exercise you analyzed two essays that addressed the question of whether elementary and secondary schoolteachers' salaries should be based on students' academic performance. Now select the essay you decided was more reasonable and evaluate it for persuasiveness, using as your guideline the strategy for persuasive writing presented in this chapter. If you see any room for improvement in persuasiveness, explain what changes you would make.

6.7. Describe a situation in which you attempted to be persuasive, for example, a situation at work or in college. Revisit that situation, apply the guidelines for persuasion, and explain how you would approach the situation if it were occurring now. (Feel free to substitute a present situation for a past one if you wish.)

6.8. Contemporary feminism is divided into two broad and conflicting viewpoints, which Christina Hoff Sommers terms "gender" feminism and "equity" feminism. Some feminists consider these terms inaccurate; nevertheless, the terms have become representative of the ongoing debate and are therefore useful search terms. Feminists generally included in the "gender" camp include Gloria Steinem, Andrea Dworkin, Catherine MacKinnon, and Patricia Ireland. "Equity" feminists include Christina Hoff Sommers, Tammy Bruce, Wendy McElroy, and Camille Paglia. Apply the W.I.S.E. approach to the controversy, and write a persuasive composition presenting your view. Be sure to list the sources you consulted.

6.9. A popular idea in America today is "redistributing wealth." The basic idea is that government can solve the problem of inequality by taxing the rich and creating "entitlement" programs for the poor. (Note that the word "entitlement" supports the idea of *having a right* to what is received.) Economist Henry Hazlitt challenged this idea more than 60 years ago in his book *Economics in One Lesson*. He argued that, though government should "create and enforce a framework of law that prohibits force and fraud," it should never attempt to redistribute wealth because such actions make matters worse. Use the W.I.S.E. approach and decide whether redistributing wealth is a sensible approach to economic inequality. Write a brief essay supporting your view.

6.10. A number of individuals and groups are promoting international monitoring of questionable practices within individual nations. One way to do this, some argue, is to expand the powers of the United Nations to include the authority to enter a country and investigate alleged violations of human rights and to monitor elections to ensure fairness. Critics of this idea point to the fact that most of the U.N.'s member nations are not democracies, to the organization's record of discrimination, notably its anti-Semitism, and to its own acknowledgment of its deficiencies. Using the W.I.S.E. approach, determine whether the idea of globalization has merit and, if so, whether the U.N. is the right organization to manage it. Explain your conclusions in a brief essay.

6.11. In light of what you have learned in this chapter about persuasion, what would you say is your greatest difficulty in persuading others? Think of one or more occasions on which you have experienced this difficulty. Then meet with a group of two or three classmates and discuss your individual difficulties and the ways in which this chapter will help to overcome them. During this meeting make a special effort to apply the strategy for group discussion.

6.12. What lessons can you draw from the Good Thinking profiles of Dorothea Dix, Dale Carnegie, and George Orwell presented in this chapter? Explain how you can use each of those lessons in your career and/or personal life.

QUIZ

1. Define persuasion as the chapter defines it.

2. Name four places where you can find opportunities to be persuasive.

3. The strategies of persuasion guarantee that you will be successful. True or false? Explain.

4. If persuasion occurs at all, it occurs immediately after you present your ideas. True or false? Explain.

5. Why is it important to eliminate errors in grammar and usage from your persuasive writing and speaking?

6. The challenge of persuading others is greater in spoken communication than in written communication. True or false? Explain.

7. People who are quiet by nature should be content to let others talk during group discussions. True or false?

8. The leader of a group discussion has special obligations. True or false?

9. In what ways is persuasive speaking more difficult than persuasive writing?

10. List the five steps for persuasive writing.

Answers to this quiz are available at www.cengagebrain.com.

Applying Your Thinking Skills 7

IN THIS CHAPTER

Thinking critically about . . .

▶ Relationships	*Improve your relationships.*
▶ Careers	*Make sensible career decisions.*
▶ Ethical judgments	*Master the use of ethical criteria.*
▶ Commercials	*Evaluate the impact of TV commercials.*
▶ Print advertising	*Assess the quality and honesty of ads.*
▶ Television programming	*Determine the effects of TV on people.*
▶ Movies	*Examine characters, plot, setting, and theme.*
▶ Music	*Decide if popular music is antisocial.*
▶ Magazines	*Decide whether the sensational is glorified.*
▶ Newspapers	*Evaluate the views in editorials and letters.*

Note that the exercises in this chapter are presented after each area of application rather than at the end of the chapter.

THINKING CRITICALLY ABOUT RELATIONSHIPS

A relationship is a significant association between or among people. Relationships differ in intensity. You may visit your bank, grocery store, and post office at least once a week, yet your relationship with the people who work there is probably casual. On the other hand, your relationships with old friends and former classmates are no doubt much deeper, even though you may see them only once or twice a year. Generally speaking, the most significant relationships are *teaching/learning, business, family,* and *personal* relationships. (The personal category includes both friendships and romantic and marital relationships.)

In recent years, much has been written about "dysfunctional" relationships. Dysfunctional is a fancy word for "troubled." The number of troubled relationships seems to be increasing, and if that is the case, a likely reason is that self-help books, articles, and tapes have emphasized putting self above others. They urge us to "look out for number one," to be assertive about our rights, and to resist being taken advantage of by others.

Such advice contains an element of truth. It is possible to be so concerned about other people that we do ourselves a disservice. Some individuals give up their own hopes and dreams in order to please a selfish, overly demanding parent. Others allow themselves to be taken advantage of by their children or shamelessly overworked, underpaid, and even harassed by their employers. In such cases, the advice to stand up for oneself is good. But that advice is definitely not appropriate for people who are so absorbed in themselves and their rights that they ignore other people's rights. Such people need to give *less attention to asserting their rights and more to accepting their responsibilities.*

Responsibility is an important ingredient in relationships. For example, teachers are responsible for making lessons clear and challenging, offering constructive criticism, and testing and grading fairly. Students, in turn, are

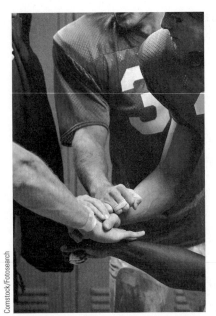

Comstock/Fotosearch

responsible for completing assignments on time, paying attention in class, and accepting criticism graciously and thoughtfully. Similarly, friends and family members have the *mutual* responsibility of giving support, encouragement, and loyalty, as well as consolation in times of sorrow.

Guidelines for successful relationships

Good relationships are not the result of chance or fortune—they are created and maintained by observing some basic guidelines. In Chapter 6 you encountered the most general and basic of these guidelines, the Golden Rule: "Do unto others as you would

GOOD THINKING!

The Story of Oprah Winfrey

Sages have always taught that hardship and suffering need not conquer us but can, instead, inspire us to achieve. There is no better example of that wisdom than the life of Oprah Winfrey. Born out of wedlock and molested as a child by a cousin, an uncle, and a friend of her family, by age 13 she became so rebellious that she was sent to a detention home. However, no beds were available, and Winfrey went to live with her father, whom she recalls as "not accept[ing] anything less than what he thought was my best." His strict discipline succeeded in bringing out her exceptional talent.

Since she got her first broadcasting job at age 17, Winfrey's life has been a series of achievements. In 1984 she began hosting *AM Chicago*; in 1985 the show was renamed *The Oprah Winfrey Show*; and by 1986 it was the number one syndicated talk show in America. The show remained at the top of the TV ratings until Winfrey decided to end it in 2011. She has won Oscar and Golden Globe nominations for her acting role in *The Color Purple*, and critical acclaim for her role in *Native Son*. She became the first woman to own and produce her own talk show. She founded a successful magazine and book club. *Time* magazine named her one of the most influential people of the twentieth century.

Oprah Winfrey's contributions to society have gone far beyond having a television show. She has been active in the movement to keep children safe from predators and has given millions of dollars to education and leadership programs in this country and around the world.

Winfrey credits her success to education and to being honest with herself. Although she is "the first African-American woman to become a billionaire," and remains one of the wealthiest women in the world, her life and work are not about making money. She says that "money has never been the focus. . . . I would do this job, and take on a second job to make ends meet if nobody paid me. Just for the opportunity to do it." Her real mission in life is to help people change their lives for the better. And her central message is, "It doesn't matter who you are, where you come from. The ability to triumph begins with you. Always."

For more about Oprah Winfrey, see www.achievement.org/autodoc/page/win0bio-1.

have them do unto you." Following are more specific guidelines that flow from this rule.

1. *Acknowledge other people.* Many people are so absorbed in their thoughts that they ignore others. When you pass someone on campus that you

recognize, make eye contact, smile, and where appropriate, offer a greeting. Do the same for the mail carrier, the waiter or waitress in a restaurant, and others with whom you have some transaction. As Frederick W. Faber wisely observed, "Many a friendship, long, loyal, and self-sacrificing, rested at first on no thicker a foundation than a kind word."

2. *Be generous with compliments, stingy with criticism and/or advice.* People like receiving compliments and are generally grateful to receive them, provided they are sincere. Similarly, most people resent unsolicited advice. Never give unsolicited advice. Even when advice is asked for, try to determine whether the person really wants it. If the person seems to want approval that you cannot, in honesty, give, say this: "I sense that you'd like me to say _____. But I really don't think that is the best response. I'll be glad to explain why if you'd like."

3. *Keep your moods to yourself.* No one likes to be in the company of people who are forever moaning or complaining. Make a special effort to be positive and upbeat in your remarks.

4. *Expect more of yourself and less of others.* Benjamin Franklin once said, "Blessed is he who expects nothing, for he shall never be disappointed." It is a valuable insight. The more you expect of others, the more you will be tempted to criticize them for their shortcomings. By setting higher expectations for yourself than for others, you will be more inclined to focus on improving *yourself.* This habit will help you to grow and develop as a person and make you more pleasant to be around. Moreover, your good example to others will be more persuasive than any lecture could be.

5. *Make allowance for differences of opinion.* Whenever you discuss controversial matters—for example, social, religious, or political issues—try to present your views clearly, not to change people's minds. If you aim for the latter, you will usually be disappointed.

6. *Be sensitive to others' feelings.* This rule can be difficult to observe because rudeness has become fashionable. We see it in homes and schools, in offices and grocery stores, on the telephone and in Internet chat rooms, at airports and on the highways. Crude and disrespectful language and behavior are also modeled in modern entertainment, including rap music, TV situation comedies, and "reality" programming. Resist these negative influences and avoid words and gestures that insult, ridicule, or humiliate others, even jokingly. (The targets of such humor may join in the laughter yet be offended at a deeper level.)

7. *Balance talking with listening.* There is no shortage of excellent talkers, but excellent listeners are rare, and therefore greatly appreciated. You'll also learn a great deal more by listening than by talking.

8. *Think before speaking.* Blurting out whatever happens to pop into your mind is a sure way to cause problems in your relationships. In contrast,

pausing to ask yourself, "What effect will saying this have? Should I say it at all, and if so, how should I phrase it?" is a sure way to avoid problems.

9. *Purge negative emotions.* Negative emotions have a way of becoming visible to other people and disrupting relationships. If they remain hidden, they can be unhealthy for you. Whenever negative emotions arise, talk yourself out of them. This will be difficult to do when they represent a response to a real offense or provocation. But even in that case, make the effort.

10. *Refrain from gossiping.* Talking about others behind their backs is a sign of disrespect and could easily damage a relationship. Keep in mind, too, that whoever is willing to gossip to you about someone else is just as likely to talk to someone else about *you*! André Maurois writes of a woman with a perfect approach to such situations. He explained that "whenever one of her intimates is attacked in her presence, [she] merely states: 'She is my friend,' and refuses to say more."

11. *Apologize when you are wrong.* Few expressions have the healing power of "I'm sorry." These words have been known to eradicate generations of animosity and resentment and restore relationships that were thought to be irreparable. Unfortunately, the longer you wait to say these words, the harder it is to say them. Develop the habit of saying them as soon as you realize you were wrong. And if you feel you were only partly wrong, apologize for that part.

12. *Forgive when you are wronged.* Forgiving others can be even more difficult than apologizing, particularly if the other person has not apologized for having wronged you. But without forgiveness, resentments remain, prevent relationships from healing, and harm you. A character in Mitch Albom's novel *The Five People You Meet in Heaven* explains why: "Holding anger is a poison. It eats you from inside. We think that hating is a weapon that attacks the person who harmed us. But hatred is a curved blade. And the harm we do, we do to ourselves" (Albom, 141).

13. *Be a peacemaker.* When people you know and care about are having difficulties in their relationship, and one or both discuss the problem with you, it is often difficult to know what to say. The wrong words may worsen the situation and even cause one or both people to resent you. If you can't say something that will promote understanding and healing, say only "I care about both of you and I hope you find a way to restore your relationship."

14. *Meet your responsibilities to others.* In all your relationships, be aware of your obligations to the other people and do your best to meet those obligations.

15. *Look for opportunities to be kind.* To be worthy of the greatest respect from those around you, follow Charles Kingsley's advice and live each

day in such a way that when you close your eyes at night you can honestly say, "I have made one human being at least a little wiser, a little happier or a little better this day."

EXERCISES

7.1. Review the fifteen guidelines for successful relationships and list those that you are in the habit of observing and those on which you still need to work.

7.2. Consider your most significant *teaching/learning* or *business* (i.e., employer/employee) relationships and decide which is *least* successful. Describe what is wrong with that relationship and explain which of the guidelines for successful relationships can help to improve it. (Note: In some situations, several rules will apply.)

7.3. No one would dispute that advancements in communications technology have been a blessing in many ways. But some say they are also a curse. For millennia, people engaged in face-to-face conversation. The philosopher Montaigne described that activity as "the most fruitful and natural exercise for our mind." But in our time, radio and TV distracted people from conversation, and computers, cell phones, iPods, and iPads have threatened it even more. Today many people are so engrossed in their gadgets and so involved with texting and tweeting that they hardly see the people around them, let alone engage them in conversation. Is the concern over the decline of conversation exaggerated? Use the W.I.S.E. approach to decide. Then write a brief essay presenting your thoughts.

THINKING CRITICALLY ABOUT CAREERS

The choice of a career is one of the most important decisions you will ever make. The reason is fairly obvious. If you are like most people, you will work 8 hours a day, 5 days a week, 48 weeks a year, for 40 or more years. That adds up to almost 77,000 hours of your life. A wise career choice will ensure that most of those hours will be satisfying and fulfilling. A foolish choice could mean self-inflicted misery.

Given this reality, it is astounding how many people put little more thought into choosing a career than they would into choosing a video game, a CD, or a DVD. Some decide on the tasks or level of remuneration they imagine to be associated with various careers: "Lawyers deal with interesting cases and make lots of money, so I guess I'll be a lawyer." Others choose on the basis of personal preference: "I love animals, so I'll be a veterinarian," or "I like to help people, so I'll be a social worker," or "I love food, so I'll be a chef."

These approaches to choosing a career are unrealistic for several reasons:

- The tasks or level of remuneration associated with a career may not be as you imagine.
- Merely loving something about a field may not qualify you for candidacy in a program of studies. You may also need to demonstrate, through academic achievement or in another way, that you have certain aptitudes or skills.
- The occupation may involve more or different tasks than you are aware of, and some of them you may find boring or unfulfilling.
- The job market in the field may be poor. Thus, after devoting many years to formal education and incurring tens of thousands of dollars in expense, you may not be able to find employment in the field.

VStock/Alamy

GOOD THINKING!

The Story of Faye Abdellah

There are many different reasons for choosing one's life's work. Faye Glenn Abdellah's was the experience of watching helplessly as the dirigible *Hindenburg* exploded in 1937, killing 36 people and severely burning many others. She was eighteen at the time, the American-born daughter of an Algerian father and a Scottish mother, and she decided right then to become a nurse. After gaining a nursing certificate, she earned her B.A., M.A., and Ph.D. degrees at Columbia University and began teaching at Yale.

Abdellah's devotion to improving the field of nursing and the care of patients was so intense that it sometimes got her into trouble. At Yale she argued for better textbooks, and when the dean refused to follow her suggestion, she organized a textbook-burning event in the Yale courtyard. (As a punishment, she was required to pay for the textbooks out of her rather meager salary.) Years later, she again got into trouble when she informed a nursing home accrediting organization that the conditions in many nursing homes were worse than the conditions for the animals at the San Diego Zoo. (The organization responded by having her escorted from the event.)

In 1949 Abdellah joined the U.S. Public Health Service, which in time became a part of the U.S. Navy. As a senior officer, she received research and consultation assignments in Japan, Australia, China, and Russia, among other countries. In the United States in the 1970s, she founded the Office of Long-Term Care, which monitored conditions in the nation's nursing homes. In time, she became Chief Nurse Officer of the Public Health Service and Deputy Surgeon General of the United States under C. Everett Koop. She holds the naval rank of Rear Admiral.

Over her long career, Admiral Abdellah has been a strong advocate for making nursing a science, raising standards in nursing homes, overcoming fetal alcoholism, and putting patients at the center of concern in the medical community. She has authored 150 research articles and several books.

For more about Faye Glenn Abdellah, see http://www.greatwomen.org/component/fabrik/details/2/1.

The practice of law is seldom as glamorous as courtroom dramas make it seem. Many lawyers spend little, if any, time in the courtroom; their jobs consist mostly of working with legal documents such as contracts. Even courtroom lawyers spend more time poring over law books than questioning witnesses or delivering dramatic summations to juries. In addition, the preparation to be a lawyer is long and demanding—four years of college, followed by the rigors of law school. Numerous careers associated with law, such as police officer, court reporter, and paralegal, require considerably less preparation. One could also be a journalist specializing in legal matters.

Not everyone who loves animals can meet the science requirements for veterinary medicine. Even those who can meet them may have difficulty gaining acceptance to a veterinary science program because relatively few colleges offer that specialty. Yet there are many other careers that people who love animals might consider—for example, animal trainer, animal breeder, or veterinary technician.

Similarly, someone who likes to help people has many more career choices than social worker, including nurse, guidance counselor, and occupational therapist. And someone who loves food should not limit his or her focus to the career of chef but also consider other food-related careers, such as nutritionist or restaurant manager, or a position in the sales or marketing division of a food company.

A sensible approach

The most sensible approach to choosing a career is to assess your interests, identify broad career areas that seem suited to your aptitudes and skills, and then investigate those areas and decide which you should consider.

Randy Glasbergen/glasbergen.com

"All of my professors told us the key to success is doing something you love. I love living at home with you and mom."

The best starting point for your investigation into career possibilities is your campus career center. Peter Vogt of MonsterTRAK.com, the college division of the career website Monster.com, offers seven reasons for becoming acquainted with your campus career center (www.quintcareers.com/campus_career_centers.html).

1. "It's staffed by professionals who are *specifically* trained to assist college students with career-related concerns.

2. Its staff members work closely with the employers who will someday hire you.

3. It's the best place on campus to help you figure out what you want to do with your life and how.

4. It's loaded with career-related resources, whether in print or on the computer.

5. The more "known" you are to the career services staff, the better the chance a staffer will refer you to an employer looking to fill a specific position.

6. It's a good place to meet other students who share your worries.

7. You're [already] paying for it!"

A number of websites are also available to assist you in your investigation into career possibilities. The standard career reference is the *Occupational Outlook Handbook* published by the U.S. Department of Labor, Bureau of Labor Statistics. The Internet address is www.bls.gov/oco/home.htm.

Another helpful resource is the Minnesota Careers website at www.iseek.org/mncareers. The interest assessment test offered there will reveal which one (or combination) of the following descriptions fits you best: Realistic, Investigative, Artistic, Social, Enterprising, or Conventional. A list of occupations for each description is also provided. For each occupation, there is information about the kind of work you would do, the educational background required, the salary range, and the job outlook.

EXERCISES

7.4. Visit your campus career center and ask for an explanation of the various services provided. Record what you learned and the name of the person you spoke to.

7.5. Visit the U.S. Department of Labor website and examine the *Occupational Outlook Handbook*. Begin by checking the "search tips" in the middle of the home page. Then examine the various features and record your findings.

7.6. Visit the Minnesota Careers website, take the interest assessment test, and read the information about the occupations associated with your descriptive term. Record your findings.

7.7. Visit the Career and College Planning Resources list at www.khake.com/page51.html, scan the links, and click on those that might be useful to you. List the ones that you decide are most useful.

7.8. Visit Google and conduct a search using the search term "personal interest assessment." Sample at least three of your findings and decide how useful they are. Describe them and explain your assessment of each.

7.9. In recent years the subject of monetary profit has been vigorously discussed in the media. Key questions have included these: Is the pursuit of monetary profit honorable? Should government focus on creating conditions that encourage individuals and companies to seek profit or on increasing taxes on profit makers? Using the W.I.S.E. approach, decide which approach government should take. Then write a brief essay explaining your position.

THINKING CRITICALLY ABOUT ETHICAL JUDGMENTS[1]

Ethical judgments, also known as moral judgments, are the decisions people make about the rightness or wrongness of human behavior. Over the last century, considerable disagreement has arisen about the basis of such judgments. Some say the basis is each person's feelings—if someone feels a certain action is morally acceptable, then it is acceptable, at least for that person. In theory,

---

[1] For a more detailed treatment of this subject, see Vincent Ryan Ruggiero, *Thinking Critically About Ethical Issues*, 6th ed. (New York: McGraw-Hill, 2004).

Flip Schulke/Corbis

this view sounds reasonable. But would it prove to be so when applied to actual events?

In the late 1930s and early 1940s, on the orders of their leader Adolph Hitler, the Nazis killed 9 million people. Most of the victims were Jews, gypsies, and physically or mentally compromised individuals, all of whom the Nazis classified as "life unworthy of life." The Nazis felt these killings were morally acceptable.

Before 1964 many U.S. restaurant owners had a policy of serving only white people. The same was true of many hotel, motel, and theater owners. These owners felt that the policy was morally acceptable—in fact, some believed that to allow "nonwhites" to mingle with white people in their establishments would have been morally wrong.

To say that the Nazis' feelings and the establishment owners' feelings justified their actions is *to ignore the feelings of the people hurt by their actions*, and that is irresponsible. That is precisely why an international court found the Nazis guilty of "crimes against humanity" and the Civil Rights Act of 1964 required the owners of establishments that serve the public to treat all patrons equally.

Many similar examples could be cited. Robbery, sexual harassment, spousal abuse, rape, child molestation, and murder may be prompted by powerful feelings, urges, and impulses. Nevertheless, they harm others and violate their rights. That is why they are against the law.

A better basis for judgment

Clearly, we need a better basis for ethical judgment than our feelings. But what, exactly, should that basis be? Let's begin by noting that all the offenses noted in the previous examples have one thing in common—they violate people's rights.

This theme of rights is found in many important documents. For example, the U.S. Declaration of Independence declares that "all Men are created equal, and they are endowed by their Creator with certain unalienable rights, that among these are Life, Liberty, and the Pursuit of Happiness." The United Nations Declaration of Human Rights claims that "human rights should be protected by the rule of law." Similarly, medical associations' codes of ethics speak of patients' rights; legal codes of ethics affirm clients' rights; and corporate codes of ethics acknowledge the rights of employees and customers.

Such acknowledgment of the rights of individuals is referred to in ethics as the *principle of respect for persons*. According to Errol E. Harris, the principle incorporates several requirements:

> First, that each and every person should be regarded as worthy of sympathetic consideration, and should be so treated; secondly, that no person should be regarded as a mere possession, or used as a mere instrument, or treated as a mere obstacle, to another's satisfaction; and thirdly, that persons are not and ought never to be treated in any undertaking as mere expendables. (Harris, "Respect for Persons," *Dædalus*, Spring 1969, 113)

GOOD THINKING!

The Story of Chiara Lubich

When the bombs were dropping on her native Trent in Italy during World War II, young Chiara Lubich and her companions sat huddled in bomb shelters reading the Gospel. Certain phrases had special meaning for them, especially "Love one another as I have loved you." They decided that love is supposed to be *lived*, and not just talked about. Thus began the Focolare ("Hearth") Movement. The name is apt, for this movement warms and nurtures the cause of brotherhood.

The movement's main focus is the "spirituality of unity." Members combine passion for their own religious beliefs with deep respect for people of different beliefs and no beliefs. The movement has developed dialog relationships not only with the members of the various Christian denominations, but also with Jews, Buddhists, Muslims, and Hindus, as well as agnostics and atheists.

These relationships go far beyond listening politely to one another. They aim at discovering common values and finding ways to express those values together.

The Focolare Movement has established little towns that serve as "models for a new humanity." There are twenty such towns, and they are found on every continent. The people who live and visit there subscribe to the "law of reciprocal love."

In Brazil and Argentina the movement developed an economic system known as "the economy of sharing." In this system, participating businesses use one-third of their profits for capital reinvestment, one-third to raise the standard of living of the less privileged, and one-third for structures such as community centers in which the values of sharing and harmonious living are taught. More than 700 businesses are now participating in those and other countries.

In 1977 Chiara Lubich was awarded the Templeton Prize for Progress in Religion.

For more information on Chiara Lubich, see www.rc.net/focolare/chiara.htm.

Criteria for ethical judgment

Over the centuries ethicists have identified three criteria helpful in deciding when actions honor the principle of respect for persons and when they do not. The three criteria are *obligations*, *moral ideals*, and *consequences*. Let's look more closely at each.

Obligations   Human relationships create various kinds of obligations, all of which place requirements or restrictions on people's behavior. Contractual obligations require people to honor whatever terms they have agreed to honor. Employment obligations make demands on both employers and employees. Professional obligations require that clients' or patients' interests be served. Obligations of friendship demand mutual support, encouragement, and the keeping of confidences. Marital obligations demand mutual love and honor and faithful devotion in sickness and in health.

Moral ideals   Moral ideals, also known as virtues, are standards of excellence in behavior. There are many such ideals, the best known of which are justice, fairness, and honesty. Other important ideals include kindness, compassion, and forgiveness.

Consequences   This is the broadest of the criteria for making ethical judgments. All actions produce consequences. Some consequences are positive, others negative. Some affect the person who takes the action, others the people who are acted upon. (The effects may be physical, emotional, spiritual, social, and/or economic.) Similarly, some consequences occur immediately, whereas others are delayed for months and even years.

Applying the criteria

The three criteria provide a sound basis for deciding whether an action is ethical. Here is how to proceed:

Step 1   Examine the situation and determine the obligations, if any, that exist; the moral ideals that are relevant; and the people who are likely to be affected by whatever action is taken.

Step 2   Determine the various actions that could be taken and the various consequences—subtle as well as obvious, long-term as well as immediate—that each action would likely have on the people involved. *Caution:* Be sure to consider all possible actions and not just the one you prefer. Also, resist the temptation to ignore unpleasant consequences.

Step 3   Decide which action honors the obligations and the moral ideals and produces the most desirable consequences for the various people involved. In cases where a conflict exists between two obligations, two ideals, or an obligation and an ideal, decide which is more important. Also, when you must choose between two good actions, choose the one that represents the greater good. Similarly, when your only choice is between two harmful actions, choose the one that does less harm.

A sample case

Luke, a senior journalism student, is facing a dilemma. Earlier this term, his final semester, he was given the major assignment of doing a feature story on an interesting person of his choosing. The assignment is due tomorrow. However, he hasn't yet decided whom to interview, let alone conducted the interview and written the story. (One reason is that he has been busy with his work in other courses; another, more significant reason is that he is socially hyperactive.)

Luke could ask his instructor for extra time, but he knows that there will be a penalty of at least one letter grade, possibly two, and he is barely passing now. Moreover, if he were to repeat the course, he could not graduate until the following year because the course is offered only in the spring semester. For these reasons, Luke is considering two alternatives. One is to search the Internet, find an obscure but well-written feature article, and, after making strategic changes to disguise it, submit it as his own. The other alternative is to create an imaginary person, conduct an imaginary interview, and write a bogus feature story. Given the difficulty of Luke's situation, would either of these alternative approaches be ethical? Let's apply the criteria and see.

Step 1   Luke has the obligation to do the work assigned to him and to submit it on time. The relevant moral ideal is honesty, which in this case prohibits both plagiarizing someone else's work and passing fiction off as fact.

Step 2   The most obvious action Luke could take would be to present his case to the instructor and hope for a lenient penalty. One clear consequence is that he could take satisfaction in his honesty and willingness to accept responsibility for his laziness. Beyond that, the consequences are uncertain. He could receive a low passing grade and graduate on time, or he could fail the course and have to wait until next year to graduate.

If Luke submits the article he found on the Internet as his own and his deception is not discovered, he would graduate on time. However, if the instructor discovered the plagiarism, Luke could fail the course and even (depending on the college's conduct code) be expelled.

Creating an imaginary person and writing a bogus feature story is more likely to fool Luke's instructor than plagiarizing an article. However, the consequences of this action could be harmful in the long term. Luke might be tempted to adopt it as a strategy for meeting deadlines after he graduates and is working as a journalist. And if he gave in to that temptation, he would run the risk of ruining his career. (If this seems overly dramatic, be assured that it is not. In recent years, a number of journalists have suffered professional disgrace when their dishonesty was discovered.)

Step 3   In this case, the ethical judgment is clear: both plagiarizing and creating a bogus story are unethical responses to the situation. Although we might *understand* how a weak person might choose one of these responses, there is no way to justify either response ethically.

EXERCISES

7.10. Select one of the following ethical issues and examine it using the three-step approach for evaluating ethical issues. Record all your work.

a) Harry and Ruth are a financially successful married couple aged 53 and 50, respectively. Harry is the president of his own company. Once a fashion designer, Ruth no longer works but maintains an active social schedule. They live in a large house on Lake Michigan in suburban Chicago. Recently, Ruth's 80-year-old mother, Angela, suffered a fall in her modest apartment, where she had lived alone for the last ten years since her husband died. Because Angela suffers from osteoporosis, the doctors have recommended that she no longer live alone. As an only child, Ruth has to decide whether to let her mother move into her home or move her to an assisted living facility. After talking the situation over with Harry, Ruth decides on the assisted living facility.

b) Lawrence Preston is a first-term congressman. The theme of the campaign that got him elected was to take government out of the hands of the special interest groups and return it to the people. Since taking office, however, he has been under considerable pressure from several special interest groups to endorse bills he believes are against the best interests of his constituents. He has asked two senior members of his party for their advice and they said: "Look at it this way, Larry. In order to represent your constituents' interests, you've got to stay in office. And you'll never get reelected without the support of the special interest groups. So you'd better do as they say for a while. Postpone being a hero for a few terms." He decides to take their advice.

    c) Ramona is a 35-year-old police officer who looks no older than 25. Her latest assignment is to go undercover and pose as a student at a university because the police suspect that a major drug operation is being run there. After a month on the job, she has made a number of friends among the students and faculty. Though she has no evidence that any of them are involved in the drug operation, she begins to feel guilty about not being able to be honest with them. Is it morally acceptable for her to continue on the assignment?

7.11. Find an ethical issue currently being discussed on campus. Analyze the issue, using the three-step approach for evaluating ethical issues. Detail your findings.

7.12. In recent years there has been increasing interest in "social justice." One idea that has arisen is that wealthy and successful people did not achieve what they have by their own efforts but rather by taking advantage of others. (Some would add that entire countries were established this way.) Those who reject this idea admit that cases of dishonesty exist, but believe that most successful people owe their achievements to a combination of hard work and good fortune. They add that lack of success is often due to lack of effort and/or poor choices. Use the W.I.S.E. approach, determine which view is more reasonable, and explain your view in a brief essay.

THINKING CRITICALLY ABOUT COMMERCIALS

Examining commercials critically doesn't require us to set aside our sense of humor. We can still laugh at the kid banished to the crib but managing to use his electronic gadgets to trade stocks, and the guy with a leg up on the competition, literally, in the La Quinta commercial. But even as we enjoy the humor, we should remember that by their very nature advertisements are, as Chesterton rightly observed, tricks intended to mesmerize us.

    Advertisers spend billions of dollars a year on commercials. The cost of just one 15-second commercial can exceed $500,000. In many cases advertising goes beyond presenting the product or service. Advertisers stimulate viewers through appeals to desires: to be youthful, sexually appealing, successful, loved, or accepted by others. In advertising language, the aim is to "sell the sizzle, not the steak."

    In *Four Arguments for the Elimination of Television*, former advertising executive Jerry Mander claims that advertising exists only to create needs for products. The trick, he says, is to make people feel discontented. The standard advertising formula for doing so is to (1) gain the audience's attention, (2) arouse their interest, (3) stimulate a desire for the product, and (4) make the sales pitch.

"**Laughter is the best medicine and now it's available
in prescription form. Ask your doctor if
Chuckle Tabs are right for you!**"

Mander explains that the design of a commercial or print ad is no casual affair. (Print ads are discussed in the next section.) Advertisers employ thousands of psychologists, behavioral scientists, perception researchers, and sociologists. These experts identify deep-seated human needs and desires, insecurities and fears. Then they determine how these can be used to the advertiser's advantage. The most basic appeals are:

1. *Self-indulgence.* The appeal here is "Don't deny yourself this [product or service]. Go ahead and treat yourself. You deserve it."

2. *Impulsiveness.* Here the appeal is "Don't delay. Don't pause to think and evaluate. Just act."

3. *Instant gratification.* This appeal is "Why wait? You can enjoy it now, and it will make you feel s-o-o-o-o good."

The techniques of advertising are the techniques of propaganda. Among the most common are the following.

Bandwagon

This technique creates the impression that everyone is buying the product or service. It appeals to the viewer's urge to conform.

Glittering generality

Here the advertiser uses words and phrases to imply excellence and uniqueness. Few specifics are offered. "Amazing new discovery," "now a stunning breakthrough," and "unheard-of softness" are examples of glittering generality.

Empty comparison

This technique uses words such as *better*, *bigger*, and *more* (as in "more economical") without completing the comparison. What, for example, does "greater cleaning power" mean? Greater than last year? Greater than the competition? Such a statement seems to make a serious claim, yet we can't hold the advertiser responsible for it because we aren't sure just what is being claimed.

Meaningless slogan

Most large companies have slogans designed to create a positive impression. These create pleasant images but promise little.

   United Airlines' slogan, "Fly the friendly skies," was designed to associate that airline with friendliness. "AT&T—The Right Choice" tried to link the act of choosing a telephone company with AT&T. Another slogan is "Michelin [pause]. . . because so much is riding on your tires," and with these words we see pictures of adorable babies. The aim: to have viewers associate buying Michelin tires with protecting their children.

Testimonial

A testimonial is an endorsement for a product or a service. Actors, musicians, sports figures, and other well-known people are paid substantial sums of money to appear in commercials, lending their credibility and celebrity status to products. The words they speak may be written by someone else, and viewers often know this. Even so, advertisers still hope we'll associate the celebrity with the product or service.

Transfer

One kind of transfer involves objects instead of people. For example, the Statue of Liberty or the flag could be shown with a product or service. These symbols arouse strong positive feelings in many people. Advertisers want viewers to transfer those feelings to the product.

   Another common kind of transfer is the voice-over. Here the celebrity never appears in the commercial but acts as off-camera narrator. Even if the viewer cannot name the speaker, the voice may be familiar and make the message more appealing.

   A less obvious use of transfer is the "party scene," in which we see people enjoying themselves. The intended message is that the featured product— a beer or wine cooler—made the occasion enjoyable.

Stacking the deck

We noted this technique in our discussion of manipulation in Chapter 4. This technique is also commonly used in advertising when comparisons are made between the advertiser's product and a competitor's product. For example, one commercial showed a competitor's fish sticks on a cookie sheet, all in black and white, looking as if they were still frozen. Then the scene shifted to the advertiser's frozen dinner appetizingly presented in vibrant color, with steam rising.

A similar approach is used in many diet commercials. For example, a "before" picture will be a fuzzy black-and-white print, with the person dressed poorly and looking sad. In contrast, the "after" picture will be sharply focused, in color, with the person well dressed and happy.

Misleading statement

This technique uses words that invite viewers to make an erroneous interpretation. Such statements appear to promise something but in reality do not. Long-distance telephone ads used to include such statements.

One such commercial promises "Eight cents a minute for calls over ten minutes. That's a 50 percent saving." That invites thinkers to conclude that they will save 50 percent on every call. But the ad does not say what calls under ten minutes cost. Is it eight cents? Eighteen cents? Twenty-eight cents? We can't be sure.

Another commercial says we can talk up to twenty minutes for 99 cents. We're tempted to think that's a rate of less than 5 cents a minute. But wait. If the 99 cents is a flat rate, then a five-minute call would cost almost 20 cents a minute, and a two-minute call would cost almost 50 cents! That's quite a difference.

The standard commercial break consists of four 15-second commercials. The average hour of television has 44 commercials. If you watch four hours of television a day you encounter 176 appeals designed to short-circuit your critical thinking and create an artificial desire or need. Your best safeguard against this manipulation is to use your critical thinking skills.

EXERCISES

7.13. Watch at least two hours of television. Pay close attention to the commercials. For this assignment the programs themselves are unimportant. If you wish, record the program first so that you can move quickly from commercial to commercial.

As you observe each commercial, note the product or service advertised, the scenes shown, and the people on camera. Also listen for the narrator, music, and other sounds.

Next, select three of the commercials you observed and answer the following questions for each:

- Does the commercial motivate the viewers to think or merely appeal to their emotions? Explain.

- What hopes, fears, or desires is the commercial designed to exploit? How?

- What attitudes and values does the commercial promote—for example, attitudes about success and happiness? How does the commercial promote them? Do you share these attitudes and values?

- Does the commercial use propaganda techniques? How?

- Would you classify this commercial as fair or unfair persuasion? What's the evidence for your view?

7.14. Calculate the average attention shifts occurring during commercials using the following approach:

1. Watch any half-hour or one-hour program. When a commercial break occurs, keep your eyes focused on the television set. Each time a new image appears on the screen, make a tally mark on a sheet of paper. When the next commercial appears, resume your tally on a new line.

2. At the end of the program, divide the number of lines (i.e., the number of commercials) into the grand total of tally marks. The answer will be the average number of attention shifts occurring during commercials for that program. Record your findings.

3. Comment on your findings. Were you surprised at the number of attention shifts per commercial? Explain. What possible reasons might advertising agencies have for changing images at that rate? Which of those reasons seems most likely? Explain.

7.15. This exercise extends the analysis of commercials you did in the previous exercise. Television commercials in the 1950s and 1960s were one minute long and contained relatively few images. Typically, one or more people talked about the product as they displayed it. In the 1970s and 1980s, commercials were thirty seconds long and contained more images. Today's commercials are fifteen seconds in length and contain considerably more images. What effect, if any, could this change have had on academic performance? Job performance? Personal relationships? Explain your thoughts carefully.

7.16. In past years the following slogans were popular. Reflect on them and decide if any of them are in any way objectionable. For each one you object to, write a brief explanation of your reaction.
"Just do it." (Nike slogan)
"Image is everything." (Canon slogan)
"Life is short—play hard." (Reebok slogan)
"On planet Reebok there are no rules."
"Why ask why? Try Bud Dry." (Budweiser slogan)
Voice asks, "What should I drink?" Narrator says, "Give your brain a rest. Try some Sprite."
"Though we carry over 160,000 passengers a day, we serve each of them one at a time." (US Airways slogan)
"Red Wolf is here. Follow your instincts." (Red Wolf beer slogan)
"We measure success one investor at a time." (Dean Witter slogan)

THINKING CRITICALLY ABOUT PRINT ADVERTISING

Like television commercials, print advertising is designed to sell a product, a service, or an idea. Such advertising may appeal to the desire for happiness or the need for belonging, acceptance, or love. However, the techniques that print ads use are more limited. They cannot use sound or depict motion. They are strictly visual and static.

Advertisers know how to make a print ad effective. Every detail must contribute to the overall message. They take great care in choosing every word and picture. Analyzing print ads involves studying these choices.

Always ask yourself whether the statements made in print ads make sense. Suppose an auto ad says, "Due to unprecedented demand, we are discounting hundreds of cars in our lot." But think about it. If the demand were high, the prices wouldn't be changed. The reality must be that *too few people* are buying.

Also read the fine print. No doubt you've gotten more than one credit card ad that says: "Why pay an adjustable rate of 17.9 percent or 18.9 percent when you can pay a low FIXED rate of only 4.9 percent?" You may even have gotten some that say "NO INTEREST." Both offers certainly sounds like great deals . . . until you look at the fine print and learn that the rate is "fixed" for three months. And after that? Presumably the sky's the limit.

Look critically at the pictures in print ads, too. Their effect can be even more powerful than words. Cigarette ads have been especially clever in depicting smokers as physically attractive people having a wonderful time as they puff.

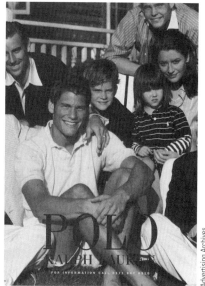

Other ads are equally clever. A perfume ad pictured a man and a woman in a highly aroused state. The caption read, "Unleash your fantasies." The unspoken promise was that using the perfume would heighten sexual fulfillment.

Some ads are truly offensive. Another perfume ad showed a beautiful but frightened woman with several men clinging to her. The caption read "No one could protect her from herself." And a jeans ad showed a woman being backed into a fence by cowboys. The implied meaning of these ads was that women enjoy being assaulted.

Some critics say most advertising is dishonest at best. They are especially troubled by the ads directed at the most vulnerable individuals, children. Defenders of advertising deny the charge, claiming that advertising is simply honest persuasion.

EXERCISES

7.17. Visit the magazine section of your campus library. Skim at least a half-dozen magazines, looking for interesting print ads. Don't limit yourself to magazines you already know. The wider your assortment, the more varied the ads you'll find. Next, select two ads and describe each one.

Then analyze them by answering the questions that follow. If you wish, attach a photocopy of the ads.

- Does the advertisement motivate the viewers to think or merely appeal to their emotions? Explain.
- What hopes, fears, or desires, if any, is the ad designed to exploit? How does it appeal to them?
- What attitudes or values, if any, does the ad promote—for example, attitudes about success? How does it promote them?
- Do you share those attitudes and values?
- What propaganda techniques, if any, are used? Explain how they are used.
- Would you classify this ad as fair or unfair persuasion? What's the evidence for your view?

THINKING CRITICALLY ABOUT TELEVISION PROGRAMMING

By high school graduation the average American has spent 11,000 hours in the classroom and 22,000 hours watching television. All things being equal, television has twice as much impact on a person's mind as formal education.

Yet all things are not equal. Television producers have more means to maintain audience attention. They can use music to manipulate emotions. Directors can shift scenes to sustain interest and use applause tracks to cue responses. All this is evidence for television's impact. The question continues to be debated: Is that impact mainly positive or negative?

In 1961 Newton Minow, then chairman of the Federal Communications Commission, called television a "vast wasteland." Twenty-five years later his judgment was essentially the same. In Minow's view and those of other critics, television seriously underestimates the viewer's intelligence.

Other critics of television programming argue that it also creates mental habits and attitudes that hinder learning. These critics advance the following arguments:

- By keeping young people away from books, television denies them opportunities to develop imagination.
- Television aims programming at the lowest common denominator. This deprives young people of intellectual challenge.
- By feeding young people a steady diet of slang and clichés, television hinders their language skills.
- Television limits game show questions to who? what? where? and when?—seldom how? and never why? This creates the impression that knowledge of trivia is the only knowledge worth having. It also implies that careful analysis of issues is unnecessary or boring.
- Television uses the narrative approach for most of its programming. Examples are soap operas, sitcoms, movies, and dramatic series. By doing so, television denies young people exposure to critical thinking. (Such thinking is more commonly expressed in analysis than in narrative.)
- Television fills the roster of talk shows with celebrities rather than authorities. By doing so, television creates the impression that it's not what you know but how well you are known that's important. It also promotes misinformation. For example, a television interviewer asked an actress, "Did your role in that television drama give you any insights into adoption fraud?" (That's about as sensible as asking an actor who played a surgeon how to perform an appendectomy, or asking an actor who played an auto mechanic how to overhaul an engine.) Not surprisingly, the actress did not hesitate to offer her opinion.

Jerry Mander has analyzed why television has failed to live up to expectations. In *Four Arguments for the Elimination of Television*, he claims that television has a number of inherent limitations that cannot be easily overcome. For one thing, it is an artificial environment that viewers have no hand in creating. Even on newscasts, we see only what others decide to show us, and always from their particular perspective and according to their priorities. For every item included in the news, thousands are excluded.

Another limitation is that less dramatic things don't play as well on television as more dramatic ones. That is why we see more angry expressions than happy ones, more fistfights and shootings than calm discussions, more car chases and explosions than tranquil scenes, more passionate sexual encounters than gentler expressions of friendship, caring, and tenderness.

A third limitation, according to Mander, is that the everyday pace of reality is not well suited to television. To make their stories interesting, programmers have to compress events. TV heroes are confronted by one dangerous situation after another, whereas in real life many tedious hours of inactivity intervene. Regular television viewing can create the unrealistic expectation that real life ought to be one peak experience after another.

The expectation is reinforced by the news. Reporters prefer to cover sensational stories. When they are forced to cover an ordinary event they often seek out the most dramatic or sensational aspect—for example, the single angry outburst in an otherwise calm and productive city council meeting. Antisocial behavior is deemed more newsworthy than social behavior.

The inherent limitations of television result in a number of biases in selecting program material. Mander finds more than thirty, including the following:

A bias for war over peace and violence over nonviolence

A bias for superficiality over depth, simplification over balance

A bias for feelings of conflict over feelings of agreement

A bias for dissatisfaction over satisfaction, anger over tranquility, jealousy over acceptance

A bias for competition over cooperation

A bias for materialism over spirituality

A bias for the bizarre over the commonplace, the fixed over the evolutionary, the static over the dynamic

If these charges by Mander and others are valid, television may be responsible for a number of social problems. For example, it may cause or aggravate many of the difficulties students experience in school, some of which cause them to drop out before graduating. Television may also be responsible for the tendency of many people to settle for mediocrity rather than strive for excellence.

The following exercises direct your critical thinking to these questions: Is television programming harming our country and its citizens? If so, what can be done to correct that? If not, what can be done to make television programming an even more positive influence?

EXERCISES

7.18. Select a television game show and watch it one or more times. Note the way the game is played, the kinds of questions asked, and the time allowed for responses. Also note background effects such as music, lights, or revolving wheels and any other significant details about the show. Then analyze what you've seen. Answer these and any other relevant questions:

- How intellectually demanding is the show? What is its appeal to viewers?

- What habits or attitudes could this show develop or reinforce in regular adult viewers? In children? Will these habits and attitudes help or hinder life in school, on the job, and at home?

Then write a composition of at least several paragraphs expanding on your findings.

7.19. Select a television sitcom and watch it for one or more episodes. Then analyze what you saw. Answer these and other relevant questions:

- How original was the story line? Can you remember any other show you've seen with a similar plot?
- What attitudes and values did the show encourage? Do you share them?
- Did the characters rise above stereotypes: the dumb blonde, the know-it-all teenager, and so on? Explain.
- Would you have laughed if the show had had no laugh track? How original were the jokes?

Finally, write a composition of at least several paragraphs expanding on your findings.

7.20. Choose a television drama—a soap opera, a detective or western show, or a movie. To help yourself think critically, pick a show you don't normally see. Watch the show and then analyze what you saw. Answer these and any other relevant questions:

- Which characters did the show present favorably? What was the main action taken by each of those characters during the show?
- Think about the characters you chose in the previous question. What view would each express on the following topics?
  Reasoning with others
  Violence
  Sexual relationships
  Marriage
  Authority
  Success
- Did the show include any incidents of violence or destruction? If so, describe them, and explain whether their depiction was essential to the plot.
- Were people or principles betrayed during the show? If so, describe each incident, and explain whether the betrayal was presented in a positive or a negative light.
- Did the show emphasize antagonism or harmony? Were issues resolved peacefully or violently? Explain.

Finally, write a composition of at least several paragraphs explaining whether the show you watched promoted desirable attitudes and habits.

7.21. Skim the television talk show listings. Then select a show and watch it. Analyze what you saw, answering these and any other relevant questions:

- What was the show's theme or discussion topic?

- What fields did the guests represent: show business, education, particular professions, or others? Are the guests associated with specific attitudes, values, or behaviors? If so, describe those attitudes, values, or behaviors.

- Why did each guest appear on the show? For example, an author may have published a new book or an actress may have starred in a just released film.

- What kinds of questions did the host ask? Professional questions? Personal questions? Questions that seemed outside the person's expertise?

- Were any specific attitudes and values encouraged? If so, what were they?

- How much time did the host allow for each answer? Did the guest have an opportunity to elaborate on answers? How much time was devoted to each guest?

- How many times was the discussion interrupted by commercial breaks?

Finally, write a composition of at least several paragraphs, focusing on this question: Would regular viewing of talk shows like the one you watched be good preparation for the probing discussions conducted in college classrooms?

7.22. Watch the evening newscast on FOX News Channel (this is not the same as the Fox channel that shows situation comedies and movies). Then watch the newscast on one of the following: CNN, CBS, NBC, or ABC. Compare their presentations of the news. Answer these and any other relevant questions:

- How much time, on average, was given to each news story?

- What details did the newscasters focus on? What questions did they pass over? Did you want answers to any of the latter questions?

- How were the newscasts similar? Look, for example, at the numbers and genders of the newscasters, construction of the studio sets, and each show's format. How were the shows different?

- How many commercial breaks occurred during the newscast?

- Did the news reports offer different perspectives on the events reported on?

- What other types of stories might have been included?

Finally, write a composition explaining which network you would recommend to someone looking for a fair and objective presentation of the news. Be sure to offer reasons for your choice.

7.23. Consider the observations and judgments of the various kinds of television programming from the previous exercises. Decide what changes would improve television programming. Then write a persuasive letter to the Federal Communications Commission. State your ideas for improving programming and give reasons for acting on those ideas.

THINKING CRITICALLY ABOUT MOVIES

Some people believe critical thinking has little application to movies because movies are an art form—representations of life designed to give pleasure rather than arguments offered to persuade people.

This view is an example of either/or thinking. It assumes that entertainment and persuasion are mutually exclusive. They are not. Moviemakers often want both to create a work of art *and* to influence people's thinking. In some cases, the persuasive intention takes precedence.

It is true that movies almost never present ideas directly in the manner of nonfiction writing. Nevertheless, ideas are embedded in the stories. Simply said, they show the ideas rather than tell them. The effect is more emotional than intellectual, but no less potent for that.

If a filmmaker wants to hold an idea up to ridicule, for example, he need only create a character who holds that idea and make him or her appear ridiculous.

In order to think critically about movies, you must understand the basic elements, which are the same as those in short stories, novels, and plays.

Characters

Every story has one or more main characters, and often a number of secondary ones. The way the characters are presented will influence the audience's reaction to them.

Setting

The elements of setting are time, place, and the circumstances in which the story takes place.

Plot

The plot is the sequence of events that occur in the story. The essential element in a movie plot is *conflict*. A challenge or problem confronts the characters, and they struggle to solve it. The conflict may be external or within the character's mind.

Theme

The theme of a movie is the message or lesson it offers. The theme is almost never stated directly, though the dialogue may contain statements that clearly imply it.

In addition to the basic elements, movies have three other elements not found in written literature: the performances of the actors, sound effects, and visual effects. Sound effects include background music as well as dialogue. Visual effects are created by moving the camera in for close-up shots or out for distance shots, as well as by varying the lighting and camera angles.

In thinking critically about movies, it is important to evaluate each of the elements and make a balanced judgment. Seldom will a movie be uniformly excellent in all elements. The characters, for example, may be richly drawn and the plot plausible and ingenious. Yet, the acting may be poor and the theme an insult to the viewer's intelligence.

The Golden Globe and Academy Awards reflect these distinctions. Rarely will a film "sweep" the awards. And even when it succeeds in doing so, or comes close, critical thinking will sometimes reveal serious weaknesses.

Consider, for example, the film that won a host of Academy Awards in the year 2000, *American Beauty*. (The awards included Best Picture, Best Actor, Best Screenplay, and Best Cinematography.)

The film is the story of Lester Burnam (played by Kevin Spacey) in the throes of a midlife crisis. He quits his job, becomes obsessed with and nearly seduces his daughter's teenage girlfriend, and begins smoking marijuana purchased from his daughter's boyfriend. Only after he dies does he gain the (unoriginal) "insight" that our lives are quite small and insignificant compared to the vastness of the cosmos.

In the opinion of some reviewers, all four adults are seriously disturbed. Lester's neighbor is a homophobic marine with secret homosexual urges. The neighbor's browbeaten wife is nearly catatonic. Lester's wife puts work above family and cheats on her husband with a fellow real estate agent, who is shallow and self-absorbed.

In contrast, all the teenagers are both pure of heart and wise. In fact, the drug pusher boyfriend has the controlling insight of the film, which Lester has to die to realize.

To sum up, *American Beauty* portrays adults as contemptible if not corrupt, especially those who represent discipline, order, and responsibility. Teenagers, on the other hand, are wonderful. Among the questions critical thinking raises about this film are these: Are the characterizations of adults and teenagers plausible? How reasonable is the theme?

EXERCISES

7.24. Visit the Rotten Tomatoes website (www.rottentomatoes.com) or another site that reviews current movies. Then follow the directions for *either* A or B below.

    A. Access the complete list of current box office film titles. Scan the list of films and find one that you have seen. Click on that title and access the excerpts from reviews. Find two that agree with your assessment of the film and two that disagree. Then click on each of the review excerpts, access the full review, and read it. Write a brief paper answering these questions: Did the reviews help you deepen your insight into the meaning and quality of the film? What are your strongest points of agreement and disagreement with the reviewers?

B. Click on the various film titles and read the plot synopses. (Note: The synopses are available in both brief and full format.) Then write a brief composition that answers this question: Do you find more similarities or dissimilarities of plot and theme? Explain your answer with specific references to the films.

7.25. Select a movie you have recently seen, or rent a video and watch it. Then evaluate the film, following this format:

1. State the name of the film.
2. Identify the main and important secondary characters and the setting.
3. Explain the plot and identify what you believe to be the theme.
4. Judge the film's strengths and weaknesses.

THINKING CRITICALLY ABOUT MUSIC

Ridiculing another generation's music has long been a popular pastime. Someone once defined an opera as an art form in which anything that is too dumb to be spoken is sung. Another person observed that classical music threatens to develop a tune with every other bar and then disappoints us. A third termed jazz an appeal to the emotions by an attack on the nerves. Another, writing of rock music, suggested that the proper pitch for most electric guitars is right out the window, followed by the player.

Yet the fact that each generation prefers its own music does not mean that all criticism is without merit. It is important to keep this in mind in evaluating contemporary music.

Music has changed greatly in the past half-century, perhaps more so than in any comparable period in history. In the late 1940s, two older musical traditions continued in vogue. One was big band music, played for ballroom dancing ranging from the elegant foxtrot to frenetic jitterbugging. The other was jazz.

The 1950s brought rock and roll with its different beat, both literally and figuratively. It may have lacked the refinement and style of jazz, but there was no doubting its raucous energy. From the days of Elvis Presley's "Blue Suede Shoes" to the present, rock and roll has undergone several transformations, notably to acid rock and then heavy metal. Other music forms have also become popular—reggae, for example, and rap.

The differences between 1940s music and today's music go beyond the overall sound or

Tim Mosenfelder/Corbis

the beat. Because no amplification existed then, the loudest jazz band was much quieter than today's groups. In those days, too, singers still crooned ballads in the manner of Bing Crosby and Frank Sinatra. Lyrics were meant to be understood, and the singer's voice was regarded as another fine instrument to be used with precision to produce pleasant, melodious sounds. Singers wore hairstyles no different from those of businesspeople. All that has changed.

A more significant difference than these is the ideas and attitudes conveyed by the lyrics and the mannerisms that accompany them. Today's lyrics and stage antics would have been unimaginable 50 years ago. Many popular videos celebrate the destruction of property, rape, child abuse, incest, sadism, murder, and suicide. Onscreen images depict these behaviors in graphic detail. And the average age of the audience that watches them is between fourteen and sixteen.

Critics of contemporary music have charged that it is undermining the fundamental values of society and causing antisocial attitudes and behavior, including crime. Spokespeople for the music industry tend to dismiss such criticism, claiming that musicians are only exercising their right of free expression, and no one can be harmed by that. The exercises that follow will give you an opportunity to examine this issue.

EXERCISES

7.26. Go to iTunes or another online music store and examine a selection of new releases. Note the cover designs, song titles, and lyrics. Listen to releases from major groups. Then list each group you examined and record your observations.

7.27. Analyze your findings about the music you researched. Answer these and any other relevant questions:

- On the basis of your inquiry, would you say the music conveys positive values and attitudes? Why or why not?

- Suppose that people applied the messages in the song lyrics to their lives. In what specific ways would their behavior be affected? Would the consequences be desirable or undesirable?

On the basis of your analysis in the previous two exercises, write a brief composition that answers the following questions: Are the complaints against popular music justified? If not, why not? If so, what action do you recommend? Who should take that action? Government? The music industry?

THINKING CRITICALLY ABOUT MAGAZINES

Literally hundreds of magazines are available on a variety of subjects, including animals, art, investment, computers, entertainment, hobbies, home and garden, nature, religion, science, and travel. Among the most widely read are newsmagazines such as *Time* and *U.S. News and World Report*. Also popular are the general interest tabloid magazines such as *People*, *The Star*, and *The National Enquirer*.

Some magazines publish only staff-written articles. Others solicit articles from freelance writers. Every magazine has its own specific areas of interest, format, editorial requirements, and point of view.

A magazine's target audience may be broad, as in the case of most newsmagazines, or narrow. There are magazines for political conservatives and magazines for liberals, some for men and others for women. Age, marital status, and work status are further areas of specialization. *McCall's*, for example, is published for women in general; *Redbook*, for young mothers, ages 25–44; *Cosmopolitan*, for working women, 18–35, who are single, married, or divorced.

Among the most common criticisms of news and general interest magazines are the following:

- The editorial biases of newsmagazines often result in a lack of objectivity in reporting, particularly on issues related to the bias. A secular bias, for example, might prejudice the treatment of religion; a liberal political bias might prejudice the treatment of conservative proposals or programs.

- General interest magazines often promote shallowness and superficiality by focusing on the details of celebrities' lives, particularly scandalous details.

- Many magazines allow their choice and treatment of subject matter to be influenced—and often compromised—by their advertisers.

- Many magazines tend to reinforce the values of popular culture—in particular, impulsiveness, self-indulgence, and instant gratification—rather than the values of traditional culture.

The following exercises invite you to apply critical thinking and decide whether these charges are valid. To complete these assignments you may decide to visit a newsstand, a library, or a bookstore.

EXERCISES

7.28. Examine the current editions of several newsmagazines, such as *Time* and *U.S. News and World Report*, or one written from a particular ethnic perspective. Select a single news item and compare the treatment it is given in each magazine. Decide which magazine's treatment is most biased and which is least biased. Support your findings. Present your decision and explanation.

7.29. Check the covers of the current issues of magazines such as *Cosmopolitan*, *McCall's*, *Esquire*, *Redbook*, and *Psychology Today*. (Feel free to include any other magazine to which you subscribe or in which you are interested.) Compare the titles of the articles listed on the covers. Do these titles raise any questions about the magazines' themes, focuses, or editorial perspectives? Explain your findings.

7.30. Examine an edition of each of the following publications: *The Star*, *The National Enquirer*, and *People*. Read the articles, the special sections, and the advice columns. Sample the ads and look closely at the photographs. Then answer these questions:

- Suppose that a stranger to this country were to draw a conclusion about our society's attitudes and values just from reading these publications. What conclusion do you think he or she would draw? What is it about these periodicals leads you to this conclusion?

- Do you think these publications merely reflect our society's attitudes and values, or do they also help shape those attitudes and values? Explain.

   Finally, write a brief composition explaining what changes in format and emphasis you would recommend to improve these publications.

THINKING CRITICALLY ABOUT NEWSPAPERS

The newspaper is an ancient form of communication that can be traced back to about 59 B.C. when the Roman *Acta Diurna* was posted in public places. Its greatest development, however, occurred after the invention of printing in the fifteenth century. More recently, the invention of the telegraph, the photocomposition process, and the communications satellite have made news gathering and publication faster and more efficient.

Other inventions, however, have challenged the newspaper's position as the leading provider of information. The most notable of these inventions have been radio, television, and the Internet. Smartphones and other wireless devices have recently become popular media for news. All these make news available at the flip of a switch or tap on a screen, whereas the newspaper is available, in most cases, only once a day.

The newspaper has a further disadvantage—it requires the effort of reading. In contrast, broadcast news is obtained effortlessly, and in a conveniently rapid pace, in moving pictures. In reaction to this handicap, the newspaper industry has simplified and shortened stories. A good example of this approach is the *USA Today* format.

Another change in print journalism over the past few decades concerns the treatment of fact and opinion. Traditionally, news stories presented only facts, objectively and without comment. A special place was reserved for commentary—the op-ed page (the term is short for opinion-editorial). There the reader would find editorials presenting the newspaper's official point of view on issues of the day, letters expressing readers' reactions to previous news stories, and opinion essays written by professional columnists.

Today's newspapers still have op-ed pages, with editorials, letters, and columns. But opinion is not always carefully screened out of news stories. Many journalists blend their interpretations and personal judgments into the news. Only the alert reader will understand where reporting ends and editorializing begins.

EXERCISES

7.31. Choose the largest newspaper in your area or a newspaper serving a large audience, such as *USA Today*. Read the main editorial of the day. Also read any news story mentioned in the editorial. Then answer the following questions:

- What position does the editor take on the issue? What support does he or she offer for this position?
- What other positions could be taken on the issue? How might those positions be supported? Before answering these questions, you may wish to research the issue by visiting the library or interviewing experts.
- What are the editorial's strengths and weaknesses?
- What position is most reasonable in light of the evidence? Present your response in a composition of at least several paragraphs. Another option is to write your response as a letter to the editor. If you do this, consider sending the letter to the newspaper.

7.32. Select an opinion column or a letter to the editor that interests you, apply the W.I.S.E. approach, and then write a persuasive composition of at least several paragraphs stating and supporting your position on the issue. You may agree with the article or letter in the newspaper, disagree with it, or agree in part. Attach either a summary or a copy of the original article or letter.

7.33. What lessons can you draw from the Good Thinking profiles of Oprah Winfrey, Faye Abdellah, and Chiara Lubich presented in this chapter? Explain how you can use each of those lessons in your career and/or personal life.

QUIZ

1. How many guidelines are offered for successful relationships? Briefly explain the one you find most helpful to you personally.

2. In choosing a career, only one factor is important—what you would like to do. True or false? Explain.

3. State and briefly explain each of the three criteria for making ethical judgments.

4. Newton Minow believes that television has improved significantly over the past quarter-century. True or false? Explain.

5. Explain two common criticisms of magazine publishing.

6. The first newspaper was published in the nineteenth century. True or false? Explain.

7. Identify two criticisms commonly made of popular music.

8. Define each of the following terms:

   Bandwagon

   Glittering generality

   Empty comparison

   Meaningless slogan

   Testimonial

   Transfer

   Stacking the deck

   Misleading statement

9. Explain two criticisms commonly made of print advertising.

10. Name the elements to examine when evaluating a movie.

Answers to this quiz are available at www.cengagebrain.com.

MAKE THE END A BEGINNING

You've finished reading this book and completed its exercises and other opportunities to practice critical thinking. Now you have a choice. You can decide that this moment will mark the end of one more academic experience. If this is your choice, just consign the book to a box in your basement and let it gather dust. As memory fades, the experiences you had with this book will be lost.

On the other hand, you can decide to make this book and critical thinking skills a vital part of your life. You can choose to make the end a beginning. One strategy is to buy a notebook and continue the journal you began here. If you use an actual notebook, as opposed to a computer document, use the left pages for recording observations and reserve the right pages for reflecting on those observations. Since your reflections are likely to be lengthier than your observations, leave appropriate space between observations.

Here is a collection of quotations to help you get started. Some apply in many situations; others, in a limited number. A few may need qualification. All will provide excellent food for thought. *Bon appétit!*

If I am not for myself, who will be? If I am only for myself, what am I?
  —*Rabbi Hillel*
Someone's boring me . . . I think it's me. —*Dylan Thomas*
A great many people think they are thinking when they are merely rearranging their prejudices. —*William James*
Each morning puts a man on trial and each evening passes judgment.
  —*Roy L. Smith*
There are two ways of exerting one's strength: one is pushing down, and the other is pulling up. —*Booker T. Washington*
Happiness is not a state to arrive at, but a manner of traveling.
  —*Margaret Lee Rumbeck*
How glorious it is—and how painful—to be an exception.
  —*Alfred de Musset*
The man who most vividly realizes a difficulty is the man most likely to overcome it. —*Joseph Farrell*
You can tell the ideals of a nation by its advertisements. —*Norman Douglas*

That man is the richest whose pleasures are the cheapest.
    —*Henry David Thoreau*
To read without reflecting is like eating without digesting. —*Edmund Burke*
Remember, no one can make you feel inferior without your consent.
    —*Eleanor Roosevelt*
Trend is not destiny. —*Lewis Mumford*
Success is a journey, not a destination. —*Ben Sweetland*
Many people's tombstones should read "Died at 30. Buried at 60."
    —*Nicholas Murray Butler*
Victory has a hundred fathers, but defeat is an orphan. —*Count G. Ciano*
A cathedral, a wave of a storm, a dancer's leap, never turn out to be as high
    as we had hoped. —*Marcel Proust*
Men are not punished for their sins, but by them. —*Elbert G. Hubbard*
Never has a man who has bent himself been able to make others straight.
    —*Mencius*
Free will does not mean one will, but many wills in one [person].
    —*Flannery O'Connor*
The offender never forgives. —*Russian proverb*
No matter which side of an argument you're on, you always find some peo-
    ple on your side that you wish were on the other side. —*Jascha Heifetz*

Adler, Mortimer J. *The Great Ideas: A Lexicon of Western Thought*. New York: Macmillan, 1992.

Albom, Mitch. *The Five People You Meet in Heaven*. New York: Hyperion, 2003.

Antonio, Michael D. *The State Boys Rebellion*. New York: Simon & Schuster, 2004, 5, 18.

Carnegie, Dale. *How to Win Friends and Influence People*. New York: Pocket Books, 1990.

Cerf, Christopher, and Victor Navasky. *The Experts Speak*. New York: Villard, 1998.

Curtsinger, Bill. "Close Encounters with the Gray Reef Shark." *National Geographic,* January 1995, 45–67.

Dyer, Wayne. *Your Erroneous Zones*. New York: Funk & Wagnalls, 1976, 90–1.

Fischer, David Hackett. *Historians' Fallacies: Toward a Logic of Historical Thought*. New York: Harper Perennial, 1970, 283 f.

Frankl, Viktor. *Man's Search for Meaning*. 3rd ed. New York: Simon & Schuster, 1984, 84–6.

Gilovich, Thomas. *How We Know What Isn't So: The Fallibility of Reason in Everyday Life*. New York: Free Press, 1991, 77.

Glaser, Edward M. *An Experiment in the Development of Critical Thinking*. New York: Bureau of Publications, Teachers College, Columbia University, 1941.

Hagen, Margaret A. *Whores of the Court: The Fraud of Psychiatric Testimony and the Rape of American Justice*. New York: HarperCollins, 1997, 39.

Harris, Errol E. "Respect for Persons." *Dædalus,* Spring 1969.

Henslin, James M. *Sociology: A Down-to-Earth Approach*. 7th ed. New York: Pearson, 2005, 144.

Iles, George. *Inventors at Work*. New York: Doubleday & Page, 1906, 370.

Kohn, Alfie. "The Truth about Self-Esteem." *Phi Delta Kappan,* December 1994, 272–283.

Larrabee, Harold A. *Reliable Knowledge*. Rev. ed. New York: Houghton Mifflin, 1964.

L'Amour, Louis. *Education of a Wandering Man*. New York: Bantam Books, 1989.

Liebert, Robert M., and Joyce Sprafkin. *The Early Window: Effects of Television on Children and Youth*, 3rd ed. New York: Pegammon Press, 1988.

Loftus, Elizabeth. *Eyewitness Testimony*. Cambridge, MA: Harvard University Press, 1996.

Loftus, Elizabeth, and Katherine Ketcham. *Witness for the Defense*. New York: St. Martin's Press, 1991.

Mander, Jerry. *Four Arguments for the Elimination of Television*. New York: Quill, 1978.

Marshall, Ray, and Marc Tucker. *Thinking for a Living: Education and the Wealth of Nations*. New York: Basic Books, xvi–xviii.

Moore, T. J., J. Glenmullen , C. D. Furberg, (2010). "Prescription Drugs Associated with Reports of Violence Towards Others," *PLoS ONE* 5(12): e15337. doi:10.1371/journal.pone.0015337.

Osborn, Alex. *Applied Imagination*. New York: Scribner's Sons, 1957, 115.

Rogers, Carl. *On Becoming a Person*. Boston: Houghton Mifflin, 1961.

Rossman, Joseph. *The Psychology of the Inventor*. Washington, DC: The Inventor's Publishing Co., 1931, 57.

Samenow, Stanton. *Inside the Criminal Mind*. New York: Times Books, 1984.

Schlesinger, Arthur, Jr. *The Disuniting of America: Reflections on a Multicultural Society*. New York: Norton, 1992.

Seligman, Martin. *Authentic Happiness*. New York: Free Press, 2002.

———. *Learned Optimism*. New York: Free Press, 1990.

Steele, Shelby. *White Guilt: How Blacks and Whites Together Destroyed the Promise of the Civil Rights Era*. New York: HarperCollins, 2006, 45, 58, 59, 60, 62.

Stevenson, Harold, and James Stigler. *The Learning Gap*. New York: Simon & Schuster, 1992.

Strasburger, Victor C. *Adolescents and the Media: Medical and Psychological Impact*. Thousand Oaks, CA: Sage Publishing Co., 1995.

Sutherland, Stuart. *Irrationality: Why We Don't Think Straight!* New Brunswick, NJ: Rutgers University Press, 1994, 240.

———. *The Mismeasure of Woman*. New York: Simon & Schuster, 1992.

Tavris, Carol. *Anger: The Misunderstood Emotion*. New York: Simon & Schuster, 1982.

Underhill, Jack. "New Age Quiz." *Life Times*, 1988, 6.

Vitz, Paul. *Faith of the Fatherless*. Dallas: Spence, 1999.

Wood, Peter. *Diversity: The Invention of a Concept*. San Francisco: Encounter Books, 2003.

The following books on critical thinking and related subjects can help you deepen your understanding and expand your skill.

Adams, James. *Conceptual Blockbusting.* New York: Norton, 1979.

Adler, Mortimer. *How to Read a Book.* New York: Simon & Schuster, 1972.

————. *Intellect: Mind over Matter.* New York: Macmillan, 1990.

Alexander, Janet E., and Marsha Ann Tate. *Web Wisdom: How to Evaluate and Create Information Quality on the Web.* Mahwah, NJ: Lawrence Erlbaum Associates, 1999.

Barker, Evelyn M. *Everyday Reasoning.* Englewood Cliffs, NJ: Prentice-Hall, 1981.

Barry, Vincent E., and Joel Rudinow. *Invitation to Critical Thinking.* New York: Harcourt Brace, 1998.

Browne, M. Neil, and Stuart M. Keely. *Asking the Right Questions: A Guide to Critical Thinking.* 7th ed. Englewood Cliffs, NJ: Prentice-Hall, 2004.

Cederblom, J. B., and David W. Paulsen. *Critical Reasoning.* 5th ed. Belmont, CA: Wadsworth, 2001.

Chaffee, John. *Thinking Critically.* 8th ed. New York: Houghton Mifflin, 2006.

Damer, Edward. *Attacking Faulty Reasoning.* 5th ed. Belmont, CA: Wadsworth, 2005.

DeBono, Edward. *Lateral Thinking.* New York: Harper & Row, 1970.

Engel, Morris S. *With Good Reason: An Introduction to Informal Fallacies.* 6th ed. New York: St. Martin's Press, 2000.

Feynman, Richard P. *"Surely You're Joking, Mr. Feynman!"* New York: Bantam Books, 1985.

————. *The Pleasure of Finding Things Out.* Cambridge, MA: Perseus Publishing, 1999.

Fischer, David Hackett. *Historians' Fallacies: Toward a Logic of Historical Thought.* New York: Harper Perennial, 1970.

Fisher, Alec. *The Logic of Real Arguments.* New York: Cambridge University Press, 2001.

Gilovich, Thomas. *How We Know What Isn't So: The Fallibility of Reason in Everyday Life.* New York: Free Press, 1991.

Goldberg, Bernard. *Bias.* Washington, DC: Regnery, 2002.

Gould, Stephen Jay. *The Mismeasure of Man.* New York: Norton, 1981.

Govier, Trudy. *A Practical Study of Argument.* 5th ed. Belmont, CA: Wadsworth, 2001.

Halpern, Diane. *Thought and Knowledge.* Hillsdale, NJ: Lawrence Erlbaum, 2002.

Hoaglund, John. *Critical Thinking.* Newport News, VA: Vale Press, 1995.

Hofstadter, Richard. *Anti-Intellectualism in American Life.* New York: Vintage, 1963.

Johnson, Ralph, and J. A. Blair. *Logical Self-Defense.* New York: McGraw-Hill, 1994.

Kohn, Bob. *Journalistic Fraud: How The New York Times Distorts the News and Why It Can No Longer Be Trusted.* Nashville, TN: WND Books, 2003.

Kytle, Ray. *Clear Thinking for Composition.* 5th ed. New York: McGraw-Hill, 1988.

Langer, Ellen J. *Mindfulness.* Reading, MA: Addison-Wesley, 1989.

Lazere, Donald. *American Media and Mass Culture.* Berkeley: University of California Press, 1987.

Mander, Jerry. *Four Arguments for the Elimination of Television.* New York: Quill, 1978.

Mayfield, Marlys. *Thinking for Yourself: Developing Critical Thinking Skills through Reading and Writing.* 5th ed. Boston: Heinle & Heinle, 2003.

Moore, Noel, and Richard Parker. *Critical Thinking.* New York: McGraw-Hill, 2003.

Moore, W. Edgar, et al. *Creative and Critical Thinking.* Boston: Houghton Mifflin, 1984.

Nickerson, Raymond S. *Reflections on Reasoning.* Hillsdale, NJ: Lawrence Erlbaum, 1986.

Nisbett, Richard, and Lee Ross. *Human Inference: Strategies and Shortcomings of Social Judgment.* Englewood Cliffs, NJ: Prentice-Hall, 1980.

Paul, Richard, and Linda Elder. *Critical Thinking.* Englewood Cliffs, NJ: Prentice-Hall, 2001.

Perkins, David. *Archimedes' Bathtub: The Art and Logic of Breakthrough Thinking.* New York: Norton, 2000.

Postman, Neil. *Amusing Ourselves to Death.* New York: Oxford University Press, 1985.

Rosenthal, Peggy. *Words and Values.* New York: Oxford University Press, 1984.

Ruggiero, Vincent Ryan. *The Art of Thinking*. 4th ed. New York: HarperCollins, 2004.

————. *Beyond Feelings: A Guide to Critical Thinking*. Mountain View, CA: Mayfield, 2004.

————. *Thinking Critically about Ethical Issues*. Mountain View, CA: Mayfield, 2004.

————. *Warning: Nonsense Is Destroying America*. Nashville, TN: Thomas Nelson, 1994.

Scriven, Michael. *Reasoning*. New York: McGraw-Hill, 1997.

Seech, Zachary. *Open Minds and Everyday Reasoning*. 2nd ed. Belmont, CA: Wadsworth, 2005.

Siegel, Harvey. *Relativism Refuted*. Norwell, MA: Kluwer, 1987.

Sutherland, Stuart. *Irrationality: Why We Don't Think Straight!* New Brunswick, NJ: Rutgers University Press, 1994.

Thornton, Bruce S. *Plagues of the Mind: The New Epidemic of False Knowledge*. Wilmington, DE: ISI Books, 1999.

Toulmin, Stephen. *The Uses of Argument*. New York: Cambridge University Press, 2003.

Toulmin, Stephen E., Richard Rieke, and Alan Janik. *An Introduction to Reasoning*. Englewood Cliffs, NJ: Prentice-Hall, 1997.

Von Oech, Roger. *A Kick in the Seat of the Pants*. New York: Harper & Row, 1986.

————. *A Whack on the Side of the Head*. New York: HarperCollins, 1993.

Weaver, Richard. *Ideas Have Consequences*. Chicago: University of Chicago Press, 1948.

Weddle, Perry. *Argument*. New York: McGraw-Hill, 1978.

INDEX